Encyclopaedia of
Rugby League Football

Other Sports Encyclopaedias published by Robert Hale Limited

Association Football
BY MAURICE GOLESWORTHY

Athletics
BY MELVYN WATMAN

Bowls
BY KEN HAWKS AND GERARD LINDLEY

Boxing
BY MAURICE GOLESWORTHY

Chess
BY ANNE SUNNUCKS

Cricket
BY MAURICE GOLESWORTHY

Flat Racing
BY ROGER MORTIMER

Golf
BY WEBSTER EVANS

Motor Cycle Sport
BY PETER CARRICK

Motor Racing
BY ANTHONY PRITCHARD AND KEITH DAVEY

Mountaineering
BY WALT UNSWORTH

Rugby Union Football
BY J. R. JONES
  (Second edition edited by Maurice Golesworthy)

Show Jumping
BY CHARLES STRATTON

Steeplechasing
BY PATRICIA SMYLY

Swimming
BY PAT BESFORD

Encyclopaedia of
Rugby League Football

Compiled by
John Huxley and David Howes

Based on the First Edition
Compiled by A. N. Gaulton

Foreword by
The Earl of Derby, MC
President of the Rugby Football League

ROBERT HALE · LONDON

© *A. N. Gaulton 1968*
© *John Huxley, David Howes and*
Robert Hale Limited, 1980

First Edition 1968
Second Edition 1980

ISBN 0 7091 8133 7

Robert Hale Limited
Clerkenwell House
45-47 Clerkenwell Green
London EC1R 0HT

PHOTOSET BY
PHOTOBOOKS (BRISTOL) LTD,
PRINTED AND BOUND IN GREAT BRITAIN
BY REDWOOD BURN LTD, TROWBRIDGE
AND ESHER

Foreword

by

THE EARL OF DERBY, MC

President of the Rugby Football League

I was very pleased in 1968 to do a foreword for Mr A. N. Gaulton's *Encyclopaedia of Rugby League Football*. I am delighted to do this once again for the new edition of the Encyclopaedia. It could not be coming out at a more appropriate moment as over the past eleven years Rugby League has seen immense changes, all of which I am glad to say are for the better. Attendances are once again on the increase, and the image and mood of Rugby League are at a high level, ready for the challenge of the 1980s. This new edition is packed with facts and figures which will provide a ready reference for the Rugby League purists and the converts to this great game of Rugby League.

Knowsley,
Prescot,
Merseyside.

List of Illustrations

Raymond Fletcher

Records featured in this Encyclopaedia have been researched or verified by Raymond Fletcher, eminent Rugby League record keeper and Rugby League correspondent for the *Yorkshire Post*.

which games former professionals and permit players are allowed to compete in. They are ruled out of any of the Association-controlled games, for example, the National Cup, the National Inter-League competition, inter-county games and internationals.

Effectively they are restricted to playing in normal League matches and in any cup competition the local league organisation cares to admit them to.

See also BRITISH AMATEUR RUGBY LEAGUE ASSOCIATION.

ALL FOUR CUPS

Until recently the ambition of every club was to perform the extremely difficult feat of winning " All Four Cups " in a single season. The four major trophies to be won were:

The Northern RL Championship
The Rugby League Challenge Cup
The Lancashire (or Yorkshire) Challenge Cup
The Lancashire (or Yorkshire) League Championship

Only three clubs achieved this distinction. They were:

Hunslet 1907-08
Huddersfield 1914-15
Swinton 1927-28

One player, J. W. Higson, was associated with both Hunslet and Huddersfield during their " All Four Cups " seasons. He was a member of Hunslet's pack and then joined Huddersfield in 1910.

The County League Championships were abolished in 1970, but though the traditional " All Four Cups " feat is not now possible the introduction of sponsored competitions and other trophies has made it even more difficult for clubs to sweep the board.

See also TROPHIES.

AMATEURS

The British Amateur Rugby League Association's definition of an amateur is: A person who has not been paid for playing rugby.

Under their constitution, however, they will allow people to play amateur Rugby League as long as they are not being paid to play the game.

This allows former professionals and players registered by a professional club on a permit to play in the amateur game.

But the Association has strict rules about

AMERICA

Michael Mayer was totally unknown in the Rugby League world before 1977. Then he burst onto the scene in devastating style by suggesting that the game should be introduced on an organised basis to the United States and that he was prepared to lead the way. In fact former grid-iron footballer Mayer had started to lay his plans for importing the game when, on 12 Oct. 1976, he instituted a corporation called, significantly, the "United States Rugby League".

At this stage Mayer had not seen a live game of Rugby League. His inspiration had been some television films of League games and an interest stimulated by the fictional film *This Sporting Life* which featured Richard Harris in a Rugby League situation. Mayer's first-hand experience of Rugby League started when he visited Britain in May 1977. He undertook a brief tour of the North of England and watched the Challenge Cup final between St Helens and Widnes. He then flew to Australia to watch the World Championships and outline his plans, to the International Board.

Encouragement without commitment was Mayer's only reward. The giant American was undaunted, and he returned to America to develop his idea further. He established his headquarters at 6414 Copps Avenue, Madison, Wisconsin.

Mayer returned to Europe in spring 1978. He tried to interest the British League in taking a financial stake in the adventure, but he received a cautious reception and no money. This was put down to the fact that the council were still wary of international expansion after the gallant, but ill-fated, attempts to take the game into Italy and South Africa during the 'fifties and 'sixties. The basis of his plans are a 12-team league spread throughout the United States playing a thirteen-week season.

He launched his scheme on the American public and sporting Press at another historic meeting, a Press conference at Gallagher's Restaurant 228 West 52nd Street, New York, on 15th August 1978. He was trying to attract businessmen to take up franchises for the proposed clubs on the same kind of basis as American football, baseball, basketball, and to a lesser extent, soccer. Mayer, who had adopted the title of League President, appointed Jim Taylor as the League Commissioner. A partner to Mayer in the adventure, Taylor is a former Green Bay Packers grid-iron star who was elected to the American Football Hall of Fame.

A coaching session for a number of Americans was staged at Great Lakes Naval Base near Chicago during Autumn 1978 and coaches in charge were Britain's Albert Fearnley and Doug Nye from Sydney's Newtown Club.

It was hoped to start the league during 1979, but various problems have delayed the projected start.

In 1980, the British League offered to send England and Wales to America for three promotional matches during June but the Americans failed to raise the necessary £50,000 tour costs.

Rugby League, however, was not entirely unknown in America before Mayer's arrival. In 1953 a team calling themselves the "American All Stars" made a 26-match tour of Australia and New Zealand. In New Zealand they won four of their eight matches with victories over Taranaki, Wellington, North Auckland and South Auckland. They scored 153 points, but conceded 210. They had found the going a great deal harder in Australia where they won 3, lost 13 and drew 2 in their 18 matches. In Australia they scored 306 points and had 560 registered against them.

The All Stars were captained by Vince Jones, and managed by Mike Dimitro. They had some preliminary coaching from former Leeds and Salford player Cliff Evans and, while they were in Australia, they were coached by Australian official N. Robinson and referee G. Bishop. One unfortunate feature of the tour was that one of the forwards, Jack Bonetti, contracted polio in Queensland and had to be flown home.

G. Kerkorian was the team's leading scorer with 78 goals and 5 tries (171 points). He played in 17 of the 18 Australian games and scored in every one. The leading try scorer in New Zealand was A. E. Kirkland with 13 in Australia and 5 in New Zealand.

Various Australian and New Zealand players assisted the All Stars to strengthen the team. They made up the numbers in New Zealand because of injuries and the failure of some American players to undertake that part of the tour.

The full record for the All Stars tour was:

In Australia

Opponents	Venue	Points For–Against
Southern and Monaro Divisions	Canberra (4,827)	34-25
Sydney	Sydney (65,453)	25-52
New South Wales	Sydney (32,554)	41-62
Combined Country	Wollongong (11,787)	9-35
Western Division	Dubbo (4,717)	21-24
Newcastle	Newcastle (14,160)	19-10
Northern and North Coast Districts	Cape Harbour (5,400)	18-26
Queensland	Brisbane (24,397)	36-39
North Queensland	Cairns (6,042)	17-17
Central West Queensland	Longreach (1,635)	21-26
Central Queensland	Rockhampton (5,332)	26-33
Brisbane	Brisbane (7,000)	26-39
Toowoomba	Toowoomba (5,778)	15-29
Ipswich	Ipswich (3,155)	16-15
Wide Bay	Maryborough (6,166)	33-33
Riverina	Gundagai (2,560)	14-30
New South Wales	Sydney (19,686)	18-27

In New Zealand

Opponents	Venue	Points For–Against
Auckland	Auckland	28-54
Taranaki	New Plymouth	21-18
Wellington	Wellington	17-8

In New Zealand			Points
	Opponents	*Venue*	*For Against*
West Coast		Greymouth	10-27
Canterbury		Christchurch	8-39
Northland		Whangarei	25-6
Maoris		Auckland	26-40
South Auckland		Hamilton	22-19

During December 1953 and January 1954 another American Rugby League team played five matches in France. They won one match but lost the remaining four scoring 70 points against 121. At the time France was celebrating the twentieth anniversary of the game's introduction to their country and three of the Americans played in a special match in which France defeated the Rest of the World 19-15. The game was played in a snow storm at Lyons on 3 Jan. 1954 and the Rest of the World team included Italian, Australian and British players.

In November 1954 the Australian and New Zealand World Cup teams played each other in two games at Long Beach Memorial Stadium and the Coliseum, Los Angeles. Australia won both matches, the first 30-13 before 1,000 people and the second 28–18 before 4,554. Both attendances were affected by foggy weather. Keith Holman of Australia won the Dick Hyland Trophy awarded by the Helms Athletic Foundation to the outstanding player.

Americans have, at various stages, been connected with League clubs in both Britain and Australia. Chuck Wiseman played for Blackpool Borough in the early 'sixties and in season 1963-64 topped their try-scoring lists with 19 before going to Australia. A. E. Kirkland played several games for Leeds and distinguished himself by scoring a try on his first senior appearance against Blackpool.

In the early 'seventies two American Rugby Union players from California, Sam Moore and Chris Machado, attempted to break into Rugby League with Oldham and then moved on to Blackpool. They did not last long, however, after a dispute over financial arrangements. Blackpool, however, have maintained their transatlantic links and, encouraged by their part-time general manager-director Albert Fearnley, the seaside town's business community were persuaded to finance the recruiting of two former grid-iron football players Ural Jackson and Bob Harrison. During 1978 Sydney club Newtown signed a grid-iron player Manfred Moore on a limited con-

tract. He played five games, all first grade matches, and scored one try.

APPEARANCES

The longest sequence of successive appearances for a club is 190 by Gilbert Austin, a Hull Kingston Rovers winger. Austin made his debut for Hull KR at home to Wakefield on 25 Jan. 1919 and did not miss a match until 8 Dec. 1923 when he played for Yorkshire against Lancashire.

ARROWFAST EXPRESS TROPHY

Introduced in the 1977-78 season to reward the top try-scorers in League football. Sponsored by Arrowfast Express, a United Kingdom haulage company, the award scheme provides a trophy and a four-figure cash prize to the club who score most tries in either the First or Second Division campaigns.

The first holders were St Helens who scored 142 tries during their 30-match 1977-78 season.

The all-time record for tries in a League season is held by Huddersfield with 240 touchdowns in 39 matches in the 1911-12 season.

The roll of honour is:

1977-78:	St Helens	142
1978-79:	Hull	145
1979-80:	Featherstone Rovers	142

ARTIST

In 1979-80 season, Ashton-in-Makerfield artist Chris Brady (23) was challenged by State Express of London to capture on canvas the spirit of Rugby League, particularly the State Express Challenge Cup.

It was believed to be the first time a sport had been designated its own full-time artist.

Brady's completed portraits were put on exhibition throughout the country.

"A" TEAMS

The majority of professional clubs also field a reserve team, known in Rugby League as "A" teams.

"A" teams west of the Pennines play League matches in the Lancashire Combination and are eligible to compete in a knockout competition, the Lancashire County Challenge Shield.

East of the Pennines, " A " teams take part in the Yorkshire Senior Competition, with entry to the Yorkshire Senior Competition Challenge Cup.

Highest attendance at an " A " team fixture was the 12,000 fans who watched the Yorkshire Senior Competition Challenge Cup Final between Hull and Hull Kingston Rovers at the Boulevard, Hull, on 5 May 1949.

ATHLETES

The switch from top grade athletics to professional Rugby League has met with starkly contrasting results—from a one-match career to representing Great Britain on an Australasian Tour!

Emmanuel McDonald Bailey, 32-year-old joint holder of the world record for 100 metres, signed for Leigh in July 1953 at a reported fee of £1,000, plus two further instalments of £1,000. A crowd of 14,996 witnessed his one and only appearance in a friendly match against Wigan, when he scored one of Leigh's three tries. Two months after that floodlit encounter on 16 Dec. 1953, Bailey announced his retirement.

Olympic sprinter Alf Meakin joined Leeds in Nov. 1964 but was not retained after taking part in three trial games. Meakin signed for Blackpool Borough, topping their try scoring list with 12 touchdowns in the 1965-66 season.

The most successful convert was Berwyn Jones, at the time Europe's fastest man over 100 yards. His first game for Wakefield Trinity was in Mar. 1964. In the same year he scored two spectacular tries to help Trinity capture the Yorkshire Cup. In Dec. 1964, he made his debut for Great Britain against France in Perpignan, playing in the return match at Swinton in the following January. In the Aug. 1965, Jones represented a Commonwealth XIII against New Zealand at Crystal Palace. His third and final Great Britain appearance was against France in Perpignan in January 1966, although he toured Australia and New Zealand in that summer, leading the try scorers with 24 touchdowns in 15 games, but not gaining Test selection. Jones signed for Bradford Northern in Feb. 1967.

Arthur Rowe signed for Oldham in July 1962 after breaking his own European record with a putt of 64ft 3in. The reported fee was £1,500, with a further payment of £1,500 after ten first team appearances. His Rugby League debut was in an " A " team game against Leigh in the September. After a further three reserve team outings, Rowe quit the 13-a-side code.

Olympic sprinter Ken Anderson played for Liverpool City in 1953, while Kiwi Peter Henderson, a 1950 Empire Games runner and New Zealand Rugby Union International, played for Huddersfield from 1950-57, scoring 214 tries in 258 matches, plus gaining International honours.

ATTENDANCES

The record crowd for any Rugby League match is 102,569 at Odsal Stadium, Bradford, for the RL Challenge Cup replay between Warrington and Halifax on 5 May 1954. It was a midweek evening match.

The biggest crowd at a League match is 47,747 at Central Park when Wigan played St Helens on 27 Mar. 1959.

Since the reintroduction of two divisions in 1973 the biggest crowd at a League match is 16,745 for the Hull v Hull KR Division One game on 7 Oct. 1979.

During the same period, the biggest gate for a Second Division match is 12,424 for the Hull v New Hunslet clash in April 1979.

In the current spell of two divisions, the record aggregate attendance for home league matches is Hull's 150,978 (average 10,065) from 16 matches in 1979-80 season.

The biggest total for a season of League matches is 4,950,000 in 1949-50 when 29 clubs each played 36 matches. That season Wigan averaged just under 23,000 for their home League matches.

On Saturday, 19 Feb. 1949 a record total for one day of 210,000 spectators attended 16 RL Challenge Cup first round, second leg matches.

AUSTRALIA

As in Great Britain Rugby Union's reluctance to allow either broken-time payments or assistance with medical expenses caused dissatisfaction in Australia and two important events brought the Northern Union game as an answer to this unhappy state of affairs.

First was the formation of A. H. Baskerville's New Zealand tourists in 1907 (See NEW ZEALAND) and second was the broken collar-bone of Rugby Union player Alick Burdon. He sustained the injury playing for New South Wales against Queensland and was left to pay his own medical expenses. He also failed to get any compensation for his injury.

News of his problems reached Victor Trumper, the famous Australian cricketer. The item of news was passed on to him by his friend Sep Carter, the Test wicketkeeper, and because Trumper's shop in Market Street, Sydney, was a favourite meeting place for top Australian sportsmen, Burdon's plight was soon well known. At this time a report on Baskerville's plans appeared in the Sydney newspapers and it could not have come at a more opportune moment. Discussions at Trumper's shop led to an invitation being sent to Baskerville to bring his team to Australia on the way to England.

Sydney sports follower Jim Giltinan, one of the Trumper-shop conversationalists, knew New Zealand pioneer George Smith and sent a cable suggesting that three matches should be played at the Sydney Agricultural Ground with a guarantee of £500. The Australians gave the venture a flying start when Giltinan and Trumper took a taxi-ride out to Double Bay and persuaded Rugby Union star Herbert Henry (Dally) Messenger to join the rebels for the not inconsiderable fee of £300. He played in each of the three matches against the "All Golds" the nickname the New Zealanders were given because they played for money, and made such an impression that he was invited to play with them in England.

The matches were played on 17, 21 and 24 Aug. 1907 and the New Zealanders won all three, 12-8, 19-5 and 5-3. To complete the successful experiment the £500 guarantee was taken through the turnstiles and there was an added bonus of a £180 profit.

That success, however, brought a number of teething problems. First there was the £180. The leaders of the new code were not sure how to spend it. They were faced with sharing the money between the players or investing it in more publicity for the venture. They eventually decided to follow the latter course.

The next drama surrounded the formation of the Sydney Premiership and the adoption of Northern Union laws. The decision to change over from Rugby Union laws was made only after the president Henry Hoyle had used his casting vote. The competition's first committee consisted of Hoyle (president), Trumper (treasurer), Giltinan (secretary) and H. R. Miller (assistant secretary).

Besides Messenger other converts from Rugby Union were Burdon, whose injury inspired the first approach to Baskerville, Peter Moir and winger Albert Rosenfeld, who later joined English club Huddersfield and set up a sensation try-scoring record of 80 in a season which has still to be beaten.

Eight clubs were formed for the Premiership's first season in 1908. They were Balmain, Cumberland, Eastern Suburbs, Glebe, Newcastle, Newtown, North Sydney and South Sydney. Progress was rapid. In that same season the game spread to such an extent that the first New South Wales v. Queensland match was staged and playing standards improved so quickly that it was agreed to send a touring team to England.

That first team included one or two New Zealanders and for that reason the team was named Australasia. It was not until 1921-22 that the first all-Australian party made the trip across the world and in 1948, when England changed their name to Great Britain, before New Zealanders were prevented from qualifying for the Australian tour.

The first Australian tourists, however, hit England at a bad time. The mother country was in the middle of a depression and strikes and hard times kept attendances at the matches low. It was reported that the English League had to give financial help to the Australians when they returned home.

The financial blow, however, was the worst thing that happened on the tour. The Australians played their first Test matches against England. The first was staged in London on 12 Dec. 1908 and it ended in a 22-22 draw. The Australians lost the next two 15-5 in Newcastle-upon-Tyne and 6-5 in Birmingham. Their complete tour record was: played 45, won 18, lost 21 and drawn 6.

Australia's increasing power in the game was recognised in 1910 when England sent out their first touring team downunder. England won the first Test 27-20 in front of a massive 50,000 Sydney crowd and then went on to make sure of the series by winning the second Test in Brisbane 22-17.

Australasia returned to England in 1911 and they put one over on the country of Rugby League's birth by winning the three-match series 2-0 with one match drawn.

In 1914 England made their second tour and gained revenge for defeat on their own soil by beating the Australians 2-1 in a series, which included one of the most famous Rugby League matches of all-time,

"Rourke's Drift". Named after a famous Boer War battle when a handful of British soldiers held out against overwhelming odds, the English RL team battled their way into the last Test drawing 1-1 with the Australians. The raw courage of the injury-savaged English team carried the day, and despite their terrible problems they won 14-7 in front of an admiring 40,000 Sydney crowd.

The First World War came and went and Rugby League thrived in Australia; New South Wales country areas joined the code, Queensland Rugby League boomed and, because they played League throughout the war, the Australasians were able to beat the English when tours resumed in 1920. For the second Test in that series in Sydney 65,000 people poured through the gates.

The 1920s was a period of great growth for Rugby League in Australia. In Queensland, the Bulimba Cup competition was started in 1925. This was a three-way clash between Brisbane, Ipswich and Toowoomba. Discontent within the Brisbane clubs led to the formation of an independent Brisbane League in 1922 and, despite repeated attempts by the Queensland Rugby League to regain control, they retained their independence. Today Brisbane Ipswich and Toowoomba have their own Leagues within the QRL.

Back in New South Wales City v. Country games were instituted in 1928. With the growth of the Australian game the transfer fee system was introduced to stop poaching of players but this system was to prove a problem until it was abolished after a legal struggle in years to come.

The Second World War had more affect on Rugby League than the First World War. Inter-State matches were abandoned between 1941 and 1945 and the internal competitions were severely disrupted. A three-grade Sydney competition struggled through. City v. Country matches continued at a reduced level, Brisbane League played on and the Bulimba Cup was abandoned.

The War, however, was responsible for the spread of Rugby League in Australasia. Servicemen continued to play the game while they were stationed away from home and the code became established in places as far apart as Western Australia and Papua New Guinea. In Papua the first competition was formalised in 1949. The English touring team played a match in Fremantle, W. Australia and Darwin from Northern Territory entered the Australian

RL fold in 1950. Australian Rugby League was marching into the future. From this point it is easier to understand the development and progress of Australian RL at state level.

New South Wales

Sydney and New South Wales are the major growth centres for Rugby League. Since 1951 they have moved into a system of complete professionalism which is heavily covered by written media, television and radio.

During 1951 the first French team visited Australia and interest was such in Sydney that there were attendances of 60,160 for the first Test and 67,009 for the third Test. St George set up a world club championship record by winning the Sydney premiership eleven successive times from 1956 to 1966 and producing, at the same time, all-time great players such as second row forward Norm Provan, centres Graeme Langlands and Reg Gasnier, Kangaroo captain Ian Walsh, and swashbuckling lock-forward Johnny Raper.

Other major highlights before 1970 were the all-time Sydney attendance record 78,056 for the 1965 Grand Final between St George and South Sydney, the first Sunday game in June 1966 at Sydney Cricket Ground when Balmain beat Souths in front of 55,934. And in 1969 the famous South Sydney full-back Eric Simms, one of the best-ever goalkickers, created a new record points aggregate for the Sydney Premiership competition of 265 points.

The 1970s have been a period of considerable importance. The laws of the game were altered with the yardage play-the-ball changed, the introduction of first four-tackle and then six-tackle restrictions and the reduction of the drop, or in Australian terms "field", goal to one point.

In 1974 the Sydney League abandoned its Match-of-the-day at Sydney Cricket Ground every weekend and switched to a home-and-away policy. This has improved the club ground facilities and several new attendance records have been created.

In 1975 the third grade was switched from open age to under-23 years and this has helped ensure a steady supply of players for the future.

The Amco Cup floodlit television competition involving clubs from Sydney, New South Wales, Brisbane and New Zealand, were started in 1974 and the final is staged each year at Leichhardt Oval, Sydney. (See "Amco Cup")

One of the most important, and popular, competitions in Sydney is the sponsored pre-season knockout Wills Cup. Players too can earn high financial rewards and incentives, such as the Rothmans' Medal, and these contribute to Sydney's high standards of competition. One of the major events of the 1970s, was the Dennis Tutty affair, which saw the end of the transfer fee system and introduction of players' freedom of contract. The transfer system was challenged in court by Tutty, who had played for Australia against New Zealand. He sought a release from his contract with Balmain at the end of his agreed period and, under the rules that applied at the time, Balmain refused to let him go. After a two-year fight, the High Court ruled that this amounted to a restraint of trade and this had massive repercussions in the Australian transfer system. The floodgates were opened for a while, and Australian clubs, who grew rich on the proceeds of fruit or gaming machines, imported players from England (for example, Castleford's Malcolm Reilly joined Manly Warringah for £16,000) and paid their players up to £6,000 per season plus another £100 per match.

The gold-rush, however, has slowed down to a more sensible rate and the 1977 international signing ban has prevented Australian clubs importing further players from England, France or New Zealand. It has also put an end to close-season loan transfers which British players enjoyed for a spell in the mid-seventies but which caused much heart-searching for the British clubs and League. Tutty, meanwhile has returned to Balmain, the club he fought in the court room and, in 1978, he was their reserve grade coach.

Today the powerful Sydney Premiership is made up of twelve clubs Balmain, Canterbury-Bankstown, Cronulla-Sutherland, Eastern Suburbs, Manly-Warringah, Newtown, North Sydney, Parramatta, Penrith, South Sydney, St George and Western Suburbs. After the founder members, University joined the league in 1920, St George in 1921, Canterbury-Bankstown 1935, Parramatta and Manly-Warringah in 1947. Glebe, a founder member, withdrew in 1929 followed by University in 1937. Cronulla Sutherland and Penrith were both admitted to the First Grade in 1967.

The Premiership, the Sydney championship, is not decided in the European League fashion. The top five clubs in the League at the end of the season qualify for the play-off system which is made up of various semi-finals and finals.

The first round in the play-off is called the preliminary semi-finals. For this round the League winners, called the minor premiers, are not brought into the draw. The second club plays the third club and the fourth club the fifth. At the end of the round the loser of the fourth v. fifth tie is eliminated. For the next stage the minor premiers are brought into the draw. They play the winners of the second v. third match in the major semi-final, while the loser of the second v. third match plays the winner of the fourth v fifth encounter in the minor semi-final.

The winner of the major game qualifies direct for the Grand Final, while the winner of the minor has to play the loser from the major for the second place in the Grand Final. The match is known as the final.

The present system of deciding the Premiership was instituted in 1954 and the play-off for fourth place was added in 1974. Until 1926 the Premiership was conducted on a first-past-the-post principle with the minor premiers having a right to challenge in the Grand Final if they were beaten in the semi-final or final.

Country League
One of the major strengths of Australian Rugby League is the well organised system of leagues outside the Sydney metropolitan area in New South Wales. This organisation is called the Country Rugby League and it controls 23 separate competitions, 21 groups and the Illawara and Newcastle Leagues. The groups and leagues are made up in the following manner (as in 1978):
Group One: South Grafton, Casino RSM South Lismore, Marist Brothers Western Suburbs, Lower Clarence, Ballina, Mid-Richmond, Grafton, Kyogle.
Group Two: Sawfell, Kempsey, Bellingen, Macksville, Smithtown, Nambucca Heads, Jetty Beach, Woolgoolga, Coff's Harbour.
Group Three: Wingham, Taree Old Bar, Foster-Tuncurry, Taree United, Wauchope, Port Macquane, Gloucester.
Group Four: Gunnedah, Tamworth City, North Tamworth, West Tamworth, Narrabi, Weeris Creek, Manilla, Walcha.
Group Five: Moree, Glenn Innes, Guyra, Armidale, Warialda, Inverell, Tenterfield.
Group Six:: Campbelltown Warriors, Collegians, Camden, Oakdale, Ingleburn, Campbelltown City, The Oaks, Bowral, Picton, Moss Vale.

Group Seven: Nowra, Warilla, Milton-Ulladulla, Jamberoo, Batesman Bay, Bombaderry, St Michaels, Kiama, Albion Park, Shellharbour, Gerringong, Berry.

Group Eight: Canberra Tigers, Woden Valley, West Belconnen, North Canberra, Queanbeyan United, Yass Yass, Queanbeyan Kangaroos, Crockwell, Goulbourn United, Goulburn Workers.

Group Nine: Wagga Kangaroos, Junee, Harden-Murrimburrah, Tumut, Temora, Wagga Magpies, Gundegai, Turvey Park, Cootamundra, Young.

Group Ten: Mudgee, Cowra, Lithgow Workmans, Bathurst Railways, Blayney, Bathurst St. Patricks, Bathurst Charlestons, Orange CYMS, Lithgow Shamrocks, Oberon, Orange Ex-Services.

Group Eleven: Narromine, Dubbo Macquarie, Canowindra, Dubbo CYMS, Forbes, Parkes, Condobolin, Wellington.

Group Twelve: Woy-woy, Gosford, Erina, The Entrance, Unina, Wyong, Ourimbah, Terrigal.

Group Thirteen: Albury Blues, Tumbarumba, Albury Roos, Lockhart, Holbrook, Batlow, Terrigal.

Group Fourteen: Coonamble, Dunedoo, Gilgandra, Baradine, Coonabararan, Coolah.

Group Fifteen: Walgett, Bourke, Brewarrina, Nyngan, Cobar, Goodaga.

Group Sixteen: Coomba, Narooma, Candelo-Bemboka, Snowy River Bears, Eden, Bega, Delegate, Merimbula, Tathra, Bambala.

Group Seventeen: Hillston, Barellan, Hay, Gollgowi, Rankin Springs, Deniliquin.

Group Eighteen: Old Boys, Tweed Head Seagulls, South Murwillumbah, Byron Bay, Mullumbimby, Brothers, Cudgen, Bimambil.

Group Nineteen: Belconnen United, Lakes United, South Woden, Tuggerannong United, South Canberra, East Canberra.

Group Twenty: Leeton, Griffith, Griffith Waratahs, Yanco-Wamoon, Narrandera, Darlington Point, Coleambally, Yenda, Lakes United, West Wyalong.

Group Twenty-one: Scone, Singleton, Quirindi, Denmah, Muswellbrook, Merriwa.

Illawarra League: Thirroul, Port Kembla, Helensburgh, Collegians, Wollongong, Dapto, Corrimal.

Newcastle League: First Division: Western Suburbs, Macquarie United, Cessnock, South Newcastle, Kurri-Kurri, Maitland, Northern Suburbs, Central Charlestown Lakes United, Waratah-Mayfield. Second Division: " A " Grade: Cardiff, Beresfield, Hexham, Raymond Terrace, Swansea, West United, South Lakes, University Windale, Wallsend. " B " Grade: Wangi, Shortland, Nelson Bay, West Wallsend, Belmonth, South Newcastle, Lambton-Jesmond, Stockton, Karuah, Kotara, Gateshead.

Country Rugby League is a world on its own. Competition is fierce and many of their players have gone to reach international status via the Sydney Premiership. The top country League competition is the Caltex Cup. It is run on two levels, the first, which is called the Caltex Divisional Cup, and the second, a pre-season competition, which is known as the secondary Caltex Cup. For the main competition, the divisional, the Newcastle and Illawarra Leagues field teams against six other divisions, North Coast, Northern, Western, Southern, Riverina and Monaro.

Sydney Metropolitan League (previously known as Second Division)

This secondary competition in Sydney assumed a position of some importance in Rugby League but it had a comparatively short life. It was founded in 1963 as the Inter Districts Competition and, in 1964, changed its name to the Second Division. During the early part of the 1970s the League made a third change of name to become the Sydney Metropolitan League, but even this could not give security for in 1976 it folded up.

Its clubs were distributed throughout the New South Wales Country League system but, during 1978, there were rumours that the competition would be reformed under the banner of Second Division. Before it disappeared a number of famous clubs Wentworthville, for many years the home of former Leeds star Lewis Jones, University of New South Wales, Sydney University, Ryde, Northern Districts, Blacktown and others, played in the League.

Queensland

Although Rugby League was played in the northern state after 1907 it took them until 1922 to beat New South Wales in an inter-state match 25-9 and, at first, their main competition was the three-way Bulimba Cup. Today the Queensland Rugby League is made up of six major leagues, Brisbane, Ipswich, Toowoomba Wide Bay, Central Queensland and the North Queensland.

The North Queensland competition encompasses most of the State's larger towns and it has grown considerably since its inception in 1948. The championship is called the Foley Shield and the winners have included Babinda, Townsville, Ayr, Herbert River, Cairns, Mackay, Innisfail, Eacham, Tully and Mount Isa. The shield final is played in Townsville each September, approximately one week before the Brisbane Grand Final.

1972 saw the end of the Bulimba Cup. Toowoomba won it first in 1925 and since then Brisbane have had the most wins with 19, Toowoomba 16 and Ipswich 11. It was replaced by the Carlton Cup and it involves another three-way split Toowoomba, Ipswich and Wide Bay.

The Queensland League's trial series which they use to pick their representative teams have changed considerably over the years. They have taken the form of City v. Country, Queensland v the Rest with a Possibles v. Probables follow up and then they were run on the same basis as New South Wales with Country I and II v. City I and II.

Today's trials start with qualifying matches in the country. From them emerge a team which is called Combined Country which faces a team selected from the Brisbane clubs.

The Brisbane League is made up of eight clubs, Norths, Souths, Easts, Wests, Valleys, Brothers, Wynnum and Redcliffe. But, in spite of all these selection methods, Queensland have never been able to match up to New South Wales for long in the inter-state matches. In the early 1970s a state coaching programme was instituted. This did not achieve the desired results and in 1978 the programme was changed with the appointment of a state coaching director and panel. The first man appointed to the post was Barry Muir the state coach, 1974-78.

Northern Territory

Historically the progress of Rugby League in Northern Territory can be divided into two periods: 1950-1974 and 1974 to present day. The divisive factor was a meterological disaster called "Cyclone Tracy"!

In 1956 the State League staged its first inter-state trip to Western Australia, they played matches against the French touring team at Darwin in 1960 and 1964 and Great Britain in 1966, 1970 and 1974. Between 1970 and 1974 Darwin played host to sides from North Queensland, Papua-New Guinea and Sydney's Parramatta Club.

A regular inter-state visit started with Western Australia in 1969 and, in the four subsequent years, nine matches were played with six wins to Western Australia.

Just prior to "Tracy" the Northern Territory League acquired its own floodlit ground, Richardson Park. But "Tracy" set Rugby League back years and in 1978 the League was just beginning to recover. The hurricane devastated Darwin and most of the players left. Those who did return were too busy with the rebuilding programme to devote their time to Rugby League. Finance was also a problem as all available sources were being channelled into rebuilding.

There are signs that a recovery is being made. The State entered the Pacific Cup competition in 1975 and 1977, and their performances in the cup have demonstrated that there is hope for the future.

Northern Territory are trying to re-establish what was once a thriving junior scene and they are confident that is the key to more success. Presently Rugby League is played in five centres in Northern Territory, Darwin, Gove, Katherine, Tennat Creek and Alice Springs.

The considerable distances involved in Australian sport can be appreciated in Northern Territory where one team, Katherine who field a side in the Darwin Reserve grade, travel 420 miles each week for their game.

Darwin has four first grade clubs and an established centre at Richardson Park.

Western Australia

In 1948 four Rugby Union clubs decided to change their loyalties and Rugby League was born in Western Australia. Their switch proved very successful and they were followed by more (if you'll pardon the expression) conversions. By 1957 the League had grown to such an extent that the French touring side visited the League.

Belmont Oval was Perth's major ground until 1975 when a change in the local government administration resulted in a local soccer club taking over the ground. In 1976 activities were switched to a new ground, Wilson Park, the home of Victoria Park-Cannington club. This ground had limited spectator facilities and, in 1977, the Western Australian Rugby League moved yet again, this time to Cannington Central, a million-dollar greyhound stadium. Here they even have their closed circuit television service at the ground and on Saturday evenings the 8,000 to 10,000 greyhound crowds can see rival coaches interviewed about Sunday's matches.

Western Australia were one of the original members of the Pacific Cup competition and as 1979 is the 150th anniversary of the Western Australian state, the League are due to act as hosts if the competition continues following the heavy financial losses in New Zealand in 1977.

Junior Rugby in Western Australia started in 1975 and in 1977 the League's 16-year-olds side went to New Zealand at the same time as the professional World Cup series and achieved great success against Kiwi junior sides.

Four new clubs joined the Western Australia League in 1976 and there are now eight clubs in their first grade competition. The League has become so popular that a recent survey revealed a " participation growth " of 95 per cent. It has also established its own permanent headquarters and full-time secretary.

Besides being played in Perth, Rugby League has other centres in Western Australia, the Goldfields area Kalgoorlie, Boulder, Kambalda, and Norsman; the Pilbarra area, Karratha and Dampier and, the newest added in 1978, at Newman, Tom Price and Port Hedland.

South Australia
Although Rugby League was played in South Australia in the early 1950s, it existed on a " social match " basis until 1 Feb. 1976 when there was a public meeting at the State Government Administration Theatre, Adelaide. The meeting gave the go-ahead for the re-introduction of RL on an organised basis and almost 200 attended the first trial matches on 22 Feb. at Railway Oval, Adelaide.

The Australian Rugby League promised their support, and, despite a limited budget of approximately £30, organised Rugby League fought its way back into the state. Six district clubs were formed: North Adelaide (now Northern Districts) Norwood, South Adelaide, Port Adelaide, Glenelg and Central Districts and, in 1976, all the matches were played at West Beach Reserve. The pre-season competition was won by South Adelaide but they were beaten 19-18 in the first grand final by Central Districts.

In ti.:ir first reconstituted season the League played representative matches

against Broken Hill, Victoria and Whyalla (twice). They won one of the matches against Whyalla, but lost the others.

In 1977 home-and-away matches were re-established at suburban centres although the Central Beach site was still used for a double-header (two matches) match-of-the-day. These games, together with some exhibition matches, helped popularise the game in Adelaide again.

As well as gaining spectator support, Rugby League in Adelaide has attracted players from Rugby Union and Australian Rules football. Although the relationship with Rugby Union remains the same, League enjoys friendly relations with both soccer and Rules organisations and have, in fact, used their facilities for representative games.

Standards clearly improved for in 1977 the South Australians beat Broken Hill and were narrowly beaten by Victoria and Northern Territory. Establishing the junior game became a priority and in 1977 a Sunday morning league was established for the youngsters and they undertook representative games against Whyalla and a visiting Sydney team.

By 1978 the League had added two more clubs Southern Vale, (a southern Adelaide area) and Tea Tree Gully (an outer Adelaide district). The League obtained the lease of Sturt Baseball Ground and they still stage the " match of the day " at headquarters together with a home-and-away programme.

In June 1978 Mr Peter Corcoran, the Rothmans Australian Rugby League coaching director, visited South Australia to institute the formation of a state coaching panel.

More success on the field came South Australia's way when they beat Victoria and Broken Hill in 1978 and this progress is reflected by the sport becoming one of the States most important sports.

Victoria
Club competition existed in Victoria in the 1920s and a famous Australian administrator Harry Sunderland was involved. But the competition suffered because the Victorians were " Aussies Rules mad, " and it never got beyond a " social stage " game. It was revived in the 1940s and it reached peak in the early 1950s with several well established clubs, Moorabbin, Preston, Ballarat and Bendigo. The year 1955 turned out to be a critical one, and after the

League's team was involved in several unsavoury incidents with the French touring team in front of a crowd of 3,000 at Punt Road Oval, Melbourne, the game declined seriously. By the 1960s the competition was reduced to district club Moorabbin, several RAAF sides at Port Cook, Waverton and Tottenham and one or two ethnic sides, for example, the Kia Toa Maori club. By 1976 there were just three teams left playing Rugby League in Melbourne. This serious decline prompted the Victorian Rugby League to re-organise the competition on district lines with games on a home and away basis.

In the two years since then the League has built up to six clubs with ten teams. Boys are being coached in the outer high schools and it is hoped that 1979 will bring a junior competition. Australian National coaching director Corcoran has helped the Victorian League establish a coaching panel and Australian Rugby League Authorities believe this will be the key to Victoria's future in the game.

The Victorian League was able to hold its Grand Finals matches at Melbourne's top ground, Olympic Park, and it is hoped that the State side will be admitted to the Amco Cup during 1979. They competed in the Pacific Cup in New Zealand during 1977 and were beaten by eventual finalists Western Australia.

During 1978 two top Sydney clubs, Western Suburbs and Manly-Warringah, played an exhibition game at St Kilda Victorian Football ground and the code benefited from the exposure the game received.

Administration

Rugby League in Australia is overseen by the Australian Rugby League. The League, originally formed as the Board of Control, was instituted in 1954 and it is responsible for organising tours to and from Australia, referees for Test matches, captains and vice-captains of Australian Test teams and is the game's final authority in the country. Three of its members come from New South Wales, three from Queensland. It must have a president from New South Wales with a casting vote in case of deadlock.

The New South Wales League, Australia's biggest and most important State League, is made up of 41 delegates, two each from the Sydney first-grade clubs, ten vice-presidents (all former club officials), a president, four from the Country League

and two from the Referees' Association.

Referees are appointed on a week-by-week basis following reports on their displays in the previous weekend matches. The Referees' Board, which chooses the referees, is made up of four former referees, plus a chairman from the League general committee, who must have passed a referees' examination.

Regional Rugby Leagues Association:

To look after the interests of the States not represented on the Australian Rugby League (see Administration) the Regional Rugby Leagues Association was loosely formed at a meeting in Perth in 1976.

The Association was formally organised at a second meeting, this time held in Adelaide, during 1977. Mr Frank Geddes was installed as chairman, Mr Ian Carnachan as secretary, and its headquarters were established in Subiaco, Perth, Western Australia.

As yet formal recognition has not been granted by the Australian Rugby League. The Australian Association's long-term aims are to gain recognition and aid from the Australian Rugby League and to establish voting power on the national body.

Coaching

Coaching has been vital to Australian Rugby League, particularly in the last two decades. The modern scheme had its beginnings when former Kangaroo captain Dave Brown was given the job of assisting schools coaches in 1961 and, like Topsy, the scheme just grew. Today, New South Wales Rugby Football Leagues scheme is the best in Australia. Their coaches have spread their net to American and European centres seeking new ideas which would benefit Rugby League, especially in the fields of physical fitness, sports medicine and a greater knowledge of coaching psychology. The scheme is under the control of a National director, Peter Corcoran and its aim will be to place every piece of available information about modern coaching before all the code's coaches senior, junior and schools.

Each State is being encouraged to set up its own coaching panel and coach directorships. New South Wales and Queensland are leading the field as they do at the top level in the game and other States are already in the process of setting up their schemes.

Players and Officials

A separate book is really needed to talk about the great Australian players but here are a selection who have made a mark on World Rugby League either in Test football, with Australian clubs or by playing in Britain.

H. H. Messenger, better known as "Dally" or "the Master", was among the first Australian Northern Union players and even today, 70 years later, his name and memory are still cherished. He learned to kick barefooted and is reputed to have been able to land goals from the half-way line.

Before the Second World War *Dave Brown* from the mighty Eastern Suburbs club in Sydney was the King. Besides being Australian captain he established two individual records that still stand today—45 points in one game in 1935 and also in 1935 the most tries in a first grade season—38. He rightly earned his nickname as "the Don Bradman of Rugby League". He also played with Warrington between 1936 and 1938.

Albert Rosenfeld was one of the first Australian tourists to arrive in Britain and he stayed with Huddersfield to set a try-scoring record, 80 in one season, that still stands. In England the golden period for Australians playing with English clubs was in the post-Second World War years when such players as forwards *Harry Bath* (Barrow and Warrington) and *Arthur Clues* (Leeds) were at their best.

Huddersfield's great team of the 1950s contained three outstanding Australian players in *Lionel Cooper, Pat Devery* and *Johnny Hunter*. Ironically one of the best of them all, *Brian Bevan*, was never properly seen in his native country. The bald, bandy winger was with Eastern Suburbs for a short while and after the outbreak of war joined the Navy. After the war he went to England and was signed by Warrington where he was an outstanding success.

To stop the drain of Australian players leaving the country a ban was instituted. This prevented such magnificent players as full-back *Clive Churchill*, who was nicknamed the "little master", playing British club football despite some massive offers.

A similar case was that of the prince of centres, *Reg Gasnier*, who it was confidently expected would have realised £25,000 from British clubs.

The mighty St. George team that won 11 First grade Sydney premierships in the late 1950s and early 1960s had a galaxy of stars in their sides, second-row *Norm Provan*, who played in 10 of those 11 Grand Finals, *Johnny Raper*, Gasnier, *Graeme Langlands* and *Ian Walsh*, who skippered Australia.

Today there are a host of Australian stars, prop *Artie Beetson*, who after a short spell with England's Hull KR became one of the all-time greats, English-born stand-off half *Bobby Fulton*, star of the 1973 and 1978 tours of Great Britain, and his scrum-half partner *Tom Raudonikis*.

Of the top officials from Australia probably best remembered is *Harry Sunderland*. A magnificent organiser, he started his career in Queensland and then moved to Britain where he was a respected radio commentator. He died in 1964, but is remembered with a trophy named after him for the man-of-the-match award in the English end-of-season premiership competition. The award is sponsored by the Rugby League Writer's Association.

Other top men were *Harry Flegg, S. George Ball, John Quinland* and *Bill Buckley*. Today the Australians have such giants as Australian Rugby League president *Kevin Humphries*, a former Balmain prop, and Senator *Ron McAuliffe* from Queensland, the Australian Rugby League vice-chairman.

AUSTRALIAN ROLL OF HONOUR

Sydney—First Grade Premierships

Year	Winners	Runners-up
1908	South Sydney	Eastern Suburbs
1909	South Sydney	Balmain
1910	Newtown	South Sydney
1911	Eastern Suburbs	Glebe
1912	Eastern Suburbs	Glebe
1913	Eastern Suburbs	Newtown

Year	Winners	Runners-up
1914	South Sydney	Newtown
1915	Balmain	Glebe
1916	Balmain	South Sydney
1917	Balmain	South Sydney
1918	South Sydney	Western Suburbs
1919	Balmain	Eastern Suburbs
1920	Balmain	South Sydney
1921	North Sydney	Eastern Suburbs
1922	North Sydney	Glebe
1923	Eastern Suburbs	South Sydney
1924	Balmain	South Sydney
1925	South Sydney	Western Suburbs
1926	South Sydney	University
1927	South Sydney	St George
1928	South Sydney	Eastern Suburbs
1929	South Sydney	Newtown
1930	Western Suburbs	St George
1931	South Sydney	Eastern Suburbs
1932	South Sydney	Western Suburbs
1933	Newtown	St George
1934	Western Suburbs	Eastern Suburbs
1935	Eastern Suburbs	South Sydney
1936	Eastern Suburbs	Balmain
1937	Eastern Suburbs	South Sydney and St George
1938	Canterbury-Bankstown	Eastern Suburbs
1939	Balmain	South Sydney
1940	Eastern Suburbs	Canterbury-Bankstown
1941	St George	Eastern Suburbs
1942	Canterbury-Bankstown	St George
1943	Newtown	North Sydney
1944	Balmain	Newtown
1945	Eastern Suburbs	Balmain
1946	Balmain	St George
1947	Balmain	Canterbury-Bankstown
1948	Western Suburbs	Balmain
1949	St George	South Sydney
1950	South Sydney	Western Suburbs
1951	South Sydney	Manly-Warringah
1952	Western Suburbs	South Sydney
1953	South Sydney	St George
1954	South Sydney	Newtown
1955	South Sydney	Newtown
1956	St George	Balmain
1957	St George	Manly-Warringah
1958	St George	Western Suburbs
1959	St George	Manly-Warringah
1960	St George	Eastern Suburbs
1961	St George	Western Suburbs
1962	St George	Western Suburbs
1963	St George	Western Suburbs
1964	St George	Balmain
1965	St George	South Sydney
1966	St George	Balmain
1967	South Sydney	Canterbury-Bankstown
1968	South Sydney	Manly-Warringah
1969	Balmain	South Sydney
1970	South Sydney	Manly-Warringah
1971	South Sydney	St George
1972	Manly-Warringah	Eastern Suburbs

Year	Winners	Runners-up
1973	Manly-Warringah	Cronulla-Sutherland
1974	Eastern Suburbs	Canterbury-Bankstown
1975	Eastern Suburbs	St George
1976	Manly-Warringah	Parramatta
1977	St George	Parramatta
1978	Manly-Warringah	Cronulla-Sutherland
1979		

Reserve Grade
Balmain: 1915-16-28-30-33-41-44-46-50-57-58-65-67
Canterbury-Bankstown: 1939-71-72
Cronulla-Sutherland: nil
Eastern Suburbs: 1908-09-10-11-35-37-49
Glebe: 1912-18-19-20-21
Manly-Warringah: 1954-60-69-73
Newtown: 1922-47-48-51-70-74
North Sydney: 1940-42-55-59
Parramatta: 1975-77
Penrith: nil
South Sydney: 1913-14-17-23-24-25-26-27-29-31-32-34-43-45-52-53-56-66-68
St George: 1938-62-63-64-76
Western Suburbs: 1936-61

Under-23 Grade (1908-1972 known as third grade)
Balmain: 1915-16-19-26-34-48-50-54-55-56-60-68-73
Canterbury-Bankstown: 1971
Cronulla-Sutherland: 1975
Eastern Suburbs: 1914-17-24-29-30-31-32-41-47-70-76
Glebe: 1927
Manly-Warringah: 1952
Newtown: 1920-35-43
North Sydney: 1937-45-46-59
Parramatta: 1964
Penrith: 1978
South Sydney: 1908-12-18-25-28-33-62-69
St George: 1940-42-49-51-53-57-63-65-66-72-74
Western Suburbs: 1936-38-39-44-58-61-67-77
Other winners were: Kensington 1923;

Leichhardt 1911; Mascot 1921-22; Sydney 1910; and South Sydney Federal 1909-13

Wills Cup (Pre-season Competition)

1962	Canterbury-Bankstown
1963	St George
1964	St George
1965	St George
1966	South Sydney
1967	Penrith
1968	Balmain
1969	South Sydney
1970	Canterbury-Bankstown
1971	St George
1972	South Sydney
1973	Newtown
1974	Eastern Suburbs
1975	Parramatta
1976	Balmain
1977	Eastern Suburbs
1978	South Sydney

Club champions
(Decided after considering all the performances throughout the Sydney grades)
Balmain: 1941-43-44-47-50
Canterbury-Bankstown: 1938-39
Cronulla-Sutherland: nil
Eastern Suburbs: 1930-31-34-35-36-37-45-70-74-75
Manly-Warringah: 1972
Newtown: 1973
North Sydney: nil
Parramatta: 1976-77-78
Penrith: nil
South Sydney: 1932-33-52-53-54-67-68-69
St George: 1940-42-46-49-51-55-56-57-58-59-62-63-64-65-66-71
Western Suburbs: 1948-60-61

Brisbane Premiership
Until 1922 when the Brisbane League was formed the competition was open to a greater number of Queensland clubs. The winners of the premiership have been:

1909	Valleys	1914	Valleys
1910	Ipswich	1915	Valleys
1911	Valleys-Toombul	1916	Western Suburbs
1912	Natives	1917	Valleys
1913	West End	1918	Valleys

1919	Valleys	1950	Easts
1920	Wests	1951	Souths
1921	Carltons	1952	Wests
1922	Wests	1953	Souths
1923	Coorparoo	1954	Wests
1924	Valleys	1955	Valleys
1925	Carltons	1956	Brothers
1926	Brothers	1957	Valleys
1927	Grammars	1958	Brothers
1928	University	1959	Norths
1929	University	1960	Norths
1930	Carltons	1961	Norths
1931	Valleys	1962	Norths
1932	Wests	1963	Norths
1933	Valleys	1964	Norths
1934	Norths	1965	Redcliffe
1935	Brothers	1966	Norths
1936	Wests	1967	Brothers
1937	Valleys	1968	Brothers
1938	Norths	1969	Norths
1939	Brothers	1970	Valleys
1940	Norths	1971	Valleys
1941	Valleys	1972	Easts
1942	Brothers*	1973	Valleys
1943	Brothers*	1974	Valleys
1944	Valleys*	1975	Wests
1945	Souths	1976	Wests
1946	Valleys	1977	Easts
1947	Easts	1978	
1948	Wests	1979	
1949	Souths		

* Designated " Victory Cup " during War years.

Australian Records

Sydney Premiership
Most premiership wins:
First grade: 20 South Sydney
Reserve Grade: 19 South Sydney
Third or Under 23 Grade: 13 Balmain
Most tries in a season: 38 D. Brown
Eastern Suburbs) 1935
Most goals in a season: 131 (112 placed 19
drop) E. Simms (South Sydney) 1969
Most Individual points in a season: 265
E. Simms (South Sydney) 1969
Most Individual points in one game: 45 D.
Brown (Eastern Suburbs) 1935

National Record Attendance and Receipts
1965 Grand Final St George v South
Sydney drew 78,056 people who paid
$30,679.09A.

Australian Test Records
Most individual points v. Great Britain:
104 G. Langlands, 6 tries 43 goals
Most Test appearances v. Great Britain:
14 Keith Holman

Sydney Cricket Ground Attendance Records
Australia v. New Zealand: 56,376 in 1952
Australia v. France: 67,748 in 1955
New South Wales v. France: 50,488 in 1955
New South Wales v. New Zealand: 49, 960
in 1963
New South Wales v. Queensland: 56,487 in
1927
City v. Country: 52,366 in 1946

Inter-State (N.S.W. v. Queensland)
Queensland's first win over N.S.W.: 25-9 in
1922
New South Wales' biggest win: 69-5 in 1957
Queensland's biggest win over N.S.W.: 38-
0 in 1926
Most tries for N.S.W. over Queensland: 6
S. Goodwin
Most Goals for N.S.W. against Queens-
land: 15 G. Harwick
Most points for N.S.W. against Queens-
land: 32 H. H. Messenger.

Amco Cup
Rugby League's richest prize, in finan-

cial terms, is not, surprisingly, the British Challenge Cup or the Sydney Premiership but an Australian television inspired floodlit tournament, the Amco Cup.

Inaugurated in 1974 the competition is very similar to the British BBC 2 Floodlit Tournament but it is run on a much wider geographic scale with teams from Sydney, Brisbane, the New South Wales Country League, Northern Territory, Western Australia and New Zealand competing.

A massive prize of 225,000A dollars was the incentive in 1977 and at the time of writing, plans were reported to increase it to 250,000A dollars. Besides the cash incentives for the clubs, prizes such as cars, boats and trips to Europe have been offered for various types of individual performances.

In the 1977 campaign the following teams were entered: Auckland (New Zealand), Balmain (Sydney), Brothers (Brisbane), Canterbury-Bankstown (Sydney), Canterbury (New Zealand), Central Queensland, Cronulla-Sutherland (Sydney), Eastern Suburbs (Sydney), Eastern Suburbs (Brisbane), Illawarra (New South Wales), Ipswich (Queensland), Manly-Warringah (Sydney), Monaro (New South Wales), Newcastle (New South Wales). Newtown (Sydney), North Coast (New South Wales), North Liverpool (New South Wales), North Sydney, North Queensland Northern Territory, Northern Division (New South Wales), Penrith (Sydney), Parramatta (Sydney), Redcliffe (Brisbane), Riverina (New South Wales), St George (Sydney), South Sydney, Southern Suburbs (Brisbane), Southern Division (New South Wales), Toowoomba (Queensland), Valleys (Brisbane), Western Australia, Western Suburbs (Sydney), Wide Bay (North Queensland) Wynnun (Brisbane).

So far the Amco Cup roll of honour is: 1974 Western Division; 1975 Eastern Suburbs; 1976 Balmain; 1977 Western Suburbs; 1978 Eastern Suburbs.

The competition is still expanding with the 1979 series including entries from Wellington (New Zealand) and Gold Coast (New South Wales). The tournament has grown considerably since 1974 when 21 teams fought it out for 15,000 dollars. Papua-New Guinea are known to be interested in entering the event but they are not being encouraged because of the huge increase in travelling costs that have been estimated.

Amco Shield

The Amco Shield, which is sponsored by the same company as the Amco Cup for senior RL teams, is for well-coached school and college teams. Much new talent has been unearthed by the competition which rivals the senior tournament in appeal.

Since it was first played for in 1975 the winners have been Patrician Bros High School, Fairfield, New South Wales; 1976 Blacktown Senior High School, New South Wales; 1977 Ashcroft High School; and 1978 Patrician Bros High School.

Australian Tour Teams to England and France

1908-9

D. Lutge (capt.), H. H. Messenger (vice-capt.), T. Anderson, J. Abercrombie, A. Anlezark, L. Bailey, M. Bolewski, A. Burdon, A. Butler, W. A. Cann, F. B. Cheadle, E. Courtney, A. Conlon, J. Davis, S. Deane, J. Devereaux, A. Dobbs, J. Fihelly, R. Graves, A. Halloway, W. Hardcastle, C. Hedley, W. Heidke, A. S. Hennessy, L. Jones, T. McCabe, P. Moir, A. Morton, W. S. Noble, L. O'Malley, S. Pearce, A. A. Rosenfeld, J. Rosewell, P. Walsh.

Tour manager: J. J. Giltinan.
Played 46, Won 18, Lost 22, Drawn 6, Pts for 568, Pts against 477.

1911-12

C. McKivat (capt.), T. Berecry, A. Broomham, P. Burge, W. A. Cann, E. Courtney, R. Craig, S. Darmody, V. Farnsworth, W. Farnsworth, A. R. Francis, C. Fraser, D. Frawley, H. Gilbert, G. Gillett, H. Hallett, A. Halloway, P. A. McCue, J. Murray, C. McMurtie, W. Neill, W. Noble, C. Russell, C. Savory, R. Stuart, C. Sullivan, R. Williams, F. Woodward.

Tour managers: J. Quinlan and C. Ford.
Played 36, Won 29, Lost 5, Drawn 2, Pts for 673, Pts against 287.

1921-22

L. Cubbitt (capt.), C. Blinkhorn, N. Broadfoot, E. S. Brown, F. Burge, H. Caples, G. Carstairs, J. Craig, C. Fraser, B. Gray, H. Horder, J. C. Ives, A. Johnson, B. Laing, R. Latta, E. McGrath, R. Norman, S. Pearce, H. Peters, N. Potter, C. Prentice, W. Richards, F. Ryan, W. Schultz, D. Thompson, R. Townsend, J. Watkins, R. Vest.

Tour managers: G. Ball and W. A. Cann.
Played 36, Won 27, Lost 9, Pts for 763, Pts against 253.

1929-30

T. Gorman (capt.), V. Armbruster, G. Bishop, W. Brogan, J. Busch, A. Edwards, C. Fifield, H. Finch, A. Henderson, J. Holmes, A. Justice, H. Kadwell, J. Kingston, F. Laws, P. Madsen, P. Maher, F. McMillan, D. Dempsey, W. Prigg, A. Ridley, E. Root, L. Sellars, W. Shankland, W. Spencer, H. Steinohrt, G. Treweeke, J. Upton, E. Weissel.
Tour managers: H. Sunderland and J. L. Dargan.
Played 35, Won 24, Lost 9, Drawn 2, Pts for 708, Pts against 347.

1933-34

F. McMillan (capt.), D. Brown, F. Curran, D. Dempsey, H. Denney, F. Dooner, J. Doyle, A. Folwell, F. Gardner, J. Gibbs, F. Gilbert, M. Glasheen, V. Hey, F. Laws, J. Little, M. Madsen, L. Mead, F. Neumann, F. O'Connor, C. Pearce, S. Pearce, W. Prigg, A. Ridley, V. Thicknesse, W. Smith, R. Stehr, J. Why. (Ray Morris, a centre three-quarter died from an ear infection in a Malta hospital while on the way to England with the touring team.)
Managers: J. Sunderland and W. Webb.
Played 37, Won 27, Lost 10, Pts for 754, Pts against 295 (One game placed in France.)

1937-38

W. Prigg (capt.), J. Rearden (vice-capt.), J. Beaton, E. Collines, F. Curran, L. Dawson, P. Fairall, J. Gibbs, F. Gilbert, F. Griffiths, C. Hazelton, L. Heidke, E. Lewis, G. MacLennan, R. McKinnon, D. McLean, H. Narvo, F. Nolan, E. Norman, A. Norval, J. Pearce, H. Pierce, H. Robison, R. Stehr, R. Thompson, L. Ward, G. Whittle, B. Williams, P. Williams, (J. Pearce broke a leg on the journey to England and H. Narvo was sent as a replacement.)
Tour managers: H. Sunderland and R. E. Savage.
Played 34, Won 21, Lost 12, Drawn 1, Pts for 534, Pts against 309.

1948-49

C. Maxwell (capt.), W. Tyquin (vice-capt.), F. de Belin, I. Benton, E. Brosnan, V. Bulgin, C. Churchill, L. Cowie, R. Dimond, K. Froome, A. Gibbs, J. Graves, D. Hall, N. Hand, J. Hawke, J. Holland, B. Hopkins, J. Horrigan, F. Johnson, R. Lulham, P. McMahon, D. McRitchie, N. Mulligan, W. O'Connell, L. Pegg, J. Rayner, K. Schubert, W. Thompson.

Tour managers: W. G. Buckley and E. J. Simmonds.
Played 37, Won 24, Lost 13, Pts for 627, Pts against 346.

1952-53

C. Churchill (capt.), D. Hall (vice-capt.), F. Ashton, R. Bull, B. Carlson, A. Collinson, H. Crocker, B. Davies, C. Donohoe, R. Duncan, D. Flannery, C. Geelan, C. Gill, G. Hawick, N. Hazzard, K. Holman, K. Kearney, K. McCaffery, D. McGovern, A. Paul, N. Pidding, J. Rooney, T. Ryan, K. Schubert, F. Stanmore, T. Tyrrell, H. Wells, R. Willey.
Tour managers: D. B. McLean and N. Robinson.
Played 40, Won 33, Lost 6, Drawn 1, Pts for 1,117, Pts against 373.

1956-57

K. Kearney (capt.), C. Churchill (vice-capt.), D. Adams, R. Banks, R. Bull, G. Clifford, G. Connell, B. Davies, L. Doyle, D. Flannery, D. Furner, E. Hammerton, K. Holman, I. Johnston, W. Marsh, D. McGovern, I. Moir, K. O'Brien, B. Orrock, K. O'Shea, T. Payne, R. Poole, N. Provan, B. Purcell, T. Tyquin, A. Watson.
Tour managers: C. W. Fahy and C. J. Connell.
Played 28, Won 18, Lost 9, Drawn 1, Pts for 542, Pts against 406.

1959-60

K. Barnes (capt.), R. Mossop (vice-capt.), D. Beattie, R. Boden, A. Brown, R. Budgen, P. Burke, B. Carlson, D. Chapman, B. Clay, W. Delamare, R. Gasnier, B. Hambly, K. Irvine, N. Kelly, E. Lumsden, B. Muir, G. Parcell, D. Parish, J. Paterson, J. Raper, E. Rasmussen, J. Riley, I. Walsh, H. Wells, W. Wilson.
Tour managers: J. N. Argent and E. F. Keefer.
Coach: C. Churchill.
Played 37, Won 26, Lost 11, Pts for 876, Pts against 547 (Two games played in Italy.)

1960 World Cup

K. Barnes (capt.), B. Muir (vice-capt.), D. Beattie, R. Boden, A. Brown, R. Budgen, B. Carlson, R. Gasnier, R. Hambly, K. Irvine, N. Kelly, L. Morgan, R. Mossop, G. Parcell, J. Raper, E. Rasmussen, W. Rayner, H. Wells.
Managers: J. O'Toole and P. Duggan.
Played 5, Won 3, Lost 2, Pts for 86, Pts against 64.

1963-64

A. Summons (capt.), I. Walsh (vice-capt.), J. Cleary, M. Cleary, K. Day, P. Dimond, P. Gallagher, R. Gasnier, J. Gleeson, R. Hambly, E. Harrison, K. Irvine, L. Johns, N. Kelly, G. Langlands, J. Lisle, B. Muir, P. Quinn, J. Raper, B. Rushworth, K. Ryan, K. Smyth, F. Stanton, K. Thornett, R. Thornett, G. Wilson.
Managers: J. E. Lynch and A. Sparkes.
Played 36, Won 28, Lost 7, Drawn 1, Pts for 707, Pts against 312.

1967-68

R. Gasnier (capt.), J. Raper (vice-capt.), A. Branson, R. Coote, N. Gallagher, P. Gallagher, J. Gleeson, K. Goldspink, J. Greaves, L. Hanigan, K. Irvine, L. Johns, K. Junee, N. Kelly, J. King, G. Langlands, R. Lynch, D. Manteit, J. McDonald, B. Moore, E. Rasmussen, R. Saddler, J. Sattler, W. Smith, A. Thompson, E. Walters.
Managers: J. Drewes and H. Schmidt.
Played 27, Won 16, Lost 9, Drawn 2, Pts for 398, Pts against 249.

1970 World Cup

R. Coote (capt.), R. Brannigan, J. Brown, J. Cootes, R. Costello, R. Fulton, M. Harris, R. McCarthy, B. McTaggart, J. O'Neill, R. O'Reilly, D. Pittard, P. Sait, E. Simms, W. Smith, G. Sullivan, R. Turner, E. Walters, L. Williamson.
Managers: K. R. Arthurson and J. Quinn.
Coach: H. Bath.
Played 4, Won 2, Lost 2, Pts for 51, Pts against 46.

1973-74

G. Langlands (capt.), A. Beetson, R. Brannigan, M. Cronin, G. Eadie, R. Fulton, E. Goodwin, W. Hamilton, J. Lang, R. McCarthy, K. Maddison, J. O'Neill, R. O'Reilly, W. Orr, T. Pickup, G. Pierce, T. Randall, T. Raudonikis S. Rogers, P. Sait, G. Starling, G. Stevens, D. Waite, E. Walters, D. Ward, L. Williamson.
Managers: A. L. Bishop and C. Gibson.
Played 16, Won 14, Lost 2, Pts for 364, Pts against 141.

1975 World Championship
(European section)

A. Beetson (capt.), G. Eadie, A. McMahon, M. Cronin, S. Rogers, I. Schubert, J. Peard, J. Mayers, G. Piggins, G. Veivers, T. Randall, R. Higgs, J. Quayle, J. Porter, I. Mackay, J. Rhodes, J. Brass, J. Lange.
Manager: R. Abbott.
Coach: G. Langlands.
Played 8, Won 7, Lost 1, Pts for 268, Pts against 51.

1978-79

R. Fulton (capt.), G. Pierce (vice-capt.), G. Eadie, A. McMahon, K. Boustead, L. Corowa, C. Anderson, I. Schubert, M. Cronin, S. Rogers, A. Thompson, S. Martin, J. Gibbs, T. Raudonikis, G. Oliphant, R. Price, R. Reddy, G. Olling, B. Walker, G. Gerard, S. Kneen, L. Boyd, R. Morris, C. Young, I. Thomson, G. Peponis, M. Krilich, R. Hilditch.
Managers: P. Moore and J. Caldwell.
Coach: F. Stanton.
Played 16, Won 13, Lost 3, Pts for 375, Pts against 117.

BARROW RLFC

Founded in 1878. Joined the Northern Union in 1897. Ground: Craven Park. Colours: Royal blue jersey, blue shorts.
RL Cup Winners, 1954-55.
Beaten Finalists, 1937-38, 1950-51, 1956-57, 1966-67.
Lancashire Cup Winners, 1954-55.
Beaten Finalists, 1937-38.
War League Championship Winners, 1917-18, 1918-1919.
Division Two Champions: 1975-76.
Club Records:
Attendance: 21,651 v. Salford (League) 15 Apr. 1938.
Goals: 135 by J. Ball, 1956-57.
Tries: 50 by J. Lewthwaite, 1956-57.
Points: 305 by I. Bell 1979-80.

BATLEY RLFC

Founded in 1880. Founder member of Northern Union. Ground: Mount Pleasant. Colours: Cerise and fawn hooped jerseys, cerise shorts.
RL Championship Winners, 1923-24.
RL Cup Winners, 1896-97, 1897-98, 1900-01.
Yorkshire League Winners, 1923-24.
Yorkshire Cup Winners, 1912-13.
Beaten Finalists, 1909-10, 1922-23, 1924-25, 1952-53.
Club Records:
Attendance: 23,989 v. Leeds (RL Cup) 14 Mar. 1925.
Goals: 120 by S. Thompson, 1958-59.
Tries: 29 by J. Tindall, 1912-13.
Points: 281 by J. Perry, 1950-51.

BBC2 FLOODLIT COMPETITION

Launched in 1965, the BBC2 Floodlit Competition has allowed Rugby League's stars to shine in midweek encounters which have attracted a television audience of millions.

Open to professional clubs with permanent floodlights, the tournament comprised of preliminary, first and second rounds, semi-final and final, the last tie being staged in early December.

Twelve of the matches were featured on BBC2. The traditional format was to screen " live " the second half of a match at 8.10 p.m. on a Tuesday evening. This pattern was changed in 1978 when edited highlights of the match were shown at 10.30 p.m., a switch which heralded a trebling of the television audience to three million viewers and a further 33% rise in "live" attendances.

Eight clubs took part in the first competition, the figure climbing to 22 clubs in recent years. The prize money has risen from £9,000 in 1965 to £30,000 in 1978. The Floodlit Final is always staged at the ground of one of the finalists, the venue being determined by a draw. Castleford dominated the mid-week tournament for the first three years, notching a memorable hat trick of victories over St Helens, Swinton and Leigh.

The 1973 campaign provided the stage for one of Rugby League's most romantic dramas—unfashionable Bramley's first cup success in a 94-year history. The Villagers fully deserved their first trophy since formation in 1879 by pulling off an against-the-odds victory at Widnes. The record-making win also created another Rugby League first, for the match was the only Floodlit Trophy Final to be played in daylight, because of a national power strike.

The traditional format was scrapped after the 1979-80 season because of the BBC financial cut-backs.

BBC2 Floodlit Trophy Finals
1965 St Helens 0, Castleford 4.
1966 Castleford 7, Swinton 2.
1967 Leigh 5, Castleford 8.
1968 Wigan 7, St Helens 4.
1969 Wigan 6, Leigh 11.
1970 Leeds 9, St Helens 5.
1971 St Helens 8, Rochdale Hornets 2.
1972 Leigh 5, Widnes 0 (at Wigan).
1973 Widnes 7, Bramley 15.
1974 Salford 0, Warrington 0.
Warrington 5, Salford 10.
1975 St Helens 22, Dewsbury 2.
1976 Leigh 4, Castleford 12.
1977 Hull Kingston Rovers 26, St Helens 11
1978 St Helens 7, Widnes 13.
1979 Hull 13, Hull Kingston Rovers 3.

BLACKPOOL BOROUGH RLFC

Founded 1954. Joined Northern Rugby League 1954. Ground: Borough Park. Colours: Tangerine jersey with black and white bands, white shorts.
Player's No. 6 Beaten Finalists: 1976-77.
Club Records:
Attendance: 7,614 v. Castleford (RL Cup Mar. 14, 1964. There was an attendance of 21,000 in an RL Cup-tie against Leigh on Blackpool AFC ground in 1957.
Goals: 89 by J. Maughan, 1958-59.
Tries: 22 by J. Johnson, 1970-71.
Points: 201 by P. Fearis, 1957-58.

BOTTOM FOURTEEN PLAY-OFF

Two-division football having been rejected for the second time in the game's history, the single division league structure was reintroduced for the 1964-65 season.

The traditional top four play-off to decide the Championship was replaced by a new-style top sixteen format. To compensate the lowly clubs, an unattractively named Bottom Fourteen Competition was introduced. Staged in April and May 1965, the tournament attracted an average gate of under 2,000 and was scrapped. The final, on a Tuesday evening, attracted 2,479 people, who saw Huddersfield beat Doncaster 13-3 at Tattersfield.

BRADFORD NORTHERN RLFC

Founded in 1907. Disbanded and reformed in 1964. Ground: Odsal Stadium. Colours: White jersey with red, amber and black hoops, white shorts.
Note: A Bradford club was formed in 1863 and became founder members of the Northern Union. In 1907 this club switched to Association Football and a new club, Bradford Northern, was formed.
Club records since 1907:
RL Cup Winners, 1943-44, 1946-47, 1948-49.
Beaten Finalists, 1944-45, 1947-48, 1972-73.
RL Championship beaten finalists, 1947-48, 1951-52.
Yorkshire League Winners, 1939-40, 1940-41, 1947-48.
Yorkshire Cup Winners: 1940-41, 1941-42, 1943-44, 1945-46, 1948-49, 1949-50, 1953-54, 1965-66, 1978-79.
Beaten Finalists, 1913-14.
Premiership Winners: 1977-78.

Beaten Finalists, 1978-79, 1979-80.
John Player Competition Winners: 1974-75, 1979-80.
Division One Champions: 1979-80.
Division Two Champions: 1973-74.
War-time Emergency League Championship winners: 1939-40, 1940-41.
Club Records:
Attendance: 102,569 Warrington v. Halifax (RL Cup Final replay) 5 May 1954.
Goals: 173 by E. Tees, 1971-72.
Tries: 63 by J. McLean, 1951-52.
Points: 364 by E. Tees, 1971-72.

BRAMLEY RLFC

Founded in 1879. Joined the Northern Union in 1896. Ground: McLaren Field. Amber jersey with black collar and black cuffs, black " V ", black shorts.
BBC2 Floodlit Trophy winners: 1973-74.
Club Records:
Attendance: 12,600 v. Leeds (League 7 May 1947)
Goals: 130 by J. Wilson, 1961-62.
Tries: 20 by A. Smith, 1972-73.
Points: 260 by J. Wilson, 1961-62.

BRITISH AMATEUR RUGBY LEAGUE ASSOCIATION

When it is realised that there are approximately 80,000 players and 350 clubs outside the professional game, it is surprising that it took until 1973 for the amateur game to establish its own identity.

Until that point the Rugby Football League had been responsible for the running of the amateur side of the sport and by 1973 the junior side of the game was declining at such an alarming rate that it was either going to die, or need serious surgery. While the Rugby Football League was still considering what action to take, a group of reformists, based in Huddersfield, decided to turn an idea for an amateur umbrella organisation into action. They called a meeting at Greenside Working Men's Club, Wakefield Road, Huddersfield on 4 Mar. 1973 and it gave birth to a new organisation called the British Amateur Rugby League Association which was to take over amateur affairs. This brought opposition from the Rugby Football League who refused to recognise the new organisation. Not all the amateur district Leagues agreed to join BARLA at first and, for a while, there was considerable turmoil.

There had been two previous phases of operation in the amateur game's administration. Until 1960-61 county committees had looked after the affairs of Lancashire and Yorkshire, while a county commission was responsible in Cumberland. This was changed so that all three counties were overlooked by five-men county commissions. The Commissioners, who were responsible for organising their county knockout cup and inter-town competitions, selecting county teams and acting as an appeal board to the district leagues, were appointed by the Rugby Football League.

That system, however, clearly did not work and the conditions were ripe for BARLA's take-over. Even though recognition was not granted by the Rugby Football League, the new amateur organisation pressed on with its own competitions and, in May 1974, Leigh Miners Welfare beat Latchford Albion (Warrington) in the first ever national Cup competition final.

BARLA's influence grew and a meeting was staged with the Rugby Football League in June 1974. It was from there that the British Amateur Rugby League was given official recognition as the governing body of their own game. This was followed, later in the summer, by recognition from the National Sports Council. Another important step forward was made in early 1975 when yet more recognition was afforded by the Central Council for Physical Recreation.

In March 1975 BARLA moved into international circuit by providing both Great Britain's youth and open age teams to face France. The French won both youth games, 20-0 at Villeneuve and 8-2 at Headingley, but the British carried the day at open age level 10-4 in France.

The next major stepping stone for BARLA was the appointment of their first full-time paid official, national administrator Maurice Oldroyd. He left his job in the Yorkshire textile industry to take over the post and it is hoped that he will be followed by another paid official within the next few years. The year was also notable for the establishment of an amateur Rugby League centre in Scotland.

Youth and Schoolboy Rugby was run under the guidance of an exiled Englishman Henry Callaghan at Hamilton near Glasgow. If 1976 had been a big year for the amateurs, then even more was to follow in 1977. In February a record crowd of 11,260 watched an amateur team, Pilkington Recs from St Helens, just lose to the professional Wigan team in the first round proper of the Challenge Cup. In May Blackpool's Borough Park was established as the permanent centre for the National Cup final and Cawoods (Hull) beat their Humberside rivals NDLB in the inaugural game at the seaside ground.

There were more important innovations when an amateur Rugby League coaching course was held at Carnegie College, Leeds, one of the foremost physical education establishments in Britain, in May and in June the first youth team to tour Australia and New Zealand was despatched.

Amateur Rugby League's growing importance was further recognised in June when five members of the Association R. R. Beal, T. E. Beautiman, J. A. Clayton, E. Hanson, and E. Houghton were awarded Queen's Silver Jubilee medals for their services to the game.

In time for the 1977-78 season the Minister for Sport, the Rt. Hon. Denis Howell MP, opened the Association's headquarters at Upperhead Row, Huddersfield, and after the official opening ceremony, a reception was given at the George Hotel, Huddersfield, the birthplace of the Rugby League code. The mood of optimism spread into October when National Cup winners Cawoods became the first amateur team to beat professionals in the John Player Cup. They beat Halifax 9-8 and were the first amateur club to reach the second round of a senior Rugby League competition at the expense of a professional club since 1909.

An unusual attempt to spread the game into the London area was started in March 1978 when a schoolboy seven-a-side tournament was staged by Stockwell Manor School at Herne Hill Stadium. Its importance to the League code can be judged by the fact that David Watkins, the Salford and Wales star, was on hand to present the prizes.

The biggest project undertaken by BARLA came later in 1978 with their open-age South Pacific tour of Papua-New Guinea, Australia and New Zealand (see " Amateur Tours " below).

Mr Tom Keaveney, of Huddersfield, who has been secretary to the Association since it was formed in 1973, was rewarded for his great service to the amateur game when he was given the MBE in the 1978 Queen's Birthday Honours List. The award, although to one man, seemed to set the seal of respectability on the organisation which had been born out of discontent.

Now the amateur game is firmly established. Its competitions attract interest throughout the Rugby League world and, gradually, it is expanding into areas which were not previously known for their interest in the sport, such as South Yorkshire. They are responsible for the running of all the amateur Rugby League functions such as the national coaching scheme, and the district leagues.

The English Schools Rugby League are members of BARLA but are completely responsible for the running of their own game. A similar situation also exists for the University and Colleges Rugby League.

ROLL OF HONOUR

National Cup

1973-74	Leigh Miners' Welfare 12; Latchford Albion (Warrington) 7
1974-75	Pilkington Recs (St Helens) 22; Mayfield (Rochdale) 4
1975-76	Ace Amateurs (Hull) 20; Ovenden (Halifax) 12
1976-77	Cawoods (West Hull) 10; NDLB (Hull) 3
1977-78	Milford (Leeds) 22; Leigh Miners' Welfare 13
1978-79	Pilkington Recs (St Helens) 9; West Hull 3

National Youth Cup

1973-74	Milford 49; Ince (Wigan) 0
1974-75	Blackbrook (St Helens) 13; Yew Tree (Leeds) 11
1975-76	Woolston Rovers (Warrington) 15; Askham (Barrow) 6
1976-77	Widnes Tigers 13; Wath Brow Hornets (Cumbria) 3
1977-78	Castleford Supporters 22; Widnes Tigers 19
1978-79	Hunslet (Leeds) 17; Saddleworth Rangers (Oldham) 1

National Inter-League Shield

1973-74	Hull 16; Copland 12
1974-75	Hull 20; Leeds 2
1975-76	Hull Works Association 10; Heavy Woollen 8
1976-77	Hull Works Assoc 22; St Helens 5
1977-78	Leigh 19; Kingston-upon-Hull and Humberside 11
1978-79	St Helens 15; Huddersfield 10

National Inter-League Youth Shield

1973-74	Leeds 17; St Helens 7
1974-75	Castleford 8; Leeds 3
1975-76	Cumberland 12; Warrington 11
1976-77	St Helens 12; Castleford 5
1977-78	Castleford 9; Doncaster 6
1978-79	Leeds 14; Warrington 4

National Seven-a-Side

	winners	*runners up*
1973-74	Hemsworth Miners' Welfare	Ace Amateurs (Hull)
1974-75	NDLB (Hull)	Salford University
1975-76	NDLB (Hull)	Queensbury (Bradford)
1976-77	Beecroft and Wightman (Hull)	Heworth (York)
1977-78	Lock Lane (Castleford)	Pilkington Recs (St Helens)

National Youth seven-a-side

	winners	*runners-up*
1973-74	Saddleworth Rangers (Oldham)	Wath Brow (Cumbria)
1974-75	Blackbrook (St Helens)	Dalton (Barrow)
1975-76	Featherstone Supporters	Villa YC (Hull)
1976-77	Wakefield Supporters	Widnes Tigers
1977-78	Wakefield Supporters	Corpus Christi (Leeds)

Lancashire-Cumbria Cup
1973-74   Pilkington Recs (St Helens) 23; Folly Lane (Swinton) 13
1974-75   Mayfield (Rochdale) 32; Woolston Rovers (Warrington) 2
1975-76   Leigh Miners' Welfare 20; Wath Brow Hornets (Cumbria) 4
1976-77   Pilkington Recs 17; Leigh Miners' Welfare 0
1977-78   Pilkington Recs 12; Latchford Albion (Warrington) 0

Lancashire-Cumbria Youth Cup
1973-74   Wath Brow Hornets (Cumbria) 24; Whelley (Wigan) 0
1974-75   Wath Brow Hornets 15; Whelley 6
1975-76   Blackbrook (St Helens) 24; Woolston Rovers 2
1976-77   Wath Brow Hornets 24; Widnes Tigers 14
1977-78   Saddleworth Rangers (Oldham) 11; Blackbrook 5

Yorkshire Cup
1973-74   West Hull 13; Illingworth (Halifax) 10
1974-75   Dewsbury Celtic 17; NDLB (Hull) 12
1975-76   Pointer Panthers (Castleford) 13; West Hull 16
1976-77   Beecroft and Wightman (Hull) 9; Dewsbury Celtic 6
1977-78   Dewsbury Celtic 13; NDLB 7

Yorkshire Youth Cup
1973-74   Milford (Leeds) 11; Concorde (Hull) 8
1974-75   Featherstone Supporters 19; Hunslet Supporters 9
1975-76   Hunslet Supporters 23; Corpus Christi (Leeds) 9
1976-77   Featherstone Supporters 20; Shaw Cross BC (Dewsbury) 0
1977-78   Hunslet Supporters 26; Corpus Christi 8

County Championship
1973-74   Cumbria
1974-75   Cumbria
1975-76   Yorkshire
1976-77   Lancashire
1977-78   Lancashire
1978-79   Yorkshire

County Youth Championship
1973-74   Yorkshire
1974-75   Lancashire
1975-76   Lancashire
1976-77   Lancashire
1977-78   Yorkshire
1978-79   Lancashire

Player of the Year
1975-76   R. Colgrave (Ace Amateurs, Hull)
1976-77   A. Varty (Broughton Red Rose, Cumbria)
1977-78   P. Dowling (Leigh Miners' Welfare)

Youth Player of the Year
1975-76   D. Heron (Hunslet Supporters)
1976-77   I. Rudd (Wath Brow Hornets, Cumbria)
1977-78   G. Jones (Widnes Tigers)

Amateur Internationals

One of the most popular events on the amateur Rugby League calendar is the annual international against the French. France has held the upper hand in these matches, but since the birth of the British Amateur Rugby League Association the British have started to make their presence felt.

The record of open-age internationals between the two countries is:

Year					Venue
1935	France	9	England	23	Paris
1936	England	16	France	8	Halifax
1937	France	12	England	2	Bordeaux
1938	England	11	France	15	Bradford
1939	France	13	England	3	Bordeaux
1947	France	45	England	5	Carcassonne
1948	England	2	France	5	Workington
1949	France	17	England	5	Avignon
1950	England	5	France	7	Leeds
1951	France	10	England	7	Rodez
1952	England	3	France	3	Broughton
1953	France	18	England	10	Perpignan
1954	England	23	France	0	Leeds
1955	France	15	England	12	Tarbes
1956	England	22	France	19	St Helens
1957	France	32	England	23	Tonneins
1958	England	14	France	24	Hull
1959	France	24	England	7	Villeneuve
1960	England	8	France	2	Hull
1961	France	3	England	11	Villefranche-de-Rouergue
1962	England	6	France	17	St Helens
1963	France	16	England	15	Roannè
1964	England	5	France	8	St Helens
1965	France	10	England	18	St Gaudens
1966	England	32	France	13	Warrington
1967	France	9	England	8	Tonneins
1968	England	4	France	5	Hull KR
1969	France	4	England	0	La Reole
1970	England	2	France	2	Salford
1971	France	17	England	8	Cahore
1972	England	22	France	2	Barrow
1973	France	21	England	12	Tonneins
1974	England	12	France	5	Barrow
1975	France	4	England	10	Lyons
1976	England	16	France	9	Salford
1977	France	14	England	5	Bastia, Corsica
1978	England	36	France	7	Workington
1979	France	9	Great Britain	13	Avignon

Youth Internationals

Youth internationals have been played at various stages in the amateur history between England and France. Records of the matches before 1973 are sketchy but the matches since then have been:

1974-75	France	21	Great Britain	0	Villeneuve
	Great Britain	2	France	8	Leeds
1975-76	France	16	Great Britain	9	Villeneuve
1976-77	Great Britain	9	France	5	Warrington
1977-78	France	36	Great Britain	4	Castelnaudary
1978-79	Great Britain	14	France	19	Castleford

Amateur Leagues

Before the formation of the British Amateur Rugby League Association in 1973 most amateur clubs played in leagues that were based on their own towns or immediate area and they were, in turn, responsible to the County Commissions. Although that system worked satisfactorily until the mid-1960s the change in sporting and social habits during the late 'sixties and early 'seventies left it in a sad decline. When BARLA took over responsibility for the amateur game they encouraged the district leagues to allow their clubs to move into the Regional league system.

Today, the district leagues still exist, but

for a much different purpose. They are responsible for running the grass roots of the sport in their area, for example the Huddersfield League maintain control for their own local cup competitions and championship play-offs, but their clubs actually compete in the regional Pennine League. This system has two major advantages. It allows for consistent week-to-week league competition and enables enough clubs to be brought into a league with a sufficient number of divisions to provide promotion and relegation. As an example, the Pennine League, the biggest in the country in 1978, had five open-age divisions.

Regional Leagues

There are six major open-age regional Leagues, not including the Southern Amateur Rugby League, currently operating under BARLA control, the Cumbria League, the Humberside Amateur League, North West Counties League, the Pennine League, the West Yorkshire Sunday League and the Yorkshire League.

Cumbria League

After several seasons existing as separate leagues the Barrow and Cumberland Leagues joined together in 1978 to form the new Cumbria League. Barrow has been part of the Cumbria region for Rugby League purposes for some time and BARLA are hopeful of major improvement in the Furness and West Cumbria regions because of the amalgamation.

For the 1978-79 season the league in the Cumbria region comprised the following local leagues and clubs:
Barrow: Askham, Barrow Island, Corporation Combine, Dalton, Holker Pioneers, Marsh Hornets, Millom, Roose, Ulverston, Walney Central.
Cumberland Amateur League: Broughton Moor, Broughton Red Rose, Cockermouth Egremont Rangers, Ellenborough Rangers, Glasson Rangers, Grasslot Miners' Welfare, Hensingham, Kells, Lowa, Maryport, Seaton Rangers, Wath Brow Hornets.

Humberside League

Ace Amateurs, Beecroft and Wightman, Bird's Eye, BP, City Transport, College of Higher Education, Concorde, Corporation Telephones, Crooked Billet, Dram Shop, East Mount, Fenners, Greenwood Hotel, Humber Manure, Ideal Standard, Ingle Mire Club, Jackson's, Kingfisher, Lock-wood Arm's, Mysons, National Dock Labour Board, Newington, Newland Caravans, Northern Dairies, Phoenix, Reckitts, Savoy, Sizers, Southcoats, Tetley's, Van Leer, West Hull, Zetland Arms.

North-West Counties Amateur Rugby League
Leigh Amateur Rugby League: Leigh Easts, Leigh Miners' Welfare.
Manchester Amateur Rugby League: Broadwalk, Folly Borough, GEC (Trafford Park), Irlam Hornets, Langworthy Juniors, Manchester Polytechnic, Salford Juniors, Salford University Old Boys.
St Helens Amateur Rugby League: Blackbrook, Bold Hornets, Green Dragon, Hare and Hounds, Kirkby Rangers, Pilkington Recs, UGB.
Warrington Amateur Rugby League: Crosfield Recs, Latchford Albion, Ryland Recs, Tetleys, Thames Board Mills, Woolston Rovers.
Widnes Amateur Rugby League: Commercial Hotel, Farnworth ROB Runcorn, St Maries, Simm's Cross, TAC, Widnes RNA, Widnes 'B'.
Wigan Amateur Rugby League: Heinz 57, ICI Thornton, Rose Bridge, St Cuthbert's, St Patrick's, Springfield.

Pennine League
Bradford Amateur Rugby League: Clayton, Dudley Hill, International Harvesters, Queensbury, Shipley, Thornton, Victoria Rangers, West Bowling, Wyke.
Halifax Amateur Rugby League: Brighouse Rangers, Greetland All-Rounders, Illingworth, Keighley Albion, Mixenden, Ogden Engineering, Ovenden, Park Amateurs, Siddal, Worth Village.
Huddersfield Amateur Rugby League: Bradley, Britannia Works, David Brown Gears, Deighton WMC, Emley, Greenside WMC, Holset Engineering, Huddersfield Polytechnic, St Joseph's, Underbank.
Oldham Amateur Rugby League: Ferranti, Fitton Hill, Higginshaw, St Anne's, Saddleworth Rangers, Salem Hornets, Waterhead.
Rochdale Amateur Rugby League: East Ward, Mayfield, Queen Anne, Spotland Rangers, Todmorden.

Yorkshire League
Castleford Amateur Rugby League: Allerton Bywater, Featherstone Miners' Welfare, Lock Lane.
Heavy Woollen Amateur Rugby League: Batley Victoria, Banks, Dewsbury Celtic,

Fearnsides, Gate Inn, Hanging Heaton, Ossett Trinity, Shaw Cross, Staincliffe WMC.

Leeds Amateur Rugby League: Bison Sports, Brassmoulders, Belle Isle, Corpus Christi, Drighlington, Garden Gate, Middleton, Milford, Shaw Lane Social Club (Yeadon), Stanningley, Thorpe, Waterloo, Yew Tree. *Wakefield Amateur Rugby League*: Eastmoor, Stanley Rangers, Three Horse Shoes. *York Amateur Rugby League*: Heworth, York Acorn, York Albion, York Southlands.

West Yorkshire League (Sunday fixtures)
Castleford Amateur Rugby League: Crown, Ferrybridge RHP, Fryston Welfare, Garforth, Jubilee, King William IV, Kippax White Swan, Magnet (Airedale), Pointer Panthers, Pontefract Labour Club, Redhill, Rowntree Mackintosh, Sailor's Home, Sandmartin, Smawthorne Hotel, Swillington Welfare, Travelle's Saints.
Doncaster Amateur Rugby League: Askern, Barnsley, Bentley, Bullcroft, Chesterfield, Corner Pin, Moorends, Rossington Hornets, Rotherham Rangers, Selby, Sheffield Concord.
Heavy Woollen Amateur Rugby League: Dewsbury Moor, Fox and Hounds, Mirfield, Shaw's, Thornhill Lees Trinity, Woolpack All Blacks.
Leeds Amateur Rugby League: Sherburn.
Wakefield Amateur Rugby League: Combined Hospitals, Duke of York, Flanshaw Hotel, Grimethorpe, Hemsworth Miners' Welfare, Kettlethorpe Hotel, Manor SC, Normanton, Sharlston, Truck Components, Walnut Warriors, Woolpack.

Sunday Leagues
Sunday has become the major match day for the professionals, and it is acquiring the same interest for the amateur clubs. Several youth leagues stage their programme on Sunday, but the major open age interest is firmly established in Yorkshire. The most important competitions are the Leeds Sunday League, the York League and the West Yorkshire League, which has already been mentioned.

The *Leeds League* is made up of two divisions and the competing clubs in 1978-79 were:

Division I: Bramley Social, Brassmoulders " A ", Bison " A ", Burwell, Red and Kinghorn, Meanwood, Milford, Queens, Sheepscar, Thorpe " A ", Torre Road Garage.

Division II: Airedale and Wharfedale College, Belle Isle " A ", Black Dog, Camerons, Craven Gate, East Leeds, Kirksta, Halton Moor, Osmandthorpe, Pudsey Seprata, Queenswood, Royal Park, Station Hotel, and Woodway.

The *York Sunday League* operate with one division: Acorn, Fulfordgate, Heworth, INL, INL " A ", Marcia, Punchbowl, Punchbowl Recs, Rose and Crown, Tramways.

Southern Amateur Rugby League
Amateur Rugby League has established a toe-hold in the South of England thanks to the dedication of a few very determined enthusiasts.

Initially, the Southern League ran from 1949 to 1953 with teams in London and the Hampshire region, but that failed to survive. The current League was formed in 1965 and, despite Rugby Union hostility and the distance from the North of England, they have carried the banner for the amateur code ever since. Their membership has fluctuated through the years—sides have existed at Portsmouth, Reading, St Albans, Basingstoke, Hillingdon, Hornchurch, Hackney and other centres, and in 1978 their league was made up of Clapham, Ealing, Oxford University, Peckham, McEntee and London Colonials.

The League has three internal competitions, the League Championship, the Challenge Knockout Cup, and a seven-a-side tournament. They also field a representative team who have played matches against the English Universities, Northern League representative teams and, in 1971, the full New Zealand touring team.

Southern clubs also compete regularly in the BARLA National Cup. It should be recognised that although the League still struggle against Rugby Union prejudice their aim is not to re-introduce the professional game to London, but allow ordinary people to play Rugby League football for their own enjoyment.

Youth Rugby
As in other sections of the amateur game the coming of BARLA proved a watershed in the fortunes of the youth game. In Yorkshire amateur Rugby League was being played by just ten sides. In the Barrow-Cumbria area there were less than five teams, and it was virtually extinct in Lancashire.

Before BARLA's arrival the age groupings were under-19 and under-17. The latter was known for a long time as the continuation group because it was generally those teams that players joined after leaving school.

Under the British Amateur Rugby League Association the main age-group is under 18. From that stage players are considered old enough and have sufficient experience to be able to play the more demanding open-age game. There are other age-groups emerging within club amateur rugby, under 11, under 12, under 13, under 14, under 16, etc., and this is one of the most encouraging features of modern amateur Rugby League game.

Several major Leagues now exist to fill this important need and they are:

Barrow Youth League: Askham, Barrow, Island, Dalton, Millom, Walney Central.

Bradford and Keithley Youth Amateur Rugby League (run under the auspices of Bradford and District Amateur Rugby League): Batley Boys Club, Bradford Police Boys Club, Dewsbury Boys, Dudley Hill, Keithley Civic Youth Club, St George Youth Club, Sedburgh Youth Club, Siddal, West Borough High School.

Cumbria Youth League: Egremont Rangers, Grasslot Miners' Welfare, Hensingham, Kells, Wath Brow Hornets.

Humberside Youth League: Ainthorpe, Albermarle, Amy Johnson YC, Andrew Marvell, Bransholme, David Lister, East Mount, Greatfield, Hull Boys Club, Maybury, Newland, Setting Dyke, Shaw Park, South Holderness, South Hunsley, Spring Cottage, Sydney Smith, Villa YC, Wawne, Wolfreton.

Kirklees Youth League: Batley Boys Club, Dewsbury Boys Club, Dewsbury Moor, Brighlington, Eastmoor, Gildersome, International Harvesters, Ravensthorpe, Stanley, St Francis Juniors, St John Fisher School, Thornhill, Whyther Park.

North West Counties Amateur Rugby League: Leigh Miners' Welfare, Billinge Eagles, Blackbrook, Lone House, Pilkington Recs, St Helens 'B', UGB, St Helens YMCA, Crosfield Recs, Woolston Rovers Simms Cross, Widnes Tigers.

Rochdale Youth Amateur Rugby League: Fitton Hill, St Annes, Saddleworth Rangers, Shaw, Waterhead, Balderstone, Bishop Henshaw, Todmorden.

Yorkshire Youth Amateur Rugby League: Allerton Bywater, Castleford Supporters, Featherstone Supporters, Doncaster Juniors, Greetland All Rounders, Dewsbury Colts, Shawcross BC, Huddersfield Supporters, Underbank, Eastmoor, Ryhill and Havercroft, Sharlston, Stanley Rangers, Trinity Supporters, Heworth.

Youth amateur Rugby League has also been established in two small centres outside the accepted British confines of the game, London and Scotland. This is a new venture for the game because previous attempts to take it away from its northern birthplace have been at professional or open age level.

The Scots project was started in 1976 when an Englishman, Henry Callaghan, living north of the border, introduced the game for youths and schoolboys in Hamilton, near Glasgow. During 1977-78 five teams competed in the Scottish Amateur Rugby League Youth Association and they were champions Greendyke Giants, Blantyre Bulldogs, Low Waters, Chatelherault and Hamilton Saints, while other competitions were staged for Primary Schoolboys. In fact a representative match for primary schoolboys was played in Edinburgh when Edinburgh Schools beat Hamilton Schools 13-5.

In February 1978 the Southern Schools and Youth Clubs Rugby League Association was established. Some success has been enjoyed, particularly in some London schools, and one team, Daneford School from Bethnal Green, has undertaken a tour of Yorkshire. Their most successful venture was a seven-a-side run by Stockwell Manor School at Herne Hill Stadium and their major playing achievement was their first ever win over non-London opposition when Daneford beat Hamilton Lions from Scotland in a sponsored triangular tournament.

Five Year Plan

When the British Amateur League took over the running of the amateur game one of the most important aspects they introduced to the game was forward planning, a quality that had been sadly missing from the county commission system. The new controllers introduced a five-year plan of action which called for regionalisation of the district leagues, a concerted effort in youth and schools rugby, a coaching programme, a full-time professional administration and the introduction of a premier league for the top clubs. Only the last item has failed to appear.

Regionalisation has worked in spectacular fashion. Now power has devolved away from the small local leagues into such combines as the North West Counties, the Pennine, Yorkshire, West Yorkshire, and Humberside Leagues.

Youth Rugby has increased tenfold, the English Schools Rugby Leagues have affiliated themselves to the organisation and advances have been made towards the establishment of " mini rugby " for young boys who are not old enough for competitive Rugby League.

The administration of the game is now dealt with by one full-time officer, National administrator Mr Maurice Oldroyd, and staff from their headquarters in Huddersfield. West Yorkshire, and further improvements are planned, particularly additional full-time staff. Coaching now comes under amateur control, after starting life with the Rugby Football League (see COACHING SCHEME).

In turn the five-year plan has been superseded by the regional coaching-development plans which are now forming the basis of BARLA's next few years of operations. Top priority is given to the formation of youth leagues and mini-rugby while the Association is pressing for development of Sunday Leagues, Works Associations, the establishment of clubs' own facilities and expansion into towns without their own Rugby League team.

Tours

The ultimate accolade for a Rugby League player since the game spread beyond Britain's shores is to be selected for a national touring side. From 1907, for seventy years, that honour was restricted to the professional side of the game, but in 1977 the English amateurs made their presence felt on the trans-globe tour circuit.

The new ground was broken in 1977, the year of Her Majesty the Queen's Silver Jubilee, when to celebrate the happy occasion together with the thirtieth anniversary of the Shaw Cross Boys Club, Dewsbury, the British Amateur Rugby League Association sent their first team beyond Europe's boundaries. Their pioneering team was a 20-strong party of Under-18 players and officials, and they completed a five-match programme in New Zealand and Australia.

The tour was financed by a series of fund-raising schemes in England and a grant from the Sports Council. It started on 3 June when the party flew from Manchester Airport to New Zealand and they gained immediate recognition from the International Rugby League world, when they were met off the plane in Auckland by British League chairman Mr Harry

Womersley, who was in New Zealand for the World Championships.

The amateur tourist's first match against Northern Zone at Auckland's Carlaw Park had to be postponed because of heavy rain and the match was restaged at the Jack Colvin Park, Auckland, the following day, 8 June. Still finding their feet in the Southern Hemisphere the British team were beaten 22-8.

A match against a New Zealand XIII followed at the Showground, Christchurch, and the game was staged as a curtain-raiser to the New Zealand v. Great Britain World Cup encounter. In this match the British youngsters distinguished themselves by drawing 11-11.

After leaving New Zealand the British pioneers flew to Australia where they played their first match against Toowoomba District, Queensland, as a prelude to the local senior team's game against the French World Cup side. The British found the Australians' physical approach to the game too strong and were beaten 39-12. They did not allow that sizeable defeat to deter them, however, for they improved considerably, despite losing 11-9, in their next match which was against Illawarra District (New South Wales).

The highlight of the tour, however, was the British team's appearance at the Sydney Cricket Ground to play an Australian XIII as a curtain-raiser to the World Cup final between Australia and Great Britain. The English amateurs ensured that they emerged with some honour from their first visit to the famous stadium by giving an excellent display in their 21-13 defeat. Clearly they had learned several lessons.

The youth tour party was made up of T. McGovern (Simms Cross, Widnes, capt.), I. Rudd (Wath Brow Hornets, Cumbria, vice-capt.), C. Ganley (Leigh Miners' Welfare), J. Donnelly (Wath Brow Hornets), T. Worrall (Crosfield Recs, Warrington), D. Hobbs (Featherstone Supporters), A. Swift (Blackbrook, St Helens), C. Todd (Wath Brow Hornets), M. Meadows (Whelley, Wigan), N. Kiss (Saddleworth Rangers, Oldham), R. Crewe (Simms Cross), M. Lucas (Castleford Supporters), S. Kirkby (Askam, Barrow), S. Reed (Wakefield Supporters), L. Moorby (Wakefield Supporters), D. Cairns (Askam), M. Addison (Featherstone Supporters), J. Wood (Shaw Cross Boys Club, Dewsbury), G. Smith (Shaw Cross BC), R. Howarth (Leigh Miners' Welfare); Managers: A.

Lancaster (Shaw Cross BC) and D. Hird (Shaw Cross BC).

Tour record: Played 5, lost 4, drawn 1, pts for 53, against 104.

But the lessons were not just restricted to the British youth players. The British Amateur Rugby League Association absorbed a number of important points about the administration and organisation of a touring team. This was to show almost immediate results in their next effort, the first ever Open Age team tour of Papua-New Guinea, Australia and New Zealand in May and June 1978. The 38-day, nine-match tour took in the first major tour of Papua New Guinea by any governing body in the world—indeed it was a piece of international sporting history.

After a long flight from Britain, the tourists started their programme with a match against the Papua-New Guinea Islands Zone at humid Rabaul (New Britain). The conditions, however, did not deter the British players who ran out comfortably 41-13 winners. Controversy hit their next match which was against the Northern Zone at Lae. The Papuans were leading 4-2 when, in the 74th minute, a section of the 5,500 crowd invaded the pitch and attacked the British players. The match was abandoned and, although the first British reaction was to call off the rest of the tour, it was decided to continue.

The tensions of Lae were not allowed to remain for long and the action was switched back to the field of play with a narrow 26-25 victory over the Highlands Zone at Mount Hagen.

When the tourists returned to Port Moresby the Southern Zone team proved too fast and powerful and gained a 27-15 win over the Englishmen. The Southern Zone victory must have encouraged the Papuan's hopes for success in the first international against an English amateur side at Port Moresby on 21 May. The British team, however, had other ideas and emerged as 28-7 winners, much to the dismay of the impressive 14,100 crowd.

Like the 1977 youth team, the Open Age team found their rugby baptism in Australia a trial and they were beaten 28-2 by Combined Universities at the Leichhardt Oval, Balmain, Sydney. British pride was restored, when the tourists beat the cream of Australian amateur rugby, Australian Universities 23-10, in a match four days later at Macquaide University, Sydney.

With honours even in Australia, the tourists moved on to New Zealand where they encountered a problem they had not experienced in Britain, 'the sin bin'. During their first game, a 20-13 defeat by Wellington at Hutt Recreation Ground, five players, two of them British, suffered the ignominy of temporary sendings off.

In the final game of their nine-match tour Great Britain amateurs made sure they attracted the attention of the New Zealand sporting public because their game with the New Zealand representative, Waikato team at Davies Park, Huntly was televised. The tourists reacted by winning the match 7-5.

The amateur tourists were honoured when they were given a reception by New Zealand's Prime Minister, the Rt Hon. Robert Muldoon CH at Parliament House, Wellington on 30 May and it set the seal of respectability on what could be the fore-runner of more tours for amateur players.

The British touring party was: P. Glover (Pilkington Recs, St Helens), J. Power (Spotland Rangers, Rochdale), B. Southern (Folly Borough, Manchester), D. Oaten (Ace Amateurs, Hull, vice-capt.), S. Critchenson (Ace Amateurs, Hull), P. Moore (NDLB, Hull), J. Green (Latchford Albion, Warrington), C. Porthouse (Ellenbrough Rangers, Cumbria), D. Robinson (Walney Central, Barrow), R. Colgrave (Ace Amateurs, Hull, capt.), A. Varty (Broughton Red Rose, Cumbria), D. Nicholson (Blackbrook, St Helens), P. Dowling (Leigh Miners' Welfare), J. Roberts (Leigh Miners' Welfare), R. Carter (Crosfield Recs, Warrington), S. Berwick (Maryport, Cumbria), J. Hull (Pilkington Recs, St Helens), R. Blair (Seaton, Cumbria), J. Brown (Cockermouth, Cumbria), E. Lowe (Hemsworth Miners' Welfare, Wakefield), J. Eastwood (Underbank, Huddersfield), J. McCabe (Pilkington Recs), R. Lewis (Leigh Miners' Welfare), G. Catling (Dewsbury Celtic), D. Cooper (NDLB, Hull), D. Dykes (Latchford Albion, Warrington); joint managers: R. Oldfield (Barrow) and H. Swift (St Helens); coach: S. Morton (Dewsbury); physiotherapist: F. Jones; public relations officer: R. Dennett (Warrington).

The Open Age tour record was:

In Papua–New Guinea

Date	Opponents	Points for—against	Venue and attendance
Sunday, 7 May	Islands Zone	41-13	Rabaul (5,608)
Wednesday, 10 May	Northern Zone	2-4	Lae (5,500)
	(match abandoned 74 minutes, crowd invasion)		
Sunday, 14 May	Highlands Zone	26-25	Mount Hagen (7,200)
Tuesday, 16 May	Southern Zone	15-27	Port Moresby (9,300)
Sunday, 21 May	Papua-New Guinea	28-7	Port Moresby (14,500)

In Australia

Wednesday, 24 May	Combined Universities	2-28	Leichhardt Oval Sydney (1,850)
Saturday, 28 May	Australian Universities	23-10	Macquarie University (1,000)

In New Zealand

Wednesday, 31 May	Wellington	13-20	Hutt Recreation (3,500)
Saturday, 3 June	New Zealand XIII	7-5	Davies Park, Huntly (2,200)

Tour records: Played, 9 won, 5 lost, 3 result 1, Pts for 157, against 137.

Try scorers: Critchenson 10; Dowling 5; Moore 4; Varty 2; Eastwood 2; Lowe 2; Robinson, McCabe, Oaten, Power, Porthouse, Green 1 each.

Goal scorers: Glover 28, Roberts 2, Colgrave 2.

By the very nature of the clubs' amateur status it was decided when compiling this record of amateur Rugby League at the end of the 1977-78 season and beginning of 1978-79, not to include the names and addresses of any official or headquarters. The up-to-date records are held at the headquarters of the British Amateur Rugby League Association at 3 Upperhead Row, Huddersfield, West Yorkshire HD1 2DL, and they will be pleased to supply any information that is required.

BRITISH LIONS

A British Lion is a player, manager, trainer or coach appointed or selected by the Council of the Rugby Football League to tour Australia and/or New Zealand.

The first Great Britain tour down under was staged in 1910. Off-the-cuff comments on the terraces behind the posts during a match at Fartown, Huddersfield, inspired the formation of the British Lions Rugby League Association. The pioneers were Harry Sunderland, John Wilson Snr, Frank Williams and Alf Ellaby.

The first meeting of the Lions was held in the dressing-rooms at the Belle Vue ground, Manchester, on 18 Nov. 1945. The host was Mr Tom Spedding, a former Tour Manager, and then manager of Belle Vue Rangers. The association's first chairman was James Lomas, ex-Salford captain of the 1910 Great Britain Tourists. The first secretary was Harry Sunderland, an Australian journalist who had witnessed the formation of a successful association for Australian Tourists.

Originally, the Lions held their reunion to coincide with Kangaroo Tours to Britain, the dinner being staged at the Troutbeck, Ilkley. In recent years, the dinners have become annual events, being staged at the Willows, Saltford, home of Salford RLFC, during the close season.

CAPTAIN MORGAN TROPHY

The ill-fated Captain Morgan Trophy was in existence for only one season, the 1973-74 campaign.

Warrington collected the top prize of £3,000, beating Featherstone Rovers in a dour 4-0 final at Salford, the Wires' points coming from two penalties from the boot of Derek Whitehead. The final was watched by a crowd of 5,259 and was refereed by Wakefield official Fred Lindop.

Entry to the Captain Morgan Trophy was limited to 16 clubs—winners of the first round of the Yorkshire and Lancashire Cups.

CASTLEFORD RLFC

Founded in 1913. Joined the Northern Rugby League in 1926. Ground: Wheldon Road. Colours: Yellow jersey with black collar and black cuffs, black shorts.
RL Championship beaten finalists, 1938-39, 1968-69.
RL Cup Winners, 1934-35, 1968-69, 1969-70.
Yorkshire League Winners, 1932-33, 1938-39, 1964-65.
Yorkshire Cup Winners, 1977-78.
Beaten Finalists, 1948-49, 1950-51, 1968-69, 1971-72.
Eastern Division Championship beaten finalists, 1963-64.
BBC2 Floodlit Trophy Winners, 1965-66, 1966-67, 1967-68, 1976-77.
Player's No.6 Trophy Winners, 1976-77.

Club Records:
Attendance: 25,449 v. Hunslet (RL Cup) 3 Mar. 1935.
Goals: 158 by G. Lloyd, 1976-77.
Tries: 36 by K. Howe, 1963-64.
Points: 331 by G. Lloyd, 1976-77.

CHAIRMEN'S ASSOCIATION

The Chairmen's Association of the Rugby Football League was formed in 1972 to "participate in the fostering and development of Rugby League Football". Membership is open to the chairman of any professional club in membership with the League. Past chairmen of the association are Mr Tom Mitchell BSc, of Workington Town, and Mr Brian Snape JP, of Salford.

CHALLENGE CUP

The Rugby League Challenge Cup competition is one of the world's top sporting events. Since 1929 the final, whenever possible, has been staged at the Empire Stadium, Wembley, and the May final is the highlight of the Rugby League calendar.

The tournament was launched at a meeting in Huddersfield in March 1896 and the first draw for the Northern Union Cup, as it was first titled, was made in the September.

RL Challenge Cup Final
Most finals: Wigan 15.
Most wins: Leeds 10.
Highest score: 38 Wakefield T. v Hull 5, 1960.
Record attendance: 102,569 Warrington v. Halifax, 1954 replay at Bradford.
Most tries: 3 by R. Wilson (Broughton R) v. Salford, 1902; by S. Moorhouse (Huddersfield) v. Warrington, 1913; by T. Holliday (Oldham) v. Swinton, 1927.
Most goals: 8 by C. Kellett (Featherstone R) v. Bradford N, 1973.
Most points: 20 by N. Fox (Wakefield T.) v. Hull, 1960.
Most appearances: 7 by A. Edwards with Salford, Leeds, Dewsbury and Bradford N. 1938, 1939, 1942, 1943, 1945, 1948, 1949.

CHALLENGE CUP ROLL OF HONOUR

Year	Winners		Runners-up		Venue	Attendance
1897	Batley	10	St Helens	3	Leeds	13,492
1898	Batley	7	Bradford N.	0	Leeds	27,941
1899	Oldham	19	Hunslet	9	Manchester	15,763
1900	Swinton	16	Salford	8	Manchester	17,864
1901	Batley	6	Warrington	0	Leeds	29,563
1902	Broughton R.	25	Salford	0	Rochdale	15,006
1903	Halifax	7	Salford	0	Leeds	32,507

Year	Winners		Runners-up		Venue	Attendance
1904	Halifax	8	Warrington	3	Salford	17,041
1905	Warrington	6	Hull KR	0	Leeds	19,638
1906	Bradford N.	5	Salford	0	Leeds	16,000
1907	Warrington	17	Oldham	3	Broughton	18,500
1908	Hunslet	14	Hull	0	Huddersfield	18,000
1909	Wakefield Tr.	17	Hull	0	Leeds	30,000
1910	Leeds	7	Hull	7	Huddersfield	19,413
	Leeds	26	Hull	12	Huddersfield	11,608
1911	Broughton R.	4	Wigan	0	Salford	8,000
1912	Dewsbury	8	Oldham	5	Leeds	15,271
1913	Huddersfield	9	Warrington	5	Leeds	22,754
1914	Hull	6	Wakefield Tr.	0	Halifax	19,000
1915	Huddersfield	37	St Helens	3	Oldham	8,000
1920	Huddersfield	21	Wigan	10	Leeds	14,000
1921	Leigh	13	Halifax	0	Broughton	25,000
1922	Rochdale H.	10	Hull	9	Leeds	32,596
1923	Leeds	28	Hull	3	Wakefield	29,335
1924	Wigan	21	Oldham	4	Rochdale	41,831
1925	Oldham	16	Hull KR	3	Leeds	28,000
1926	Swinton	9	Oldham	3	Rochdale	27,000
1927	Oldham	26	Swinton	7	Wigan	35,000
1928	Swinton	5	Warrington	3	Wigan	33,909
1929	Wigan	13	Dewsbury	2	Wembley	41,500
1930	Widnes	10	St Helens	3	Wembley	36,544
1931	Halifax	22	York	8	Wembley	40,368
1932	Leeds	11	Swinton	8	Wigan	29,000
1933	Huddersfield	21	Warrington	17	Wembley	41,874
1934	Hunslet	11	Widnes	5	Wembley	41,280
1935	Castleford	11	Huddersfield	8	Wembley	39,000
1936	Leeds	18	Warrington	2	Wembley	51,250
1937	Widnes	18	Keighley	5	Wembley	47,699
1938	Salford	7	Barrow	4	Wembley	51,243
1939	Halifax	20	Salford	3	Wembley	55,453
1940	*No competition*					
1941	Leeds	19	Halifax	2	Bradford	28,500
1942	Leeds	15	Halifax	10	Bradford	15,250
1943	Dewsbury	16	Leeds	9	Dewsbury	10,470
	Dewsbury	0	Leeds	6	Leeds	16,000
	Dewsbury won on aggregate 16–15					
1944	Bradford	0	Wigan	3	Wigan	22,000
	Bradford	8	Wigan	0	Bradford	30,000
	Bradford won on aggregate 8–3					
1945	Huddersfield	7	Bradford N.	4	Huddersfield	9,041
	Huddersfield	6	Bradford N.	5	Bradford	17,500
	Huddersfield won on aggregate 13–9					
1946	Wakefield Tr.	13	Wigan	12	Wembley	54,730
1947	Bradford	8	Leeds	4	Wembley	77,605
1948	Wigan	8	Bradford	3	Wembley	92,500
1949	Bradford	12	Halifax	0	Wembley	95,000
1950	Warrington	19	Widnes	0	Wembley	95,000
1951	Wigan	10	Barrow	0	Wembley	95,000
1952	Workington T.	18	Featherstone R.	10	Wembley	73,000
1953	Huddersfield	15	St Helens	10	Wembley	90,000
1954	Warrington	4	Halifax	4	Wembley	83,000
	Warrington	8	Halifax	4	Odsal	102,569
1955	Barrow	21	Workington T.	12	Wembley	67,000
1956	St Helens	13	Halifax	2	Wembley	80,000
1957	Leeds	9	Barrow	7	Wembley	77,000
1958	Wigan	13	Workington T.	9	Wembley	66,000

Year	Winners		Runners-up		Venue	Attendance
1959	Wigan	30	Hull	13	Wembley	80,000
1960	Wakefield Tr.	38	Hull	5	Wembley	80,000
1961	St Helens	12	Wigan	6	Wembley	95,000
1962	Wakefield Tr.	12	Huddersfield	6	Wembley	85,000
1963	Wakefield Tr.	25	Wigan	10	Wembley	85,000
1964	Widnes	13	Hull KR	5	Wembley	85,000
1965	Wigan	20	Hunslet	16	Wembley	92,000
1966	St Helens	21	Wigan	2	Wembley	100,000
1967	Featherstone R.	17	Barrow	12	Wembley	76,290
1968	Leeds	11	Wakefield Tr.	10	Wembley	87,100
1969	Castleford	11	Salford	6	Wembley	97,939
1970	Castleford	7	Wigan	2	Wembley	100,000
1971	Leigh	24	Leeds	7	Wembley	85,514
1972	St Helens	16	Leeds	13	Wembley	89,495
1973	Featherstone R.	33	Bradford N.	14	Wembley	74,000
1974	Warrington	24	Featherstone R.	9	Wembley	80,000
1975	Widnes	14	Warrington	7	Wembley	87,000
1976	St Helens	20	Widnes	5	Wembley	89,982
1977	Leeds	16	Widnes	7	Wembley	80,871
1978	Leeds	14	St Helens	12	Wembley	96,000
1979	Widnes	12	Wakefield Tr.	3	Wembley	95,872
1980	Hull KR	10	Hull	5	Wembley	95,000

Since 1904 a number of amateur clubs have qualified for the First Round of the Challenge Cup. Today, the winners of the Lancashire and Yorkshire Cups, organised by the British Amateur Rugby League Association, qualify.

1904 Parton (Cumberland), Brookland Rovers.

1905 Leigh Shamrocks, Parton, Brookland Rovers, Ossett (Yorkshire).

1906 Brookland Rovers, Egerton, Victoria Rangers (Bradford), Leigh Shamrocks, Egremont.

1907 Whitehaven Recs., Saville Green (Leeds), Brighouse St James, Brookland Rovers, Millom, Radcliffe Rangers, Workington.

1908 Whitehaven Recs., Barrow St George, Castleford, Millom, Beverley.

1909 Beverley, Normanton, Pemberton (Wigan), Barrow St George, Egremont.

1910 York 1NL, Paurston White Horse, Millom, Wigan Highfield.

1911 Broughton Moor, Lane End United (Leeds), Pemberton, Normanton, York Grove United.

1912 Normanton St John, Lane End United, Millom, Beverley, Wigan Highfield.

1913 Barton (Manchester), Seaton, Pemberton, Elland, Normanton St John, Featherstone Rovers.

1914 Swinton Park, Elland, Millom, Glasson Rangers, Wigan Highfield, Castleford, Featherstone Rovers.

1915 Askam, Broughton Moor, Brighouse Rangers, Wardley (Swinton), Featherstone Rovers.

1920 British Oil and Cake Mills (Hull), Healey Street Adults (Oldham), Millom, Brookland Rangers, Askam, Wigan Highfield, Featherstone Rovers.

1921 Featherstone Rovers, Pendlebury, Dearham Wanderers, British Oil and Cake Mills, Elland Wanderers, Askam, Wigan Highfield.

1922 British Oil and Cake Mills, Elland Wanderers, Askam, Broughton Moor, Cadishead.

1923 Norwood (Hull), Millom, Hensingham, Cadishead and Irlam, Castleford.

1924 Dearham Wanderers, Hull St Patricks, Dalton, Wardley.

1925 Barnsley United (Hull), Flimby and Fothergill, Twelve Apostles (Leigh), Castleford.

1926 Hensingham, Pemberton Rovers, Barrow Cambridge, Barnsley United.

1927 Dearham Wanderers, Pemberton Rovers, Cottingham.

1928 Whitehaven Recs., Twelve Apostles, Cottingham, Kinsley and Fitzwilliam (Pontefract)

1929 Uno's Dabs (St Helens), Cottingham, Lindley (Huddersfield), Whitehaven Recs.

1930 Cottingham, Great Clifton, Bickershaw Hornets, Featherstone Juniors.

1931 Lindley, Featherstone Juniors, Golden Lion (St Helens), Brookland Rovers.

1932 Uno's Dabs, Lindley, Great Clifton.

1933 Barrow Marsh Hornets, Uno's Dabs, Higginshaw, Askern Colliery Welfare.
1934 Dearham Wanderers, Pendlebury Juniors, Hull St Mary, Wigan Rangers.
1935 Barrow Marsh Hornets, Astley and Tyldesley Collieries, Manchester Ship Canal (Runcorn), Sharlston Red Rose (Wakefield).
1936 Higginshaw, Seaton.
1937 Higginshaw, Goole.
1938 Glassington Colliery (Castleford), Maryport, Pendlebury Juniors.
1939 United Glass Blowers (St Helens), Higginshaw, Seaton, Sharlston Red Rose.
1946 Kells (Cumberland), Hull Juniors, Sharlston Red Rose, Langworthy Juniors (Salford).
1947 Brookland Rovers, Pemberton Rovers, Widnes Dragons, Wheldale Colliery (Castleford).
1948 Risehow and Gillhead, Pemberton Rovers, Vine Tavern (St Helens), Buslingthorpe Vale (Leeds).
1949 Normanton, Broughton Moor, Vine Tavern.
1950 Broughton Moor, Worsley Boys' Club (Wigan), Cardiff.
1951 Broughton Moor, Latchford Albion (Warrington), Cardiff, Llanelly.
1952 Rylands Recs. (Warrington)
1953 National Dock Labour Board (Hull), Orford Tannery (Warrington).
1954 Wheldale Colliery, Latchford Albion
1955 Dewsbury Celtic
1956 Stanningley (Leeds), Triangle Valve (Wigan)
1957 St Marie's (Widnes), Wakefield Loco
1958 Orford Tannery, Lock Lane
1959 Astley and Tyldesley Colliery, Kells Recreation Centre
1960 Walney Central, Lock Lane
1961 Pilkington Recs., Dewsbury Celtic
1962 Oldham St Anne's, Brookhouse
1963 Roose, Imperial Athletic
1964 Stanningley, Thames Board Mills
1965 Crosfield Recs., Dewsbury Celtic
1966 Crosfield Recs., Brookhouse
1967 Blackbrook (St Helens), British Oil and Cake Mills (Hull)
1968 Leigh Miners' Welfare, British Oil and Cake Mills
1969 Leigh Miners' Welfare, Ackworth
1970 Glasson Rangers, Lock Lane
1971 British Oil and Cake Mills, Thames Board Mills
1972 Pilkington Recs., Dewsbury Celtic
1973 Millom, Dewsbury Celtic
1974 Lock Lane, Kippax White Swan

1975 Dewsbury Celtic, Mayfield (Rochdale)
1976 Leigh Miners' Welfare, Pointer Panthers (Castleford)
1977 Beecroft and Wightman, Pilkington Recs.
1978 Dewsbury Celtic, Pilkington Recs.
1979 Ace Amateurs, Leigh Miners' Welfare
1980 Ace Amateurs, Millom
See also STATE EXPRESS AND WEMBLEY STADIUM

CHANTICLEERS
The nickname of the French Rugby League team, adopted because the official emblem of La Fédération Française de Jeu à Treize is a crowing cock perched on a rugby ball.
See also FRANCE and JEU A TREIZE.

CLUB CHAMPIONSHIP
As attendances continued on a downward spiral in the late 1960s and early 1970s, Rugby League's administrators strove to find new ways of enticing the public back onto the terraces. Often their efforts became almost panic measures and several projects lasted only one fateful season. An example was the Club Championship, an over-elaborate and highly complicated version of the traditional end-of-season competition.

At the end of the 1973-74 season, the Club Championship was lifted by Warrington, adding to their haul of the Challenge Cup, Player's No. 6 Trophy and Captain Morgan Trophy, yet another one season venture.

To select the 16 clubs to take part in the Club Championship, a system of merit points was introduced. At least three places were guaranteed for Second Division clubs by the playing of two preliminary rounds on a two-leg basis between the top 12 teams in the final Division Two league table. The remaining places in the competition were filled by the 13 clubs that gained most merit points. Three merit points were awarded for winning a tie in a knockout competition, with points also awarded for positions in the final league tables i.e. 30 points for the First Division leader, one point for the bottom of Division Two. Four points were subtracted for relegation, four added for promotion.

Warrington gained the most points with a final tally of 68, Doncaster picking up only 2.

The one and only Club Championship roll of honour is:

	Winner	Runner-up
1974	Warrington	St Helens

See also PLAY OFFS

COACHING SCHEME

Former Rugby League Secretary Bill Fallowfield introduced an organised coaching scheme, highlighted by two week-long summer courses at Lilleshall and Bisham Abbey. In late 1974 the scheme was redesigned to become more intensive and was renamed the National Coaching Scheme, Laurie Gant and Albert Fearnley being appointed as National coaches.

The scheme's main objective was two-fold: to instruct adults on the techniques of teaching the skills of Rugby League to youngsters; and to put that knowledge into practice with schoolboy coaching courses throughout the country. The scheme was planned on a "pyramid" basis with the national coaches at the apex, regional coaches in charge of six northern zones, staff coaches responsible for up to 16 urban regions and a host of qualified coaches forming the wide base of the pyramid.

A range of badges for coaches and proficiency badges for schoolboys were introduced and the scheme was immediately hailed as a modern and progressive coaching operation.

Week-long summer courses for coaches are staged at Crystal Palace and Lilleshall, with a course for teenage players at Bisham Abbey. Summer-long coaching sessions for boys were held at Butlins Holiday Centre at Filey in 1977 and 1978.

In January 1979, the administration of the National Coaching Scheme was transferred from the Rugby Football League to the British Amateur Rugby League Association.

COLTS

The Northern Rugby Football League introduced a Colts League in the 1972-73 season. The under-19 set-up was designed to bridge the gap between schools and open-age rugby, but after the advent of the British Amateur Rugby League Association in 1973, the Colts League became a semi-professional nursery for the professional clubs. The Colts League is open to any professional club and is governed by a Management Committee with eligible players being under-19 on 1 Sept. each season.

The Colts League Championship winners receive the Stanneylands Trophy. The top four clubs in the final League table contest the Colts Challenge Cup, normally held on the same dates as the Rugby League Challenge Cup.

Lancashire and Yorkshire Colts take part in an annual County Championship match, with Great Britain and France Colts meeting on a home and away basis each season.

The Colts roll of honour is:

Challenge Cup
1975-76	Wigan 24	Hull KR 12
1976-77	Hull KR 15	St Helens 13
1977-78	Castleford 19	Wakefield Trinity 10
1978-79	Hull 17	Widnes 17
Replay	Hull 22	Widnes 17
1979-80	Leeds 25	Widnes 14

Premiership
1975-76	Hull KR 26	Wakefield Trinity 12
1976-77	Bradford Northern 29	Hull KR 15
1977-78	Wakefield Trinity 23	Hull KR 20
1978-79	Hull 17	Hull KR 9
1979-80	Oldham 21	Leeds 13

League Championship
1975-76	Wigan
1976-77	Bradford Northern
1977-78	Bradford Northern
1978-79	Hull KR
1979-80	Oldham

Internationals

1975-76	France 39	Great Britain 5	Cannes
	Great Britain 31	France 12	Salford
1976-77	France 15	Great Britain 19	Avignon
	Great Britain 6	France 2	Wigan
1977-78	Great Britain 8	France 7	Widnes
	France 24	Great Britain 13	Perpignan
1978-79	Great Britain 17	France 7	Hull Kingston Rovers
1979-80	France 11	Great Britain 29	Perpignan
	Great Britain 31	France 2	Oldham

County Championship

1975-76	Yorkshire 21	Lancashire 15	Huddersfield
1976-77	Lancashire 14	Yorkshire 31	Salford
1977-78	Yorkshire 13	Lancashire 22	Wakefield
1978-79	Lancashire 29	Yorkshire 9	St Helens
1979-80	Yorkshire 23	Lancashire 15	Bramley

CONSECUTIVE SCORING

From the start of the 1972-73 season to the end of 1973-74 David Watkins played and scored in every match for Salford—an unbroken run of 92 matches in which he scored 403 goals, 41 tries and 929 points.

Watkins is the only player to have twice achieved the feat of scoring in each of his club's matches throughout a season.

Those who achieved it once were:

Jim Hoey (Widnes)	1932-33
Billy Langton (Hunslet)	1958-59
Stuart Ferguson (Leigh)	1970-71
John Woods (Leigh)	1977-78
Steve Quinn (Featherstone R)	1979-80
Mick Parrish (Hunslet)	1979-80

CORSICA

Although it is under French control, Corsica has its own league with six clubs, Ajaccio, Bastia, Corte, Bonifacio, Cervione and Balagne. Organised competition started on the island in September 1972 and, since then, the championship has been won by Ajax (1974-75), Corte (1975-76), Bonifacio (1976-77) and the Knockout Cup by Bonifacio (1975-76-77).

As far as the British game is concerned the biggest event involving the Corsicans was in 1976-77 when the British Amateur Rugby League Association's open-age international team was beaten 14-5 by France at Bastia on 3 Apr. 1977.

Some of the Corsican clubs compete outside the island in French junior league competitions.

COUNTY CHAMPIONSHIP

County matches have featured on the Rugby League calendar since the birth of Northern Union football in 1895. Inter-county results are tabulated into a league to decide the County Champions. Players are eligible to represent their native county, or the county in which they first played professional Rugby League, although a player is not allowed to represent more than one county.

The first county fixture was staged at Stockport on 21 Oct. 1895, when Lancashire beat Cheshire. On 25 Nov. Yorkshire made their debut, losing to Cheshire at Headingley. During the 1920s a Glamorgan and Monmouth team contested the County Championship, drawing on the large contingent of Welshmen in the 13-a-side code.

In a bid to inject more spectator appeal into the Championship, an Other Nationalities team was introduced for the 1974-75 and 1975-76 tournaments with success. It was then decided that the county matches would act as inter-hemisphere International trials.

Because of the lack of Australasian commitments in the 1977-78 season, the County Championship was suspended, although two matches—Yorkshire v. Cumbria and Lancashire v. Yorkshire—were staged to celebrate the Queen's Silver Jubilee.

The County Championship has been won, including joint title successes, by Lancashire on 34 occasions; by Yorkshire 23 times; by Cumbria (Cumberland) 14 times; and by Cheshire once.

The County Championship roll of honour is:

1895-96	Lancashire
1896-97	Lancashire
1897-98	Yorkshire
1898-99	Yorkshire
1899-1900	Lancashire

1900-01	Lancashire
1901-02	Cheshire
1902-03	Lancashire
1903-04	Lancashire
1904-05	Yorkshire
1905-06	{ Lancashire { Cumberland
1906-07	Lancashire
1907-08	Cumberland
1908-09	Lancashire
1909-10	{ Cumberland { Yorkshire
1910-11	Lancashire
1911-12	Cumberland
1912-13	Yorkshire
1913-14	Undecided
1919-20	Undecided
1920-21	Yorkshire
1921-22	Yorkshire
1922-23	{ Lancashire { Yorkshire
1923-24	Lancashire
1924-25	Lancashire
1925-26	Lancashire
1926-27	Lancashire
1927-28	Cumberland
1928-29	Lancashire
1929-30	Lancashire
1930-31	Yorkshire
1931-32	Lancashire
1932-33	Cumberland
1933-34	Cumberland
1934-35	Cumberland
1935-36	Lancashire
1936-37	Lancashire
1937-38	Lancashire
1938-39	Lancashire
1945-46	Lancashire
1946-47	Yorkshire
1947-48	Lancashire
1948-49	Cumberland
1949-50	Undecided
1950-51	Undecided
1951-52	Yorkshire
1952-53	Lancashire
1953-54	Yorkshire
1954-55	Yorkshire
1955-56	Lancashire
1956-57	Lancashire

1957-58	Yorkshire
1958-59	Yorkshire
1959-60	Cumberland
1960-61	Lancashire
1961-62	Cumberland
1962-63	Yorkshire
1963-64	Cumberland
1964-65	Yorkshire
1965-66	Cumberland
1966-67	Cumberland
1967-68	Lancashire
1968-69	Yorkshire
1969-70	Lancashire
1970-71	Yorkshire
1971-72	Yorkshire
1972-73	Yorkshire
1973-74	Lancashire
1974-75	Lancashire
1975-76	Yorkshire
1976-77	Yorkshire
1977-78	Not Contested
1978-79	Lancashire
1979-80	Lancashire

COURTNEY TROPHY

The Courtney International Goodwill Trophy was donated in 1936 by Mr Roy Courtney, a well-known New Zealand sportsman. For annual award to the reigning international champions, the trophy measures 4ft high with the emblems of the four international powers—Britain, Australia, New Zealand and France—enshrined in gold, silver and enamel.

Intended to foster goodwill at international level, the trophy was originally held by a country until defeat in a Test series, when the victor took possession. In 1962, the International Board decided to award the imposing trophy to the country with the best record in Test matches over a period of five years, the first being from March 1960 to 1965.

Transport difficulties, and damage in transit, forced the trophy to be found a permanent home and after several years at the Rugby Leagues' Club in Sydney, the trophy is now on show at the new headquarters of Sydney club at Cronulla.

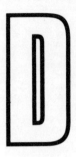

DEATHS

Patrick Collins, playing for Keighley against Batley at Mount Pleasant on 3 Dec. 1921, collapsed ten minutes from the end of the game and died shortly afterwards.

David Craven, a former Blaydon and Durham County R.U. wingman, sustained a spinal injury while playing for Halifax against Workington Town at Thrum Hall on 26 Feb. 1949. He died in hospital the following week.

Hudson Irving, a Cumberland forward who had played with Halifax for 14 years, collapsed and died during a game against Dewsbury at Thrum Hall on 12 Apr. 1947. The match, with ten minutes still to go, was abandoned by the referee, Mr. Laurie Thorpe, who was to be a victim himself six years later under similar circumstances.

Ray Morris, a member of the 1933-34 Australian Tour Team, died from an ear infection in a Malta hospital on 11 Aug. 1933, while the team was on its way to England.

Harry Myers, the Keighley captain and half back, was badly injured in a collision with a Dewsbury player at Crown Flatt on 13 Nov. 1906. He died in hospital on 19 Dec.

Dennis Norton, a Castleford prop forward, complained of pains in his chest during a game against the New Zealand Touring Team on 16 Nov. 1965. He died in hospital twelve days later.

Ralph Slater, a Rochdale Hornets second row forward, was injured in a reserve game against Oldham "A" in Oct. 1953. He died the following day.

Frank Townsend, a Wakefield Trinity three-quarter, sustained an injury in a game against Featherstone Rovers at Belle Vue on 19 Oct. 1946, and died later in hospital.

Laurie Thorpe was taken ill while refereeing the Whitehaven v. Barrow match on Christmas Day, 1953. He died the same day. Ironically enough he should not have had that fixture, but he was deputising for another referee.

Jeff Whiteside injured his spine playing on the wing for Swinton in an "A" team game at Rochdale Hornets in February 1976 and died in hospital in early May.

Chris Sanderson, the Leeds half back, died minutes after being stretchered off the field in a Salford v. Leeds First Division game at the Willows on Sunday 24 Apr. 1977. A subsequent testimonial raised more than £20,000 for his widow.

Grade One referee Joe Jackson (43) collapsed and died in the tea room at Knowsley Road after taking charge of the St. Helens v. Hull KR First Division match on 14 Oct. 1979.

DEWSBURY RLFC

Founded in 1898. Joined the Northern Union in 1898. Ground: Crown Flatt. Colours: Red, amber and black hooped jersey, white shorts.

RL Championship Winners, 1972-73.
  Beaten Finalists, 1946-47.
Division Two Champions, 1904-05.
RL Cup Winners, 1911-12, 1942-43.
  Beaten Finalists, 1928-29.
Yorkshire League Winners, 1946-47.
Yorkshire Cup Winners, 1925-26, 1927-28, 1942-43.
  Beaten finalists, 1918-19, 1921-22, 1940-41, 1972-73.
BBC 2 Floodlit Trophy beaten finalists, 1975-76.
War League Championship Winners, 1915-16, 1916-17, 1941-42.
Club Records:
  Attendance: 26,584 v. Halifax (Yorkshire Cup) 30 Oct. 1920.
  Tries: 40 by D. Thomas, 1906-07.
  Goals: 145 by N. Stephenson, 1972-73.
  Points: 368 by N. Stephenson, 1972-73.

DISCIPLINARY COMMITTEE

The Rugby League Disciplinary Committee sits in judgement on players sent off or cautioned during professional matches.

The committee consists of six members, made up of two representatives of the Rugby League Council, two from the League's Executive Committee, and one each from the Lancashire and Yorkshire County Committees.

They consider reports of misconduct during first team, "A" team and Colts matches and have the power to suspend or fine any player found guilty, bearing in mind the nature of the offence and any previous record. Meetings are normally held in the League Headquarters on the last Thursday of each month, when reported players are at liberty to make personal appearances.

A player's suspension takes effect from the day following the meeting, except for permanent suspensions which start immediately. Cautions issued by a referee to a player are recorded by the committee and if a player receives two cautions in any one season or calendar year he is liable to suspension and/or a fine. Recently the League issued referees with a yellow card, to be shown when a caution is administered.

A disciplined player has the right of appeal to the Rugby League Council.

The amateur game has its own disciplinary procedure, but any amateur club taking part in a professional competition, such as the Challenge Cup, is dealt with by the Disciplinary Committee.

DONCASTER RLFC

Founded 1951, joined the Northern Rugby League in 1951. Ground: Tatters Field. Colours: White jerseys with blue and gold bands, white shorts.

Doncaster have won no major honours.
Club Records:
  Attendance: 4,793 v. Wakefield T. (League) 7 Apr. 1962.
  Goals: 89 T. Griffiths, 1951-52.
  Tries: 17 by Brian Wriglesworth, 1957-58.
  Points: 187 by T. Griffiths, 1951-52.

DROP GOALS

The value of a drop goal was reduced from four points to two points in 1897. For the next 70 years this method of scoring became increasingly rare, being reserved for attempts to snatch a late match-winning goal.

A notable exception was in the 1962 RL Challenge Cup final at Wembley when Neil Fox's three drop goals made all the difference in Wakefield Trinity's 12-6 defeat of Huddersfield.

Drop goal attempts increased alarmingly with the introduction of the limited-tackle rule in 1966. To discourage this promiscuous outbreak it was decided that following an unsuccessful drop-goal attempt that went "dead" the defending team could retain possession with a tap kick on their own "25".

But it was not until the drop goal's value was reduced to one point at the start of the 1974-75 season that their use became more selective. Even so the number of successful kicks has gradually increased from a total of 84 in League matches during the first season of one-point drops to over 200 in 1978-79. In that season Norman Turley of Blackpool Borough scored a record 18 in all competitive matches, add the following season by Tony Dean, of Hunslet.

During the 1979-80 season Hunslet's Tony Dean, formerly of Batley and Barrow, became the first player to total 50 one-point drop goals.

The most one-point goals by a player in a match is four by Alan Agar for Hull KR at Leeds on 30 Sept. 1978, and John Blair for Halifax at home to Wakefield Trinity on 9 Mar. 1980.

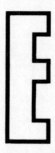

EASTERN DIVISION CHAMPIONSHIP

Season 1962-63 staged the revival of the two-division format, following its scrapping in 1905 after a three-year trial.

During this two-year venture, the traditional Yorkshire League was replaced by an Eastern Division Championship for Yorkshire Clubs. The return to a single division in 1964-65 paved the way for the reinstatement of the Yorkshire League.

Eastern Division Champions were:

	Winners	Runners-up
1962-63	Hull KR	Huddersfield
1963-64	Halifax	Castleford

See also YORKSHIRE LEAGUE CHAMPIONSHIP CUP.

ENTERTAINMENT

Rugby League has provided the subject matter for several top-class screen works.

This Sporting Life, the much acclaimed film featured shots recorded at Wakefield Trinity's Belle Vue ground, plus crowd scenes from a Wakefield Trinity versus Leeds match. Several Trinity players took part in dressing-room and close-up scenes in the film, which starred Richard Harris, who later won an actor's award at the Cannes Film Festival for his role. *This Sporting Life* was adapted from a novel by David Storey, a native of Wakefield and a former player with Leeds RLFC.

Earlier, Northern comedian Sydney Chaplin used scenes from Wembley Cup Finals in his famous film *Up for t'Cup*, in which several players had parts as extras.

David Storey put Rugby League in the spotlight again in the late 1960s when the 13-a-side code provided the backcloth for a stage play called *The Changing Room*. The highly successful production was housed at The Royal Court, London, before a run on Broadway.

In 1976, Alan Plater's stage play *Trinity Tales* was televised on BBC2, with a repeat showing. The plays were a modern version of *Canterbury Tales* and were based on the story-telling of a group of Rugby League fans making the "pilgrimage" to Wembley.

Rugby League once again figured in the drama stakes in late 1978 when Granada Television networked *Fallen Hero*, a series written by Brian Finch and starring Del Henney. The plays revolved around a former Welsh Rugby Union star whose League career was prematurely ended by a leg injury. Such was the series' popularity that a second script was ordered immediately.

ESSO YORKSHIRE CUP

Esso Petroleum provided sponsorship for the Yorkshire Cup for the first time in 1972, when the petrol company pumped £2,500 into the 16-club tournament. Retitled the Esso Yorkshire Cup, the tourney benefited by £6,000 sponsorship the following season, arising to £9,000 for the 1978 competition, ceasing after the 1979-80 campaign.

See also YORKSHIRE CUP.

EUROPEAN CHAMPIONSHIP

Several attempts to establish the European Championship as a regular feature of the fixture programme have been made since the French entered the Rugby League world in the mid-1930s, but it has never survived for long.

Its best spell came after the Second World War when it ran until 1955-56. There was a brief revival attempt in 1969-70, but it was not until 1974-75 that a serious attempt to maintain a three-cornered competition between England, France and Wales was made again.

By that time international football was considered essential to maintain interest in French and British ambitions in the Test match field.

The current competition is called the Jean Galia Cup in memory of the French Rugby League pioneer who died at the tragically early age of 44 in 1949.

Since the 1974-75 resuscitation, the competition has only missed one season, 1975-76, when it was replaced by a World Championship. The biggest threat to its future today is the erratic Welsh team strength.

In modern times not as many Welsh Rugby Union players have been tempted North and this has given the Welsh RL selectors problems particularly in the forwards. Northern-born players can qualify to play for Wales if they claim Welsh grandparents which has eased the problem slightly. Welsh-born players get preference in selection although the Anglos have performed well in the red jersey.

The European Championship since 1969 has been won by England in 1969-70, 1974-75, 1977-78, 1978-79 and 1979-80, and France in 1976-77. Before 1969 England won the title six times, France four times, Wales three times and Other Nationalities twice.

EX-PLAYERS ASSOCIATION

The formation of associations for ex-players has developed in recent years, with new bodies springing up throughout the League. Retired players band together to organise social reunions and to raise funds for former colleagues in financial distress.

Leading ex-players associations are based at Oldham, Wakefield Trinity, Humberside and Salford, known as the Red Devils. Former playing members of the now-defunct Hunslet Club also hold an annual reunion.

See also BRITISH LIONS.

FEATHERSTONE ROVERS RLFC

Founded 1902. Joined the Northern Rugby League in 1921. Ground: Post Office Road. Colours: White and blue hooped jerseys, blue shorts.
RL Cup Winners, 1966-67, 1972-73.
  Runners-up, 1951-52, 1973-74.
RL Championship beaten finalists, 1927-28.
Division One Champions, 1976-77.
Division Two Champions: 1979-80.
Yorkshire Cup Winners, 1939-40, 1959-60.
  Beaten Finalists, 1928-29, 1963-64, 1966-67, 1969-70, 1970-71, 1976-77, 1977-78.
Captain Morgan Trophy Beaten Finalists, 1973-74.
Club Records:
  Attendance: 17,531 v. St Helens (RL Cup) 21 Mar. 1959.
  Goals: 163 by S. Quinn, 1979-80.
  Tries: 31 by C. Woolford, 1958-59.
  Points: 375 by S. Quinn, 1979-80.

FIXTURES

The demanding job of arranging the season's fixture list falls on the Rugby League Secretary. Because of the unsettled fixture formula for a typical season, attempts to computerise the fixing of dates have been abortive.

Any attempt to establish an home-and-away League pattern is dented by the necessary inclusion of weekend dates for the County Cups, John Player Competition, Challenge Cup and International commitments, plus demands from clubs for lucrative derby matches to be played on certain holiday dates.

Before the start of each season, each club informs the Secretary of any agreed matches to be featured in the fixture list e.g. Boxing Day, Good Friday. With these essential dates in mind, the Secretary draws up the season's fixtures. This draft version is circulated to each club, who have a fortnight to submit amendments. At present, weekend matches are fixed for a Sunday, but the home club has the right to move the match to a Friday or Saturday without referring the matter to the visiting club.

FLOODLIGHTS

More than two-thirds of the 30 professional Rugby League clubs have installed floodlights.

Surprisingly, the first match under artificial lighting was way back in the 1870s! Two "Gramme's Lights" attached to 30ft poles illuminated the Broughton versus Swinton match on 22 Oct. 1878. A year later, "Siemens electric lights" served the clash between Halifax and Lancashire rivals Birch at Hanson Lane, Halifax. During 1896-97, Leeds experimented with a new electric system, while games were being staged with moving lights along the touch lines.

London had its first taste of floodlit Rugby League on 14 Dec. 1932, when Leeds defeated Wigan by 18-9 in an exhibition game at the White City Stadium.

Bradford Northern and Leigh were the post-1945 floodlight pioneers. Northern's first game under lights was against the New Zealand tourists at Odsal Stadium on 31 Oct. 1951, in front of 29,072 spectators, Bradford winning 13-8.

In Oct. and Nov. of 1955 the Independent Television Trophy was launched with eight teams—Featherstone Rovers, Huddersfield, Hunslet, Leigh, Oldham, Wakefield Trinity, Warrington and Wigan—taking part in matches staged on London soccer grounds. Warrington beat Leigh 43-18 in the final staged at Queens Park Rangers, Shepherd Bush, on 16 Nov. before a crowd of 3,500. Each team received £400, but television screening was restricted to the South.

In 1965, floodlighting became more widespread with the launching of the BBC2 Floodlit Trophy. At the end of the 1979-80 season, the Rugby League clubs without permanent floodlights were Batley, Blackpool Borough, Doncaster, Featherstone Rovers, Huyton, Workington Town and York. The last team, however, staged a meeting with the 1978 Australian Tourists at Wiggington Road, under mobile, temporary lights.

See also BBC2 FLOODLIT TROPHY

FORSHAWS LANCASHIRE CUP

In 1976 Burtonwood Brewery, of Burtonwood, near Warrington, entered into a four-year agreement to sponsor the Lancashire County Challenge Cup. The brewery introduced the family name of Forshaws into the title of the competition, which was renamed the Forshaws Lancashire Cup.

See also LANCASHIRE CUP

FORWARD CHEMICALS TEST SERIES

The Forward Chemicals 1978 Test Series was the first-ever sponsorship of Great Britain versus Australia matches. By injecting £17,500 into the three-match tournament, the Widnes-based company became, at that time, the second biggest sponsors in British Rugby League history.

Australia won the First Test at Central Park, Wigan, and the Third Test at Headingley, Leeds. Great Britain levelled the series in the Second Test at Odsal Stadium, Bradford.

Forward Chemicals also sponsored the Man of the Match award which, in order, went to Rod Reddy (Australia), Brian Lockwood (Great Britain) and Tommy Raudonikis (Australia).

FRANCE

In common with Australia, England and New Zealand dissatisfaction established Rugby League as an acceptable part of national sporting life in France. In March 1931 the four British members of the home Rugby Union Championship banned the French from the competition because of alleged "professionalism" and rough play.

Starved of international competition from their neighbour countries, conditions in France were just right for the introduction of Rugby League. An exhibition match was arranged between the touring Australians and Great Britain. The match, which was played in the Stade Pershing, Paris, on 31 Dec. 1933, attracted a crowd of 20,000 and the Australians ran out comfortable winners 63-13 on a frozen pitch.

Among the pioneers for this first venture were English League secretary John Wilson, English officials W. Gabbatt, J. Lewthwaite and W. Popplewell, Australian tour manager Harry Sunderland and two Frenchmen, Jean Galia, a Villeneuve and Toulouse centre who had won 20 RU caps, and M. Victor Breyer, editor of a newspaper called *Echo des Sports*.

Galia was to prove the catalyst of the French Rugby revolution. He recognised the potential offered by Rugby League and persuaded 16 of his Union colleagues to give the "new" code a chance. They made a tour of England in March 1934 playing games at Wigan, Leeds, Hull, Warrington, White City (London), and Salford.

The French won just one of those matches, at Hull, but it was enough to give them a taste for the game. The players who made the tour were: Amila, Carrere, Cassagneau, Barbazagnes, Blanc, Dechavanne, Duhau, Galia, Lambert, Mathon, Nouel, Petit, Porra, Recaborde, Samatan, Vabre and Vignials. Because they knew little about Rugby League laws two famous English internationals, Jonty Parkin and Joe Thompson, coached them.

On 2 Apr. 1934 the Fédération Française de Jeu à Treize (roughly translated it means French game for 13) was officially formed and on 15 Apr. they staged their first international game against England at Buffalo Velodrome, Paris. The Englishmen won 32-21.

The French League competition, which began on Oct. 1934, had 12 founder member clubs: Albi, Bordeaux, Côte Basque, Grenoble, La Rochelle, Lyons, Paris Celtic, Pau, Roanne, S. O. Beziers, Sport Olympique de Paris and Villeneuve-sur-Lot. During the 1934-35 season Salford and Hunslet undertook short tours and, led by Galia, Villeneuve played exhibition matches at Warrington, Broughton, Hull, Oldham and Leeds. They lost all their games, but impressed the British Rugby League public with their enthusiasm for their game.

In fact, the French were such enthusiasts for Rugby League that they suggested a world series should be played in 1935. The subject was aired, but not taken up. The French, however, retained the idea and were among the leaders when the competition was eventually introduced in 1954.

A big boost for the French game came on 1 Jan. 1935 when they achieved their first international victory, beating Wales 18-11 at Bordeaux before a crowd of 15,000.

As a gesture of goodwill the English League presented the French with the Lord Derby Trophy for use in the national knockout competition and it was put up for the first time on 5 May 1935, one day after the English final at Wembley, when Lyon beat Perpignan 22-7.

For the second season four new clubs were admitted to the League and the

French drew 15-15 with a strong English team at Buffalo Velodrome. By 1939 they had reached such strength that they were able to win the European international championship for the first time.

War clouds gathered after that triumph and Rugby League suffered a major setback in 1941 when the German-backed Vichy government of Pétain banned the game. The proclamation that brought the news was:

Secretary of State for National Education and Youth. No 5285—decree of the 19th December, 1941, bringing about the dissolution of the Association called French League of Rugby XIII. We, the Field Marshal of France, the Head of the French State, in view of the law on the 20th December, 1940, relating to sporting organisation, on the proposal of the Secretary of State for National Education of Youth, decree:

First Article—The Association called French League of Rugby XIII whose offices are at 24 Rue Drouot, Paris, is dissolved, assent having been refused it.

Second Article—The patrimony (property and money) of the Association dissolved by virtue of the preceding article, is transferred, without modification, the National Committee of Sports who assume all its charges and will be represented in the operation of liquidation by its Secretary-General M. Charles Denis.

Third article—The Secretary of State for National Education, Youth and Sports is charged with the execution of this present decree which will be published in the Official Journal. Made at Vichy, 29th December, 1941."

But, the game did not die entirely and the indomitable Frenchmen continued to play the game in villages, well away from prying German eyes. By the time France had been liberated and the European war ended in 1945, the French League faced a massive rebuilding operation. Their Paris offices had been wrecked and their records destroyed, but they were ready for a visit by England to Paris on 6 Jan. 1946, for a trip to play England at Swinton in Feb. 1946 and then an international against the Welsh in Bordeaux.

The French then entered their golden international era. They won the European Championship against England and Wales for three successive seasons and then repeated the triumph in 1950-51 when Other Nationalities competed in the championship.

Flying high after their success in Europe, the French made their first tour of Australia and New Zealand in 1951 and they continued in their winning vein by beating the Australians 2-1 in the three Test series. Just to prove that was not a fluke result they repeated the feat in 1955 and in 1960 they drew the series.

Their international decline, however, has been responsible for their last tour of Australia being in 1964, although they are scheduled to tour again in 1981.

The French international success in the early 1950s was the spring-board for another new venture, the first World Cup in 1954. Originally the brain-child of English League secretary Mr W. Fallowfield, the French were enthusiastic followers and became the first hosts. They used the centres of Bordeaux, Lyons, Marseilles, Nantes, Paris and Toulouse and Great Britain won the competition with what everybody considered, before the tournament, to be a team of "no-hopers".

Since then the state of French Rugby League has varied enormously. They have swung between finishing bottom of the European Championship and reaching the final of the World Cup. Their main strength lies in the South-west of the country with the major clubs in Carcassonne, Perpignan and Toulouse. Amateur Rugby League is widespread in France, including the capital, Paris.

Until 1974-75 the French operated a League system of 15 major clubs and, differing from most other Rugby Leagues, awarded 3pts for a victory, 2pts for a draw and one for a defeat. But after the 1974-75 annual congress in Limoux, the system was altered with a National League of two divisions, Pool " A " and Pool " B ". The major clubs in France compete in these two pools.

National League II, the less powerful clubs, play in four pools " A ", " B ", " C " and " D " which are regionalised to reduce travelling costs. The least powerful and some junior clubs play in National League III with pools " A ", " B ", " C ", " D ", " E " and " F ".

Area committees link all the clubs of varying standards. The committees are: Atlantique (Nantes area), Herault (Montpellier area), Ile de France (Paris Area), Agennais (Villeneuve area), Côte d'Argent (Bordeaux area), Languedoc (Carcassonne area), Littoral (Marseilles area), Provence (Avignon area), Pyrenees (Toulouse to Atlantic coast and Spanish border area),

Rhone-Alps (Lyon, Roanne and Grenoble areas), Rouergue (Albi-Villefranche-de-Rouergue area), Corse (Corsica) and Roussillon (Perpignan area).

In 1978-79 the French League system was made up in the following fashion:

National League I
Pool "A": XIII Catalan, Toulouse Olympique, Carcassonne, Avignon, Villeneuve, Roanne, Limoux, Lezignan, Albi, Saint-Esteve, Pamiers, Pia, Saint-Jacques, Cavallon.

Pool "B": Carprentas, Saint-Gaudens, Villefranche, Tonneins, Entraigues, La Reole, Cahors, Salon, Paris.

During 1977-78 Pool "A" was expanded to 14 clubs, while Pool "B" was left with 12 clubs. The second section was reduced to nine clubs during 1978-79 when Bordeaux, Marseilles and St Fons (Lyons) pulled out of the competition.

National League II
Pool "A": Ent Montpellier, Caumont, Ajaccio, Charlieu, La Paillade, Cavaillon, Cannes, Le Pontet.

Pool "B": Ornaisons, AS Carcassonne, Le Barcares, Aussillon, Ferrals, St Cyprien, Lezignan.

Pool "C:" Palau, Salses, La Redorte, Realmont, U.O. Albi, Auterive, Chatillon, TOAC, Clairac.

Pool "D": Lestelle Betharam, Aspet, Le Mas d'Agenais, Facture, Montrejeau Miramont de Guyenne, Tonneins, Villeneuve Tolosane.

National League III
Pool "A": PAC, Roanne, Paris XIII, Nantes, Stella St Maur, Bois d'Arcy, Fleury Merogis, Mongeron, Grigny, Ezanville.

Pool "B": Plan de Cuque, Carpentras, Bastia, Vedene, Morieres, Le Thor, Salon, Nimes.

Pool "C": Palau, Salses, La Redorte, Rieux, Toulouges, Homps, Rivesaltes, Castelnaudary.

Pool "D": Miremont, Rodez, Toulouse Jules Julien, Vill de Rouergue, Vill d'Albi, Miramont, Cardeilhac, Muret, St Jean du Falga.

Pool "E": Duras, Bias, SA Villeneuve, Trentels, Limoges, Le Mas, Cahors.

Pool "F": Ogue, Pau, Talence, Begles, Pineuilh, St Jean de Luz, Barie, Merignac.

Besides the senior league there are also a large number of junior and age-group leagues.

The French roll-of-honour is as follows:

Championship Play-Offs

Year	Winner		Runners-up	
1934-35	US Villeneuve—no play off			
1935-36	XIII Catalan	25	Bordeaux	14
1936-37	Bordeaux	23	Lyons	10
1937-38	RC Albi	8	US Villeneuve	5
1938-39	RC Roanne	9	US Villeneuve	0
	No wartime championship—see accompanying notes			
1944-45	AS Carcassonne	14	XIII Catalan	8
1945-46	AS Carcassonne	12	Toulouse Olympique	0
1946-47	RC Roanne	19	AS Carcassonne	0
1947-48	RC Roanne	3	AS Carcassonne	2
1948-49	RC Marseilles	12	AS Carcassonne	5
1949-50	AS Carcassonne	21	RC Marseilles	7
1950-51	Lyons	15	XIII Catalan	10
1951-52	AS Carcassonne	18	RC Marseilles	6
1952-53	AS Carcassonne	19	Lyons	12
1953-54	Bordeaux	7	RC Marseilles	4
1954-55	Lyons	7	AS Carcassonne	6
1955-56	RC Albi	13	AS Carcassonne	5
1956-57	XIII Catalan	14	SO Avignon	9
1957-58	RC Albi	8	AS Carcassonne	6
1958-59	US Villeneuve	24	FC Lezignan	16
1959-60	RC Roanne	31	RC Albi	24
1960-61	FC Lezignan	7	RC Roanne	4
1961-62	RC Albi	14	US Villeneuve	7
1962-63	FC Lezignan	20	RC St Gaudens	13
1963-64	US Villeneuve	4	Toulouse Olympique	3
1964-65	Toulouse Olympique	47	US Villeneuve	15
1965-66	AS Carcassonne	47	RC St Gaudens	20

1966-67	AS Carcassonne	39	RC St Gaudens	15
1967-68	SC Limoux	13	AS Carcassonne	12
1968-69	XIII Catalan	12	RC St Gaudens	11
1969-70	RC St Gaudens	32	XIII Catalan	10
1970-71	Saint-Esteve	13	RC St Gaudens	4
1971-72	AS Carcassonne	21	RC St Gaudens	9
1972-73	Toulouse Olympique	18	RC Marseilles	0
1973-74	RC St Gaudens	21	US Villeneuve	8
1975-76	AS Carcassonne	14	FC Lezignan	6
1976-77	RC Albi	19	AS Carcassonne	10
1977-78	FC Lezignan	3	XIII Catalan	0

Coupe de France (Lord Derby Cup)

Year	Winner		Runners-up	
1935	Lyon	22	Perpignan	7
1936	Côte Basque	15	Villeneuve sur Lot	8
1937	Villeneuve sur Lot	12	Perpignan	6
1938	Roanne	36	Villeneuve sur Lot	12
1939	Perpignan	7	Toulouse	3
1945	Perpignan	23	Carcassonne	14
1946	Carcassonne	27	Perpignan	7
1947	Carcassonne	24	Avignon	5
1948	Marseille	5	Carcassonne	4
1949	Marseille	12	Carcassonne	9
1950	Perpignan	12	Lyons	5
1951	Carcassonne	22	Lyons	10
1952	Carcassonne	28	Perpignan	9
1953	Lyons	9	Villeneuve sur Lot	8
1954	Lyons	17	Perpignan	15
1955	Avignon	18	Marseille	10
1956	Avignon	25	Bordeaux	12
1957	Marseille	11	Perpignan	0
1958	Villeneuve sur Lot	20	Avignon	8
1959	Perpignan	7	Avignon	0
1960	FC Lezignan	7	Carcassonne	4
1961	Carcassonne	5	FC Lezignan	2
1962	Roanne	16	Toulouse	10
1963	Carcassonne	5	Toulouse	0
1964	Villeneuve sur Lot	10	Toulouse	2
1965	Marseille	13	Carcassonne	8
1966	FC Lezignan	22	Villeneuve sur Lot	7
1967	Carcassonne	—	XIII Catalan	—
			score not known	
1968	Carcassonne	9	Toulouse	2
1969	XIII Catalan	13	Villeneuve sur Lot	8
1970	FC Lezignan	14	Villeneuve sur Lot	8
1971	Marseille	17	FC Lezignan	2
1972	Saint-Esteve	12	Villeneuve sur Lot	5
1973	Saint-Gaudens	22	Carcassonne	8
1974	Albi	21	FC Lezignan	11
1975	Pia	9	Marseille	4
1976	XIII Catalans	23	Toulouse	8
1977	Carcassonne	21	XIII Catalan	16

French teams to tour Australia and New Zealand

1951

P. Aubert, O. Lespes, G. Comes, J. Merquey, V. Cantoni, J. Dop, L. Mazon, M. Martin, A. Bernard, E. Brousse, E. Ponsinet, G. Calixte, R. Duffort, R. Contrastin, M. Andre, R. Callion, R. Perez, M. Lopez, F. Montrucolis, P. Bartoletti, A. Audobert, G. Genond, F. Rinaldi, J. Crespo, G. Delaye, M. Bellan, C. Galaup, C. Teisseire; manager: A. Blain; coaches: J. Duhan and R. Samatan.

One of the most famous pictures in Rugby League history: Odsal Stadium, Bradford, on 5 May 1954, when 102,575 spectators watched Warrington beat Halifax in the Challenge Cup Final replay by 8 points to 4. The attendance has only once been exceeded at a football match in England—at the 1923 FA Cup Final.

(*Above*) The first ever British Amateur Rugby League Association Open Age team to tour Papua New Guinea, Australia and New Zealand. Pictured at Port Moresbey, May 1978

(*Left*) Too late. Great Britain star Roger Millward prepares for the worst as Australian loose forward Ray Price pulls him out of the way during the 1978 Test series.

(*Right*) No way through. Les Dyl, Leeds and Great Britain, blocks the path of Australian Steve Rogers in the 1978 series second Test at Odsal Stadium, Bradford.

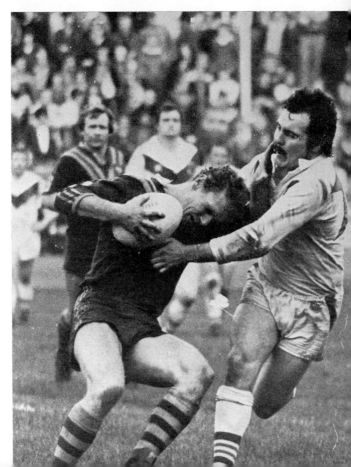

Another one for the record book. Neil Fox who broke Jim Sullivan's world points scoring record during the 1978–79 season, kicks another goal for Bradford Northern.

1955

G. Benausse, R. Contrastin, F. Cantoni, M. Voren, A. Savonne, A. Ducasse, C. Teisseire, J. Merquey, R. Rey, V. Larroude, F. Levy, A. Jiminez, A. Delpoux, J. Dop, S. Menichelli, C. Duple, R. Guilhem, F. Montrucolis, A. Save, J. Pambrun, G. Berthomieu, J. Janames, J. Fabre, J. Vanel, A. Audobert, R. Monlis, A. Carrere; manager: A. Blain; coaches: J. Duhan; trainer: R. Duffort.

1960

P. Lacaze, L. Poletti, J. Verges, R. Benausse, R. Gruppi, J. Dubon, A. Jiminez, G. Benausse, A. Foussat, J. Darrican, A. Perducat, C. Mantoulan, R. Moulinas, B. Fabre, J. Guirand, A. Lacaze, A. Marty, J. Barthe, R. Eramouspde, R. Majoral, Y. Mezard, A. Quaglio, M. Bescos, A. Boldini, F. Rossi, A. Casas, A. Vadon, G. Fages. manager: A. Blain; assistant manager: G. Vassal; coaches: R. Doffort and J. Duhan.

1964

A. Carrere, M. Boule, J. Etcheberry, R. Gruppi, C. Mantoulan, B. Fabre, captain, J. Lacompte, A. Bourreil, H. Castel, J. Villeneuve, L. Verge, R. Garnung, L. Faletti, J. Pano, P. Azlabert, F. Mas, C. Sabathier, E. Dusseigneur, J. Graciet, R. Lianas, G. Allieres, R. Erasmoupe, S. Estian, H. Larrue, M. Bardes, J. Lapotere, G. Fages, H. Chamorin, manager: J. Barres.

1968 World Cup

J. P. Clar (capt.), J. L. Cros, A. Ferren, J. Ledru, D. Pelleren, J. Gruppi, M. Moliner, J. P. Lecompte, J. Capdouze, R. Garrigues, M. Frattini, A. Alesina, F. De Nadai, H. Mazard, H. Marracq, C. Sabate, V. Gerrand, G. Alieres, Y. Begou; managers: J. Guirand and F. Soree; coach: J. Lacoste.

1975 World Championship, Southern Hemisphere section

F. Tranier, A. Dumas, A. Ruiz, R. Terrats, B. Curt, J. Calle, J. M. Imbert, M. Alglade, S. Gleyzes, M. Maique, M. Cassin, F. Kaninsky, F De Nadai, J. C. Mayorgas, C. Zalduendo, A. Gonzales, A. Moliner, G. Bonal.

1977 World Cup

J. Guieve, P. Saboureau, J. Moya, P. Chauvet, C. Laskawie, C. Bailes, J. M. Bourret, R. Terrats, A. Ruiz, J. Calle, J. M. Imbert, M. Carovala, J. Roosebrouck, J. P. Saurent, J. J. Rodriguez, J. L. Brial, J. L. Mayorgas, M. Cassin, H. Daniel, M. Chantel, M. Moussard, H. Bonet, G. Garcia.

FULHAM RLFC

The shock news that London soccer club Fulham wanted to promote Rugby League was broken in the *Daily Mail* in June 1980. Some days later at the League's AGM at the Hotel Majestic, Harrogate, on 27 June the 29 clubs present voted 26 in favour with three abstentions to accept Fulham into the Second Division for the 1980-81 season. The inaugural board of directors was Ernie Clay (Chairman), Brian Dalton, Harold Gerders, showbusiness personality Colin Wellard and ex-England soccer superstar Malcolm Macdonald. Player-coach Reg Bowden was appointed on 1 July from Widnes. They played their first match at home to Wigan on 14 September.

GALLAGHERS RESTAURANT

Situated in the West 52nd Street, New York, Gallaghers Restaurant was the venue for the historic launch of the United States Rugby League, in August 1978. A specially invited audience of nearly 100, including leading American media representatives and Rugby League hierarchy from all over the world, attended the lunch ceremony.

Rugby League match broadcasts, including highlights of the 1978 Wembley Final between Leeds and St Helens, provided the backcloth for the prestigious event, which was marked by the putting up for sale of franchises for the proposed 12-team League in the United States.

See also AMERICA.

GEORGE HOTEL

The George Hotel in the centre of Huddersfield is acknowledged as the birthplace of Rugby League. On 25 Aug. 1895, the Northern Rugby Football Union was formed at a meeting in the hotel, becoming known as the Rugby Football League in 1922.

To commemorate the historic meeting, the Rugby Football League belatedly commissioned a plaque to be mounted in the foyer of the hotel, the unveiling ceremony being held at a special dinner at the hotel on 8 Dec. 1976.

See also NORTHERN RUGBY FOOTBALL UNION.

GOALS

Most goals in a match

22 by Jim Sullivan (Wigan) v. Flimby and Fothergill (RL Cup 14 Feb. 1925).

Longest Successful Kick

Martin Hodgson (Swinton) is credited with the longest recorded successful goal kick. In a Lancashire Cup-tie against Rochdale Hornets on 13 Apr. 1940, his kick was measured at $77\frac{3}{4}$ yards.

Most goals in a career

Jim Sullivan, in a career lasting from 1921 to 1946, scored a total of 2,860 goals. All his peace-time club rugby was with Wigan. During the war he also played for Dewsbury, Bradford Northern and Keighley. Generally accepted as the greatest full back of all time, his total includes 441 scored in representative matches and on tour. He also holds the record for most centuries with a run of 18 in successive seasons.

His season-by-season record is as follows:

1921-22	101	1932-33	146
1922-23	161	1933-34	193
1923-24	158	1934-35	165
1924 tour	84	1935-36	117
1924-25	138	1936-37	117
1925-26	131	1937-38	115
1926-27	149	1938 tour	
1927-28	104	(France)	13
1928 tour	52	1938-39	124
1928-29	107	1939-40	65
1929-30	110	1940-41	40
1930-31	133	1941-42	49
1931-32	117	1942-43	49
1932 tour	110	1943-44	7
		1944-45	0
		1945-46	5

In addition he scored 95 tries for a total of 6,500 pts.

Fastest 100

At one time a century of goals before Christmas was a rare feat, but with the start of each season having fluctuated, sometimes beginning as early as August 1, it has lost its significance.

The record for the fastest 100 in terms of number of matches played is held by Bernard Ganley, David Watkins and Steve Quinn who each achieved the century in only 18 matches. In 1957 Ganley notched up 100 goals on 16 Nov. playing 17 matches for Oldham and one for Great Britain. Watkins reached his 100th goal in 1972 on 17 Nov. All his 18 matches were for Salford. Quinn equalled the feat on 16 Dec. 1979, all 18 matches being for Featherstone Rovers.

Most Goals in a Season

221 by David Watkins (Salford) in 1972-73.

1972			
Aug.	19	Leeds (h.)	5
	23	Featherstone (a.)	3
	26	Whitehaven (a.)	4
	28	Swinton (h.)	1
Sept.	1	Oldham (h.) LC	10
	9	Leeds (a.)	2
	15	Rochdale (h.) LC	11
	17	Leigh (a.)	6
	24	Barrow (a.) PNo.6	4
	29	Huyton (h.)	10
Oct.	3	Oldham (a.) BBC2	4
	6	Wigan (a.) LC	4
	8	Blackpool (a.)	5
	13	Blackpool (h.)	8
	21	Swinton (LCF)	5
Nov.	5	Huyton (a.)	8
	10	Rochdale (h.)	6
	17	Warrington (a.)	4
	19	New Zealand (h.)	10
	24	Dewsbury (h.) PNo6	4
	26	Workington (h.)	6
Dec.	1	Barrow (h.)	9
	9	Bradford (h.) PNo6	9
	13	Oldham (a.)	4
	15	Leigh (h.)	3
	24	Bradford (a.)	5
	26	Workington (a.)	3
	30	Hull KR (a.) PNo6	5
1973			
Jan.	3	Bradford (h.)	6
	7	Rochdale (a.)	2
	12	Featherstone (h.)	4
	28	Featherstone (a.) RL Cup	4
Feb.	2	Whitehaven (h.)	4
	11	Barrow (a.)	5
	23	St Helens (h.)	3
Mar.	7	Widnes (a.)	3
	9	Dewsbury (h.)	3
	16	St Helens (a.)	2
	24	Leeds (PNo6 Final)	2
	30	Warrington (h.)	1
Apr.	6	Widnes (h.)	4
	13	Oldham (h.)	3
	15	Dewsbury (a.)	2
	17	Wigan (a.)	3
	20	Swinton (a.)	7
	23	Wigan (h.)	3
	29	Rochdale (h.) (Top 16)	2

GREAT BRITAIN

To play for Great Britain in a Test or World Cup match is the highest honour a player can achieve.

The first Test match was against New Zealand at Headingley, Leeds, on 25 Jan. 1908. In the early years the team was known as the Northern Union or England until 1948 when it became Great Britain.

Matches against France did not achieve Test status until 1957 although Britain had played World Cup matches against them in 1954.

Most Appearances
46 by Mick Sullivan (Huddersfield, Wigan, St Helens and York). The total is made up of Test and World Cup matches as follows: against Australia (16), New Zealand (11) and France (19). In addition Sullivan played in two matches against France before they were given Test status.

Sullivan made his first appearance for Britain in 1954, starting record run of 36 successive Test and World Cup matches. His last match for Britain was in 1963.

Most Tries
40 by Mick Sullivan in Test and World Cup matches. In addition Sullivan scored two tries against France before they were granted Test status.

Most Goals and Points
93 goals (14 tries) and 228 points by Neil Fox (Wakefield T.) between 1959 and 1969.

Most tries in a Match
4 by Jim Leytham (Wigan) v. Australia at Brisbane, 2 July 1910.
4 by Billy Boston (Wigan) v. New Zealand, 1st Test at Auckland, 24 July 1954.
4 by Alex Murphy (St Helens) v. France, Test at Leeds, 14 Mar. 1959.

Most Goals in a Match
10 by Lewis Jones (Leeds) v. Australia, 2nd Test at Brisbane, 3 July 1954.
10 by Bernard Ganley (Oldham) v. France, Test at Wigan, 23 Nov. 1957.
10 by John Holmes (Leeds), v. New Zealand, World Cup at Pau, 4 Nov. 1972.

Most Points in a Match
26 (10 goals, 2 tries) by John Holmes (Leeds) v. New Zealand, World Cup at Pau, 4 Nov. 1972.

Highest score
53 v. New Zealand 19 (World Cup at Pau, 4 Nov. 1972.
Highest score against:
50 Australia v. GB 12, 2nd Test at Swinton, 9 Nov. 1963.
Record attendance:
70,204 1st Test v. Australia at Sydney, 6 June 1932.

Tours

Ever since A. H. Baskerville's All Gold team from New Zealand visited Britain in 1907 tours have played a very important role in the Rugby League life-style.

Financially tours have usually done well, but it took until the 1978-79 season to restore the profitability to Australian tours of Britain after a number of loss-making trips. This coincided with the recent revival in the game's fortunes at all levels.

The interchange of tours was originally on a four-year cycle, but the two world wars and various attempts to change the international format, for example the 1975 International Championship, have often interrupted that chain of events.

Today Rugby League has switched back to the tour system. In 1979 Great Britain toured Australia and New Zealand: in 1980 Australia cross the Tasman Sea to New Zealand and New Zealand play in Europe and in 1981 France will cross the equator to tour Australia and New Zealand.

P.	W.	L.	D.	G.
18	13	4	1	85

1914 Tour
A. E. Wood (Oldham), G. Thomas (Wigan), A. E. Francis (Hull), S. Moorhouse (Huddersfield), J. Robinson (Rochdale Hornets), F. Williams (Halifax), W. A. Davies (Leeds), H. Wagstaff (Huddersfield) captain, B. Jenkins (Wigan), W. Hall (Oldham), J. O'Gara (Widnes), W. S. Prosser (Halifax), J. Rogers (Huddersfield), F. Smith (Hunslet), L. Clampitt (Broughton R.), D. Clark (Huddersfield),

P.	W.	L.	D.	G.
17	14	3	–	83

1920 Tour
G. Thomas (Huddersfield), A. E. Wood (Oldham), W. J. Stone (Hull), S. Stockwell (Leeds), C. Stacey (Halifax), J. Bacon (Leeds), H. Wagstaff (Huddersfield) captain, D. Hurcombe (Wigan), E. Davies (Oldham), J. Doyle (Barrow), E. Jones (Rochdale Hornets), J. Parkin (Wakefield T.), R. Lloyd (Halifax), J. Rogers (Huddersfield), J. Cartwright (Leigh), A. Milnes

P.	W.	L.	D.	G.
25	21	4	–	111

Great Britain's teams to tour Australia and New Zealand have been:

1910 Tour
J. Sharrock (Wigan), F. Young (Leeds), C. Jenkins (Ebbw Vale), F. Farrar (Hunslet), J. Leytham (Wigan), W. Batten (Hunslet), J. Bartholomew (Huddersfield), J. Lomas (Salford) captain, B. Jenkins (Wigan), J. Riley (Halifax), F. Smith (Hunslet), J. Thomas (Wigan), J. Davies (Huddersfield), T. Newbould (Wakefield T.), T. Helm (Oldham), G. Ruddick (Broughton R.), F. Shugars (Warrington), R. Ramsdale (Wigan), E. Curzon (Salford), W. Winstanley (Leigh), F. Boylen (Hull), H. Kershaw (Wakefield T.), W. Jukes (Hunslet), W. Ward (Leeds), F. Webster (Leeds), A. E. Avery (Oldham). managers: J. Clifford (Huddersfield) and J. H. Houghton (St Helens).

18 games were played—14 in Australia and 4 in New Zealand.

For		Against		
T.	Pts.	G.	T.	Pts.
119	527	51	64	294

F. Longstaff (Huddersfield), W. Roman (Rochdale Hornets), D. Holland (Oldham), J. W. Smales (Hunslet), W. Jarman (Leeds), J. Chilcott (Huddersfield), J. W. Guerin (Hunslet), A. P. Coldrick (Wigan), A. Johnson (Widnes), R. Ramsdale (Wigan); managers: J. Clifford (Huddersfield) and J. H. Houghton (St Helens).

17 games were played—11 in Australia and 6 in New Zealand.

For		Against		
T.	Pts.	G.	T.	Pts.
123	535	44	36	196

(Halifax), J. Bowers (Rochdale Hornets), W. Cunliffe (Warrington), G. A. Skelhorne (Warrington), B. Gronow (Huddersfield), A. Johnson (Widnes), W. Reid (Widnes), G. Rees (Leeds), H. Hilton (Oldham), D. Clark (Huddersfield), F. Gallagher (Dewsbury); managers: S. Foster (Halifax) and J. Wilson (Hull KR).

25 games were played—15 in Australia and 10 in New Zealand.

For		Against		
T.	Pts.	G.	T.	Pts.
172	738	56	72	328

1924 Tour
J. Sullivan (Wigan), E. Knapman (Oldham), F. Evans (Swinton), J. Ring (Wigan), C. Pollard (Wakefield T.), W. Bentham (Broughton R.), S. Rix (Oldham), T. Howley (Wigan), C. Carr (Barrow), J. Bacon (Leeds), W. Mooney (Leigh), S. Whitty (Hull), J. Parkin (Wakefield T.) captain, D. Hurcombe (Wigan), B. Gronow (Huddersfield), H. Bowman (Hull), J.

Darwell (Leigh), R. Sloman (Oldham), W. Cunliffe (Warrington), J. Bennett (Rochdale Hornets), J. Price (Wigan), D. Rees (Halifax), J. Thompson (Leeds), W. Burgess (Barrow), A. Brough (Oldham), F. Gallagher (Batley); managers: J. H. Dannatt (Hull) and E. Osborne (Warrington).

27 games were played—18 in Australia and 9 in New Zealand.

P.	W.	L.	D.	G.	For		Against		
					T.	Pts.	G.	T.	Pts.
27	21	6	–	117	168	738	66	81	375

1928 Tour
J. Sullivan (Wigan), W. Gowers (Rochdale Hornets), A. Ellaby (St Helens), E. Gwynne (Hull), A. Frodsham (St Helens), T. Askin (Featherstone Rovers), J. Oliver (Batley), J. Brough (Leeds), M. Rosser (Leeds), J. Evans (Swinton), L. Fairclough (St Helens), W. Rees (Swinton), J. Parkin (Wakefield T.) captain, B. Evans (Swinton), W. Williams (Salford), N. Bentham (Wigan),

O. Dolan (St Helens), H. Bowman (Hull), J. Thompson (Leeds), W. Burgess (Barrow), A. E. Fildes (St Helens), W. Horton (Wakefield T.), R. Sloman (Oldham), W. Bowen (St Helens), B. Halfpenny (St Helens), H. Young (Bradford N.); managers: G. F. Hutchins (Oldham) and E. Osborne (Warrington).

25 games were played—16 in Australia and 9 in New Zealand.

P.	W.	L.	D.	G.	For		Against		
					T.	Pts.	G.	T.	Pts.
25	18	6	1	102	126	582	63	64	318

1932 Tour
J. Sullivan (Wigan), captain, A. J. Risman (Salford), B. Hudson (Salford), S. Smith (Leeds), A. Ellaby (St Helens), J. T. Woods (Barrow), A. Atkinson (Castleford), S. Brogden (Huddersfield), W. Dingsdale (Warrington), G. Robinson (Wakefield T.), I. Davies (Halifax), E. Pollard (Wakefield T.), B. Evans (Swinton), L. Adams (Leeds), J. Thompson (Leeds),

N. Silcock (Widnes), W. Williams (Salford), J. Wright (Swinton), L. L. White (Hunslet), J. Lowe (Leeds), A. E. Fildes (St Helens), N. Fender (York), W. Horton (Wakefield T.), M. Hodgson (Swinton), J. Feetham (Salford), F. Butters (Swinton); managers: G. F. Hutchins (Oldham) and R. F. Anderton (Warrington).

26 games were played—18 in Australia and 8 in New Zealand.

P.	W.	L.	D.	G.	For		Against		
					T.	Pts.	G.	T.	Pts.
26	23	2	1	136	170	782	53	51	259

1936 Tour
J. Brough (Leeds) captain, W. Belshaw (Liverpool S.), J. Morley (Wigan), B. Hudson (Salford), S. Smith (Leeds), A. Edwards (Salford), F. Harris (Leeds), A. Atkinson (Castleford), A. J. Risman (Salford), G. Davies (Wigan), E. Jenkins (Salford), S. Brogden (Leeds), W. Watkins (Salford), T. McCue (Widnes), H. Field (York), T. Armitt (Swinton), N. Silcock (Widnes), J. H. Woods (Liverpool S.), J.

Miller (Warrington), H. Jones (Keighley), A. Troup (Barrow), J. Arkwright (Warrington), M. Hodgson (Swinton), G. H. Exley (Wakefield T.), H. Beverley (Hunslet), H. Ellerington (Hull). managers: R. F. Anderton (Warrington) and W. Popplewell (Bramley).

25 games were played—17 in Australia and 8 in New Zealand. An aggregate total of 349, 493 spectators watched the 17 Australian matches.

					For			Against	
P.	W.	L.	D.	G.	T.	Pts.	G.	T.	Pts.
25	22	3	–	109	131	611	61	44	254

1946 Tour

M. Ryan (Wigan), J. Jones (Barrow), E. Batten (Bradford N.), J. Lewthwaite (Barrow), A. J. Risman (Salford) captain, E. H. Ward (Wigan), J. Kitching (Bradford N.), B. Knowelden (Barrow), E. Ward (Bradford N.), A, Johnson (Warrington), A. Bassett (Halifax), W. Horne (Barrow), W. Davies (Bradford N.), T. McCue (Widnes), D. Jenkins (Leeds), K. Gee (Wigan), F. Hughes (Workington T.), J. Egan (Wigan), G. Curran (Salford), F. Whitcombe (Bradford), R. Nicholson (Huddersfield), H. White (York), D. Phillips (Oldham), T. Foster (Bradford), H. Murphy (Wakefield T.), I. Owens (Leeds). managers: W. Popplewell (Bramley) and W. M. Gabbatt (Barrow).

27 games were played—20 in Australia and 7 in New Zealand.

					For			Against	
P.	W.	L.	D.	G.	T.	Pts.	G.	T.	Pts.
27	21	5	1	12	181	783	63	50	276

1950 Tour

J. Ledgard (Leigh), M. Ryan (Wigan), A. Daniels (Halifax), R. Pollard (Dewsbury), J. Cunliffe (Wigan), E. Ward (Bradford) captain, E. Ashcroft (Wigan), T. Danby (Salford), J. Hilton (Wigan), G. Ratcliffe (Wigan), W. Horne (Barrow), R. Williams (Leeds), T. Bradshaw (Wigan), A. Pepperell (Workington T.), K. Gee (Wigan), D. Naughton (Widnes), J. Egan (Wigan), F. Osmond (Swinton), J. Featherstone (Warrington), E. Gwyther (Belle Vue R.), F. Higgins (Widnes), H. Murphy (Wakefield T.), D. Phillips (Belle Vue R.), R. Ryan (Warrington), H. Street (Dewsbury), K. Traill (Bradford). L. Williams (Hunslet) was selected but unable to make the trip and was replaced by G. Ratcliffe.

Managers: G. O. Oldroyd (Dewsbury) and T. Spedding (Belle Vue R.).

25 games were played—19 in Australia and 6 in New Zealand.

					For			Against	
P.	W.	L.	D.	G.	T.	Pts.	G.	T.	Pts.
25	19	6	–	127	170	764	76	38	266

1954 Tour

E. Cahill (Rochdale Hornets), J. Cunliffe (Wigan), W. Boston (Wigan), A. Turnbull (Leeds), E. Ashcroft (Wigan), D. Greenall (St Helens), P. Jackson (Barrow), L. Jones (Leeds), T. O'Grady (Oldham), F. Castle (Barrow), R. Price (Warrington), R. Williams (Leeds) captain, A. Burnell (Hunslet), G. Helme (Warrington), J. Bowden (Huddersfield), J. Henderson (Workington T.), A. Prescott (St. Helens), J. Wilkinson (Halifax), T. Harris (Hull), T. McKinney (Salford), B. Briggs (Huddersfield), G. Gunney (Hunslet), C. Pawsey (Leigh), N. Silcock (Wigan), K. Traill (Bradford), D. Valentine (Huddersfield). managers: T. Hesketh (Wigan) and H. E. Rawson (Hunslet).

32 games were played—22 in Australia and 10 in New Zealand.

					For			Against	
P.	W.	L.	D.	G.	T.	Pts.	G.	T.	Pts.
32	21	9	1	170	193	919	128	92	532

1957 Tour (World Cup)

G. Moses (St Helens), W. Boston (Wigan), P. Jackson (Barrow), A. Davies (Oldham), L. Jones (Leeds), E. Ashton (Wigan), M. Sullivan (Huddersfield), R. Price (Warrington), A. Rhodes (St Helens),

J. Stevenson (Leeds), A. Prescott (St Helens) captain, T. Harris (Hull), S. Little (Oldham), G. Gunney (Hunslet), J. Whiteley (Hull), J. Grundy (Barrow), D. Turner (Oldham), T. McKinney (St Helens), man-agers: H. E. Rawson (Hunslet) and W. Fallowfield (RL Secretary).

In addition to the three World Cup matches, two other games were played in Australia and one in New Zealand.

					For		Against		
P.	W.	L.	D.	G.	T.	Pts.	G.	T.	Pts.
6	4	2	–	27	44	186	18	17	87

Note—In addition to the above, Great Britain players took part in exhibition games between combined teams in Australia. Three games were also played against France in South Africa on the way home.

1958 Tour

G. Moses (St Helens), E. Fraser (Warrington), I. Southward (Workington T.), W. Wookey (Workington T.), P. Jackson (Barrow), A. Davies (Oldham), E. Ashton (Wigan), J. Challinor (Warrington), M. Sullivan (Wigan), F. Carlton (St. Helens), D. Bolton (Wigan), H. Archer (Workington T.), F. Pitchford (Oldham), A. Murphy (St Helens), A. Prescott (St Helens) cap-tain, K. Jackson (Oldham), T. Harris (Hull), A. Ackerley (Halifax), A. Terry (St Helens), B. McTigue (Wigan), M. Martyn (Leigh), R. Huddart (Whitehaven), B. Edgar (Workington T.), V. Karalius (St Helens), D. Goodwin (Barrow), J. Whiteley (Hull). managers: B. Manson (Swinton) and T. Mitchell (Workington T.).

30 games were played—21 in Australia and 9 in New Zealand.

					For		Against		
P.	W.	L.	D.	G.	T.	Pts.	G.	T.	Pts.
30	27	2	1	190	272	1,196	120	82	486

1962 Tour

G. Round (Wakefield T.), E. Fraser (Warrington), W. Boston (Wigan), F. Carlton (Wigan), E. Ashton (Wigan) cap-tain, N. Fox (Wakefield T.), G. Cooper (Featherstone R.), P. Small (Castleford), M. Sullivan (St Helens), I. Southward (Workington T.), D. Bolton (Wigan), H. Poynton (Wakefield T.), A. Murphy (St Helens), D. Fox (Featherstone R.), J. Wilkinson (Wakefield T.), B. McTigue (Wigan), N. Herbert (Workington T.), K. Noble (Huddersfield), W. Sayer (Wigan), J. Shaw (Halifax), B. Edgar (Workington T.), R. Huddart (St Helens), J. Taylor (Hull KR), L. Gilfedder (Warrington), D. Turner (Wakefield T.), R. Evans (Wigan), man-agers: S. H. Hadfield (Wakefield T.) and A. Walker (Rochdale Hornets).

30 games were played—21 in Australia and 9 in New Zealand.

					For		Against		
P.	W.	L.	D.	G.	T.	Pts.	G.	T.	Pts.
30	24	6	–	163	224	998	88	96	464

A further three games were played in South Africa on the way home.

1966 Tour

K. Gowers (Swinton), A. Keegan (Hull), W. Burgess (Barrow), B. Jones (Wakefield T.), G. Shelton (Hunslet), F. Myler (Widnes), I. Brooke (Bradford N.), A. Buckley (Swinton), J. Stopford (Swinton), G. Wriglesworth (Leeds), A. Hardisty (Castleford), W. Aspinall (Warrington), C. Dooler (Featherstone Rovers), T. Bishop (St Helens), K. Roberts (Halifax), B. Edgar (Workington T.), P. Flanagan (Hull KR), C. Clarke (Wigan), C. Watson (St Helens), G. Crewdson (Keighley), W. Ramsey (Hunslet), J. Mantle (St Helens), W.

Bryant (Castleford), T. Fogerty (Halifax), D. Robinson (Swinton), H. Poole (Leeds) captain.

A. Murphy (St Helens) was selected but withdrew owing to business reasons and was replaced by Brooke. managers: W. Spaven (Hull KR) and J. Errock (Oldham).

30 games were played—22 in Australia and 8 in New Zealand.

					For		Against		
P.	W.	L.	D.	G.	T.	Pts.	G.	T.	Pts.
30	21	9	–	132	169	771	107	57	385

1968 Tour (World Cup)

B. Risman (Leeds) captain, D. Edwards (Castleford), C. Young (Hull KR), I. Brooke (Wakefield T.), A. Burwell (Hull KR), C. Sullivan (Hull), J. Atkinson (Leeds), R. Millward (Hull KR), T. Bishop (St Helens), M. Shoebottom (Leeds), M. Clark (Leeds), P. Flanagan (Hull KR), K. Ashcroft (Leigh), C. Watson (St Helens), R. French (Widnes), A. Morgan (Featherstone R.), J. Warlow (St Helens), R. Haigh (Wakefield T.), C. Renilson (Halifax).

N. Fox (Wakefield T.) was selected as captain, but had to withdraw owing to injury, manager: W. Fallowfield (RL Secretary), assistant-manager: C. Hutton (Hull KR).

					For		Against		
P.	W.	L.	D.	G.	T.	Pts.	G.	T.	Pts.
7	5	2	–	32	35	169	24	11	81

1970 Tour

D. Edwards (Castleford), T. Price (Bradford Northern), R. Dutton (Widnes), J. Atkinson (Leeds), A. Smith (Leeds), C. Sullivan (Hull), S. Hynes (Leeds), C. Hesketh (Salford), F. Myler (St Helens and captain), R. Millward (Hull KR), M. Shoebottom (Leeds), K. Hepworth (Castleford), A. Hardisty (Castleford), C. Watson (St Helens), J. Ward (Castleford), D. Chisnall (Leigh), P. Flanagan (Hull KR), A. Fisher (Bradford Northern), D. Hartley (Castleford), P. Lowe (Hull KR), D. Robinson (Wigan), J. Thompson (Featherstone Rovers), R. Irving (Oldham), M. Reilly (Castleford), D. Laughton (Wigan); manager: J. B. Harding (Leigh); assistant manager-coach J. Whiteley (Hull).

Mills (Widnes), G. Nicholls (St Helens), J. Bates (Dewsbury), E. Chisnall (St Helens), J. K. Bridges, J. Thompson (Featherstone Rovers), K. Ashcroft (Warrington), C. Dixon (Salford), P. Rose (Hull KR), S. Norton (Castleford), W. Ramsey (Leeds) and M. Richards (Salford) mid-to replacements, manager: R. Parker (Blackpool); coach: J. Challinor (St Helens).

			Pts.	Pts.
P.	W.	L.	for	against
28	21	7	675	313

				Pts.	Pts.
P.	W.	L.	D.	for	against
24	22	1	1	753	288

1974 Tour

D. Willicombe (Wigan), C. Hesketh (Salford, captain), P. Charlton, D. Watkins, K. Gill (all Salford), D. Eckersley (St Helens), J. Butler (Rochdale Hornets), D. Redfearn (Bradford Northern), J. Bevan (Warrington), J. Atkinson, L. Dyl (both Leeds), R. Millward (Hull KR), A. Bates (Dewsbury), S Nash (Featherstone Rovers) T. Clawson (Oldham), J. Gray (Wigan), J.

1977 World Cup Tour

G. Fairbairn (Wigan), S. Wright (Widnes), K. Fielding (Salford), L. Dyl (Leeds), J. Holmes (Leeds), W. Francis, (Wigan), K. Gill (Salford), R. Millward (Hull KR, captain), L. Casey (Hull KR), S. Lloyd (Castleford), G. Nicholls, (St Helens), S. Pitchford (Leeds), P. Smith (Featherstone Rovers), P. Hogan (Barrow), A. Hodkinson (Rochdale Hornets), J. Thompson (Featherstone Rovers), E. Bowman (Workington Town), D. Ward (Leeds), K. Elwell (Widnes), S. Nash (Salford); manager: R. Parker (Blackpool); coach: D. Watkins (Salford).

			Pts.	Pts.
P.	W.	L.	for	against
11	5	6	201	180

1979 Tour
Original Selection: Mick Adams (Widnes), John Bevan (Warrington), Len Casey (Bradford Northern), Steve Evans (Featherstone Rovers), Peter Glynn (St Helens), Jeff Grayshon (Bradford Northern), Phil Hogan (Hull Kingston Rovers), Eric Hughes (Widnes), Mel James (St Helens), John Joyner (Castleford), Ken Kelly (Warrington), Doug Laughton (Widnes), Captain until injury in Australia, Graham Liptrot (St Helens), Brian Lockwood (Hull KR), Tommy Martyn (Warrington), Jim Mills (Widnes), Roger Millward (Hull KR), Keith Mumby (Bradford Northern), Steve Nash (Salford), George Nicholls (St Helens), Captain for remainder of tour, Steve Norton (Hull), Alan Redfearn (Bradford Northern), Trevor Skerrett (Wakefield Trinity), Mike Smith (Hull KR), Gary Stephens (Castleford), Charlie Stone (Hull), David Ward (Leeds), David Watkinson (Hull KR), John Woods (Leigh), Stuart Wright (Widnes); manager: Harry Womersley (Bradford Northern); business manager: Dick Gemmell (Hull); coach: Eric Ashton MBE (St Helens); physiotherapist: Ron Barritt (Bradford Northern).

Replacements for injured players prior to departure: Roy Mathias (St Helens) for Bevan. John Holmes (Leeds) for Kelly. David Barends (Bradford Northern) for Wright.

Replacements for injured players during tour of Australia: 23/6/79—John Burke (Wakefield Trinity) for Mills. George Fairbairn (Wigan) for Martyn. 30/6/79—David Topliss (Wakefield Trinity) for Millward. Laughton and Nash also returned home at end of Australian section, but were not replaced.

P.	W.	L.	D.	Pts. for	Pts. against
27	21	5	1	559	322

Great Britain tour records in Australia and New Zealand:
Most goals and points
127 goals (8 tries)—278 points by Lewis Jones (Leeds) in 1954.
Most tries
38 by Mick Sullivan (Wigan) in 1958.
See also TESTS.

GREENALL WHITLEY/ 'SUNDAY PEOPLE' AWARDS

Introduced in the 1977-78 season, an individual award scheme sponsored by Greenall Whitley brewers and promoted by the *Sunday People*.

The Personality of the Year and individual men-of-the-month each receive a trophy and prize money, the awards being handed over at a special presentation dinner at the end of the season.

The inaugural Personality of the Year was Reg Bowden, captain of the 1978 First Division Champions, Widnes.

Personality of the Year
1978: Reg Bowden (Widnes)
1979: Doug Laughton (Widnes)
1980: George Fairbairn (Wigan)

Men of the Month
1977-78: John Woods (Leigh)
          Green Vigo (Wigan)
          Peter Fox (Bradford Northern)
          Mick Adams (Widnes)
          Bill Ashurst (Wigan)
          Eddie Cunningham (St Helens)
          John Holmes (Leeds)
          Geoff Pimblett (St Helens)
          Special Awards: Keith Fielding
          (Salford and BBC Superstars)
          Colin Welland (BBC
          Documentary)

1978-79: Jim Mills (Widnes)
          Brian Lockwood (Hull KR)
          Doug Laughton (Widnes)
          Neil Holding (St Helens)
          Charlie Stone (Hull)
          Geoff Wraith (Castleford)
          Steve Evans (Featherstone R.)
          Ken Kelly (Warrington)
          John Sanderson (Leeds)

1979-80: Ian Ball (Barrow)
          Ken Gill (Salford)
          Steve Quinn (Featherstone R.)
          George Fairbairn (Wigan)
          Roy Holdstock (Hull KR)
          Mick Adams (Widnes)
          Steve Norton (Hull)
          Geoff Munro (Oldham)
          Mal Aspey (Widnes)

GROUNDS

Barrow: Craven Park.
Formerly Parade Ground (until 1880), Cavendish Park (1913-14), Little Park Roose (1931-32).
Batley: Mount Pleasant.
Blackpool Borough: Borough Park.
Formerly The Stadium, St. Annes Road (1954-63).
Bradford Northern: Odsal Stadium.

Formerly Park Avenue (1895-1907), Green Field Stadium (1907-08), Birch Lane (1908-34).

Bramley: McClaren Field.
Formerly Pollard Lane, Whitegate Farm, Barley Mow (1890-1966).

Castleford: Wheldon Road.
Formerly "Sandy Desert", Lock Lane.

Dewsbury: Crown Flatt.
Formerly Sugar Lane (1875).

Doncaster: Tatters Field.
Formerly Doncaster Greyhound Stadium (1951-53).

Featherstone Rovers: Post Office Road.

Halifax: Thrum Hall.
Formerly Trinity Ground (1873-76), Hanson Lane Ground (1876-86).

Huddersfield: Fartown.

Hull: The Boulevard.
Formerly Ferriby, near Hull (1865), Selby (1871), West Hull (1873), Severn Street, Hull (1881).

Hull Kingston Rovers: Craven Park.
Formerly Gillett Street, known as "flad edge touch" (1883-84), Anlaby Road, Chalk Lane, Hessle Road, Locomotive Ground, Dairycoates (1887-88), Star and Garter (1889-90), Boulevard (1892), Craven Street (1895-96), Craven Park (1922).

Huyton: Alt Park.
Formerly Knotty Ash Stadium, Liverpool.

Keighley: Lawkholme Lane.

Leeds: Headingley.

Leigh: Hilton Park.
Formerly Buck's Farm Field (1878-79), Three Crown's Field, Bedford (1879-89), Frog Hall Field, later known as Mather Lane (1889-1940), Charles Street (1946-47), Kirkhall Lane, later known as Hilton Park.

Oldham: Watersheddings.
Formerly Glodwick Lows (from 1876 to date unknown), Clarksfield (for unknown period), Watersheddings (from 1889).

Rochdale Hornets: Athletic Grounds.
Formerly Rochdale Cricket Ground (Vavasour Street and Dane Street), Oakenrod.

St Helens: Knowsley Road.
Formerly Queen's Recreation, Bishops Road, Littler's Field.

Salford: Willows.
Formerly New Barns, now Salford Docks (1878-1901).

Swinton: Station Road.

Wakefield Trinity: Belle Vue.
Formerly Heath Common and Alexander Hotel Ground.

Warrington: Wilderspool Stadium.

Whitehaven: Recreation Grounds.

Widnes: Naughton Park.

Wigan: Central Park.
Formerly Folly Field (1872), Frog Lane (1877), Prescott Street (1887), Springfield Park (1901).

Workington Town: Derwent Park.
Formerly Borough Park (1944-54).

York: Wiggington Road.
Formerly Knavesmire (1868), Yorkshire Gentlemen's Cricket Ground (1883).

GUIDE

First produced in 1908, the *Rugby Football League Guide* is an annual handbook. Until the formation of the British Amateur Rugby League Association in 1973, the guide served every sector of the game.

Since the birth of BARLA, the Rugby Football League guide has been restyled to provide details of the League Council and Committees; member clubs; bye-laws; county leagues; associations; referees; laws of the game; the previous season's statistics and full fixture lists.

Affectionately known as the "little blue book", the guide is available to the public.

1966	Albert Halsall (St Helens)
1967	Ray Owen (Wakefield Trinity)
1968	Gary Cooper (Wakefield Trinity)
1969	Bev Risman (Leeds)
1970	Frank Myler (St Helens)
1971	Bill Ashurst (Wigan)
1972	Terry Clawson (Leeds)
1973	Mick Stephenson (Dewsbury)
1974	Barry Philbin (Warrington)
1975	Mel Mason (Leeds)
1976	George Nicholls (St Helens)
1977	Geoff Pimblett (St Helens)
1978	Bob Haigh (Bradford Northern)
1979	Kevin Dick (Leeds)
1980	Mal Aspey (Widnes)

HALIFAX RLFC

Founded 1873. Founder member of Northern Union. Ground: Thrum Hall. Colours: Blue and white hooped jerseys, white shorts.

RL Championship Winners, 1906-07, 1964-65.
Beaten Finalists, 1952-53, 1953-54, 1955-56, 1965-66.
Division One champions, 1902-03.
RL Cup Winners, 1902-03, 1903-04, 1930-31, 1938-39.
Beaten Finalists, 1920-21, 1940-41, 1941-42, 1948-49, 1953-54, 1955-56.
Yorkshire League Winners, 1908-09, 1920-21, 1952-53, 1953-54, 1955-56, 1957-58.
Eastern Division Championship Winners, 1963-64.
Yorkshire Cup Winners, 1908-09, 1944-45, 1954-55, 1955-56, 1963-64.
Beaten Finalists, 1905-06, 1907-08, 1941-42, 1979-80.
Player's No.6 Trophy Winners, 1971-72.
Club Records:
Attendance: 29,153 v. Wigan (RL Cup) Mar. 21, 1959.
Goals: 147 T. Griffiths, 1955-56.
Tries: 48 J. Freeman, 1956-57.
Points: 297 T. Griffiths, 1955-56.

HARRY SUNDERLAND MEMORIAL TROPHY

The trophy is awarded in memory of Queenslander Harry Sunderland, a famous Australian Tour manager, broadcaster and journalist. Donated by the Rugby League Writers' Association, the trophy is awarded to the Player of the Match in the end-of-the-season play-off final, the selection being made by a ballot of Writers' Association members at the match.

Past winners are:
1965   Terry Fogerty (Halifax)

HEADQUARTERS

The headquarters of the international authorities are:

Australian Rugby Football League
165, Phillip Street, Sydney, NWS.
Postal Address: Box 4415, GPO,
Sydney Australia 2001
Cablegrams: Rugleague Sydney.
Telephone: 232-7566

British Amateur Rugby League Association
Britannic Building, 3, Upperhead Row,
Huddersfield HD 1 2JL, England.
Telephone: 0484-44131

Fédération Française de Jeu à Treize
29 Rue Coquilliere, 75001 Paris
Telephone: 236-49-45 and 233-75-83

Rugby Football League
180, Chapeltown Road, Leeds LS7 4HT,
England
Telephone: 0532-624637

Papua New Guinea Rugby Football League
PO Box 1355, Boroko.
Telephone: Papua New Guinea 25-7827

United States Rugby League
44, East Mifflin Street, Madison,
Wisconsin 53703, USA.
Telephone: 608-221-1177

International Board Secretary
W. Fallowfield, OBE, MA
PO Box No.1, Wetherby LS22 4UZ,
England.
Telephone: Collingham Bridge 2562

HONOURS

Administrators and players have received Royal recognition by the following awards:

William Fallowfield MA, Secretary of the Rugby Football League between 1945 and 1974, was awarded the OBE in Oct. 1961.

Eric Ashton received the MBE in June 1966 while the ex-Great Britain International was player-coach of Wigan.

Geoff Gunney's 600-plus match career with Hunslet, spanning 23 years from 1951-74, featuring Great Britain on tour and in the World Cup arena, was highlighted by the awarding of the MBE in 1970.

Clive Sullivan, captain of the Great Britain side which won the 1972 World Cup, received the MBE in 1974, shortly after being featured in the television show "This is Your Life".

Former polio victim Chris Hesketh, captain of Salford and the 1974 Great Britain Tour party, was awarded the MBE in 1975.

1977, the 25th year in the reign of Queen Elizabeth II, saw Queen's Silver Jubilee Medals awarded to seven Rugby League stalwarts. From the professional sector, Mr Tom Mitchell BSc, Chairman of the Rugby Football League in 1961-62 and the longest serving current member of the Council, and National Coach Albert Fearnley were honoured. From the British Amateur Rugby League Association, medals were presented to Mr Jack Clayton, Mr Edgar Hanson, Mr Ernest Houghton, Mr Bob Beal and Mr Tom Beautiman.

On 2 Nov. 1978, the amateur game was further honoured by the awarding of the MBE to Mr Tom Keaveney, the BARLA Secretary.

Overseas honours include Mr W. G. Buckley, President of the Australian Rugby Football League, who was awarded the OBE in the 1968 New Year's Honours List.

In 1977, the MBE was awarded to former Australian Test players Keith Holman and Bobby McCarthy, and to Mr John O'Toole, secretary of the Australian Country League.

In 1953, British League Secretary Mr Fallowfield received the Medaille d'Argent d'Honneur from the French Government for services in the field of International Rugby League, with particular reference to the French sector.

Widnes referee Mr George S. Philips was awarded the BEM in 1945 for services to industry and Rugby League.

HUDDERSFIELD RLFC

Founded in 1864. Founder Member of the Northern Union. Colours: Claret and gold hooped jerseys, white shorts. Ground: Fartown.

RL Championship Winners, 1911-12, 1912-13, 1914-15, 1928-29, 1929-30, 1948-49, 1961-62.

Beaten Finalists, 1913-14, 1919-20, 1922-23, 1931-32, 1945-46, 1949-50.

RL Cup Winners, 1912-13, 1914-15, 1919-20, 1932-33, 1944-45, 1952-53.

Beaten Finalists, 1934-35, 1961-62.

Yorkshire League Winners, 1911-12, 1912-13, 1913-14, 1914-15, 1919-20, 1921-22, 1928-29, 1929-30, 1948-49, 1949-50, 1951-52.

Division Two Champions, 1974-75.

Eastern Division Beaten Finalists, 1962-63.

Yorkshire Cup Winners, 1909-10, 1911-12, 1913-14, 1914-15, 1918-19, 1919-20, 1926-27, 1931-32, 1938-39, 1950-51, 1952-53, 1957-58.

Beaten Finalists, 1910-11, 1923-24, 1925-26, 1930-31, 1937-38, 1942-43, 1949-50, 1960-61.

Club Records:

Attendance: 35,136 Leeds v. Wakefield T. (RL Cup SF) 19 Apl. 1947.

Goals: 147 by B. Gronow, 1919-20.

Tries: 80 by A. Rosenfeld, 1913-14.

Points: 330 by B. Gronow, 1919-20.

HULL FC

Founded in 1865. Founder member of the Northern Union. Ground: The Boulevard. Colours: Irregular black and white hooped jerseys, white shorts.

RL Championship Winners, 1919-20, 1920-21, 1935-36, 1955-56, 1957-58.

Beaten Finalists, 1956-57.

Division Two Champions, 1976-77.

RL Cup Winners, 1913-14.

Beaten Finalists, 1907-08, 1908-09, 1909-10, 1921-22, 1922-23, 1958-59, 1959-60, 1979-80.

Yorkshire League Winners, 1918-19, 1922-23, 1926-27, 1935-36.

Yorkshire Cup Winners, 1923-24, 1969-70.

Beaten finalists, 1912-13, 1914-15, 1920-21, 1927-28, 1938-39, 1946-47, 1953-54, 1954-55, 1955-56, 1959-60, 1967-68.

Player's No.6 Trophy Beaten Finalists, 1975-76.

BBC2 Floodlit Trophy Winners, 1979-80.

Club Records:

Attendance: 28,798 v. Leeds (RL Cup), 7 Mar. 1936.

Goals: 170 by S. Lloyd, 1978-79.

Tries: 52 by J. Harrison, 1914-15.

Points: 369 by S. Lloyd, 1978-79.

HULL KINGSTON ROVERS RLFC

Founded in 1883. Joined the Northern Union in 1897. Ground: Craven Park. Colours: White jerseys with red band, white shorts.
RL Championship Winners, 1922-23, 1924-25.
Beaten Finalists, 1920-21, 1967-68.
RL Cup Winners, 1979-80.
RL Cup Beaten Finalists, 1904-05, 1924-25, 1963-64.
Yorkshire League Winners, 1924-25, 1925-26.
Yorkshire Cup Winners, 1920-21, 1929-30, 1966-67, 1967-68, 1971-72, 1974-75.
Beaten Finalists, 1906-07, 1911-12, 1933-34, 1962-63, 1975-76.
BBC Floodlit Trophy Winners, 1977-78.
Beaten Finalists, 1979-80.
Eastern Division Championship Winners, 1962-63.
Club Records:
Attendance: 22,282 v. Hull, 7 Oct. 1922.
Goals: 146 by N. Fox, 1974-75.
Tries: 42 by G. Dunn, 1974-75.
Points: 366 by S. Hubbard, 1979-80.

HUNSLET RLFC

Founded in 1973. Joined the Northern Rugby League in 1973. Ground: Lad-brokes Stadium. Colours: Myrtle, flame and white jerseys, white shorts.
Club Records:
Attendance: 5,859 v. Warrington (RL Cup), 9 Mar. 1975.
Goals: 100 by R. Gaitley, 1975-76.
Tries: 15 by A. Griffiths, 1976-77.
Points: 208 by R. Gaitley, 1975-76.
Note: The Old Hunslet club was founded in 1882 and became a founder member of the Northern Union. It disbanded in 1973 and a few months later the new club was formed.

HUYTON RLFC

Founded in 1922 as Wigan Highfield. Joined the Northern Rugby League in 1922. Ground: Alt Park. Colours: Scarlet jerseys, sky blue shorts.
Lancashire League Winners, 1935-36.
Club Records:
Goals: 95 by J. Wood, 1954-55.
Tries: 28 by J. Maloney, 1930-31.
Points: 211 by J. Wood, 1954-55.
This club started as Wigan Highfield in 1922 and changed to London Highfield in 1933 and played under the White City, London, floodlights for a season. Other name changes were: Liverpool Stanley (1934), Liverpool City (1951), and became Huyton in 1968.

INTERNATIONALS

Unlike Test matches, which are clashes between the four main League playing nations, Australia, France, Great Britain and New Zealand, any other meeting between two countries is classed as an international fixture. These games are more common in the Northern Hemisphere where the European Championship is not afforded Test status.

The following lists illustrate the extent to which Rugby League has been played internationally at senior level.

England v. Wales

20 Apr. 1908	England	18	Wales	35	Ton-y-Pandy
28 Dec. 1908	England	31	Wales	7	Broughton
4 Dec. 1909	England	19	Wales	13	Wakefield
9 Apr. 1910	England	18	Wales	38	Ebbw Vale
17 Sept. 1910	England	25	Wales	27	Plymouth
10 Dec. 1910	England	39	Wales	13	Coventry
1 Apr. 1911	England	27	Wales	8	Ebbw Vale
20 Jan. 1912	England	31	Wales	5	Oldham
15 Feb. 1913	England	40	Wales	16	Plymouth
14 Feb. 1914	England	16	Wales	12	St Helens
19 Jan 1921	England	35	Wales	9	Leeds
11 Dec 1922	England	12	Wales	7	London
7 Feb. 1923	England	2	Wales	13	Wigan
1 Oct 1923	England	18	Wales	11	Huddersfield
7 Feb. 1925	England	27	Wales	22	Workington
30 Sept. 1925	England	18	Wales	14	Wigan
12 Apr. 1926	England	30	Wales	22	Pontypridd
6 Apr. 1927	England	11	Wales	8	Broughton
17 Jan. 1928	England	20	Wales	12	Wigan
14 Nov. 1928	England	39	Wales	15	Cardiff
18 Mar. 1931	England	23	Wales	18	Huddersfield
27 Jan. 1932	England	19	Wales	2	Salford
30 Nov. 1932	England	14	Wales	14	Leeds
10 Apr. 1935	England	24	Wales	11	Liverpool
1 Feb. 1936	England	14	Wales	17	Hull
7 Nov. 1936	England	3	Wales	2	Pontypridd
29 Jan. 1938	England	6	Wales	7	Bradford
5 Nov. 1938	England	17	Wales	9	Llanelli
23 Dec. 1939	England	3	Wales	16	Bradford
9 Nov. 1940	England	8	Wales	5	Oldham
18 Oct. 1941	England	9	Wales	9	Bradford
27 Feb. 1943	England	15	Wales	9	Wigan
26 Feb. 1944	England	9	Wales	9	Wigan
10 Mar. 1945	England	18	Wales	8	Wigan
4 Nov. 1945	England	3	Wales	11	Swansea
10 Oct. 1946	England	10	Wales	13	Swinton
16 Nov. 1946	England	19	Wales	5	Swansea
20 Sep. 1947	England	8	Wales	10	Wigan
6 Dec. 1947	England	18	Wales	7	Swansea
22 Sept. 1947	England	11	Wales	5	Wigan
5 Feb. 1947	England	10	Wales	14	Swansea
1 Mar. 1950	England	11	Wales	6	Wigan
14 Oct. 1950	England	22	Wales	4	Abertillery
19 Sept. 1951	England	35	Wales	11	St Helens

17 Sept. 1952	England	19	Wales	8	Wigan
16 Sept. 1953	England	24	Wales	5	St Helens
18 Oct. 1969	England	40	Wales	23	Leeds
24 Feb. 1970	England	26	Wales	7	Leeds
25 Feb. 1975	England	12	Wales	8	Salford
29 Jan. 1977	England	2	Wales	6	Leeds
28 May. 1978	England	60	Wales	13	St Helens
16 Mar. 1979	England	15	Wales	7	Widnes
29 Feb. 1980	England	26	Wales	9	Hull KR

England v. France

15 Apr. 1934	England	22	France	21	Paris
28 Mar. 1935	England	15	France	15	Paris
16 Feb. 1936	England	25	France	7	Paris
10 Apr. 1937	England	23	France	9	Halifax
20 Mar. 1938	England	17	France	15	Paris
25 Feb. 1939	England	9	France	12	St Helens
23 Feb. 1946	England	16	France	6	Swinton
8 Dec. 1946	England	3	France	0	Bordeaux
17 May 1947	England	5	France	2	Leeds
25 Oct. 1947	England	20	France	15	Huddersfield
11 Apr. 1948	England	25	France	10	Marseilles
28 Nov. 1948	England	12	France	5	Bordeaux
12 Mar. 1949	England	5	France	12	Wembley
4 Dec. 1949	England	13	France	5	Bordeaux
11 Nov. 1950	England	14	France	9	Leeds
25 Nov. 1951	England	13	France	42	Marseilles
11 Apr. 1953	England	15	France	13	Paris
18 Oct. 1953	England	30	France	22	Bordeaux
10 May 1956	England	9	France	23	Lyons
25 Oct. 1969	England	11	France	11	Wigan
15 Mar. 1970	England	9	France	14	Toulouse
19 Jan. 1975	England	11	France	9	Perpignan
29 Jan. 1977	England	15	France	28	Carcassonne
5 Mar. 1978	England	13	France	11	Toulouse
24 Mar. 1979	England	12	France	6	Warrington
16 Mar. 1980	England	4	France	2	Narbonne

France v. Wales

1 Jan. 1935	France	18	Wales	11	Bordeaux
23 Nov. 1935	France	7	Wales	41	Llanelli
6 Dec. 1936	France	3	Wales	9	Paris
2 Apr. 1938	France	2	Wales	18	Llanelli
16 Apr. 1939	France	16	Wales	10	Bordeaux
24 Mar. 1946	France	19	Wales	7	Bordeaux
18 Jan. 1947	France	14	Wales	5	Marseilles
12 Apr. 1947	France	15	Wales	17	Swansea
23 Nov. 1947	France	29	Wales	21	Bordeaux
20 Mar. 1948	France	20	Wales	12	Swansea
23 Oct. 1948	France	12	Wales	9	Swansea
10 Apr. 1949	France	11	Wales	0	Marseilles
12 Nov. 1949	France	8	Wales	16	Swansea
15 Apr. 1951	France	28	Wales	13	Marseilles
6 Apr. 1952	France	20	Wales	12	Bordeaux
25 Oct. 1952	France	16	Wales	22	Leeds
13 Dec. 1953	France	23	Wales	22	Marseilles
23 Oct. 1969	France	8	Wales	2	Salford
25 Jan. 1970	France	11	Wales	15	Perpignan
16 Feb. 1975	France	8	Wales	21	Swansea
20 Feb. 1977	France	13	Wales	2	Toulouse

15 Jan. 1978	France	7	Wales	29	Widnes
4 Feb. 1979	France	15	Wales	8	Narbonne
26 Jan. 1980	France	21	Wales	7	Widnes

England v. Other Nationalities

1921	England	33	Other Nationalities	16	Workington
1924	England	17	Other Nationalities	23	Leeds
1926	England	37	Other Nationalities	11	Whitehaven
1929	England	20	Other Nationalities	20	Leeds
1930	England	19	Other Nationalities	35	Halifax
1930	England	31	Other Nationalities	18	St Helens
1933	England	34	Other Nationalities	27	Workington
1949	England	7	Other Nationalities	13	Workington
1951	England	10	Other Nationalities	35	Wigan
1952	England	31	Other Nationalities	18	Wigan
1952	England	12	Other Nationalities	31	Huddersfield
1953	England	30	Other Nationalities	22	Wigan
1955	England	16	Other Nationalities	33	Wigan

France v. Other Nationalities

1950	France	16	Other Nationalities	3	Bordeaux
1951	France	14	Other Nationalities	17	Hull
1952	France	10	Other Nationalities	29	Marseilles
1953	France	10	Other Nationalities	15	Bordeaux
1955	France	19	Other Nationalities	32	Leigh

Wales v Other Nationalities

1949	Wales	5	Other Nationalities	6	Abertillery
1951	Wales	21	Other Nationalities	27	Swansea
1951	Wales	11	Other Nationalities	22	Abertillery
1953	Wales	18	Other Nationalities	16	Warrington
1953	Wales	5	Other Nationalities	30	Bradford

Wales v. New Zealand

1907-08	Wales	9	New Zealand	8	Cardiff
1926	Wales	34	New Zealand	8	Swansea
1947-48	Wales	20	New Zealand	28	Swansea
1951-52	Wales	3	New Zealand	15	Bradford

New Zealand v. South Africa

| 1963 | New Zealand | 3 | South Africa | 4 | Auckland* |

*Not recognised as an official match by New Zealand

Australia v. South Africa

| 20 July 1963 | Australia | 34 | South Africa | 6 | Brisbane |
| 27 July 1963 | Australia | 54 | South Africa | 21 | Sydney |

Papua-New Guinea v. England

| 2 July 1975 | Papua-New Guinea | 12 | England | 40 | Port Moresby |

Papua-New Guinea v. France

| 29 May 1977 | Papua-New Guinea | 37 | France | 5 | Port Moresby |

Papua-New Guinea v. New Zealand

| 30 July 1978 | Papua-New Guinea | 21 | New Zealand | 30 | Port Moresby |

Other Representative Games

| 6 May 1935 | RL XIII | 25 | France | 18 | Leeds |
| 21 Mar. 1937 | France | 3 | RL XIII | 6 | Lyons |

26 Apr. 1946	Paris	19	RL XIII	36	Parc de Princes
25 May 1946	St Etienne	13	RL XIII	22	St Etienne
26 May 1946	Roanne	9	RL XIII	0	Roanne
3 May 1951	French XIII	10	UK XIII	13	Paris
19 May 1951	Welsh XIII	16	Empire XII	29	Llanelli
19 May 1951	Great Britain	20	Australasia	23	Leeds
23 Jan. 1952	British Empire XIII	26	New Zealand	2	Chelsea
22 May 1952	France	22	Great Britain	12	Paris
24 May 1953	France	28	Great Britain	17	Lyons
3 Jan. 1954	France	19	Int Select	15	Lyons
27 Apr. 1954	Great Britain	17	France	8	Bradford
17 Nov. 1954	RL XIII	13	Australasia	25	Bradford
19 Nov. 1954	Australia	18	New Zealand	5	Leigh
13 Apr. 1955	English Serv	15	French Serv	7	Leeds
19 May 1955	France	24	Wales	11	Nantes
7 Dec. 1955	RL XIII	24	New Zealand	11	Bradford
11 Dec. 1955	France	17	Great Britain	5	Paris
11 Apr. 1956	Great Britain	18	France	10	Bradford
15 Apr. 1956	French Serv	18	English Serv	10	Marseilles
3 Oct. 1956	Great Britain	26	Rest of Lge	23	Bradford
21 Oct. 1956	France	17	Br RL XIII	18	Marseilles
29 Oct. 1956	League XIII	15	Australia	19	Leigh
16 Apr. 1958	British RL XIII	19	France	8	Leeds
22 Nov. 1958	RL XIII	8	France	26	St Helens
1 Mar. 1959	France	25	Welsh XII	8	Toulouse
22 Sept. 1960	Great Britain	21	Rest of Lge	16	St Helens
20 Sept. 1961	RL XIII	22	New Zealand	20	White City, M/cr
12 Oct. 1961	French XIII	21	RL XIII	20	Paris
1 Nov. 1962	France	16	E Select XIII	23	Carcassonne
17 Nov. 1962	England	18	France	6	Leeds
17 Feb. 1963	France	23	Welsh XIII	3	Toulouse
5 May 1966	Paris XIII	20	RL XIII	0	Paris
6 Nov. 1966	1966 Tourists	31	Rest of Lge	38	Leeds
5 Nov. 1975	England	0	Australia	25	Leeds

See also COLTS; UNDER 24s.

INTERNATIONAL BOARD

Until 1948, World Rugby League was ruled by the British Rugby Football League.

The International Board was formed in January 1948 at the first ever International Rugby League Conference in Bordeaux. The conference was staged while New Zealand were touring France after a visit to Britain, and although Australia could not attend the summit meeting, the Kangaroos backed the formation of an International Board.

Meetings of the Board are held at irregular intervals, usually to coincide with Tours in either hemisphere. The honorary secretary of the Board is former British League Secretary Bill Fallowfield, while delegates to Board meetings are appointed by each League and are not permanent positions.

As well as organising world competi-tions and tour cycles, the Board's decisions can influence domestic football including standardisation and laws and the intro-duction in 1977 of a four-year ban on the transfer of players between Britain and Australia.

ITALY

Rugby League came close to gaining another foothold in Europe after the Second World War, this time in the boot-shaped peninsula of Italy. In 1950 a number of dissident Italian Rugby Union players decided to try their hands at what they called 13-man rugby, and they made a visit to England.

The 27 strong Italian party, led by 38-year-old Vincenzo Bertolotto undertook the tour. They played six friendly matches. Not surprisingly they failed to win any of the games, but their interest in the League code was aroused.

Their record on that tour was:

1950	Opponents	Points For	Against	Attendance
26 Aug.	Wigan	28	49	14,000
30 Aug.	St Helens	38	74	14,000
2 Sept.	South Wales	11	29	2,500
6 Sept.	Huddersfield	12	28	3,737
9 Sept.	Leigh	15	58	6,500
11 Sept.	Leeds	41	56	8,500

Played 6, won 0, lost 6, Pts for 145, against 294.

That first trip to England was to reap a quick harvest. When the players returned to Italy and their home city of Turin, they formed a League team and competed in the " Latin Cup " against several French teams.

By 1954 the Italian game had spread across the country from Turin to Milan.

They had accumulated enough confidence to tour England again but they were still not strong enough technically to win a match. They played a seven-match programme, including a triangular amateur tournament against England and France.

The full return from the second tour was:

1954	Opponents	Points For	Against	Attendance
7 Apr.	Bradford Northern	18	67	7,000
10 Apr.	York	17	54	4,000
14 Apr.	Hunslet	23	40	3,300
16 Apr.	France (at Huddersfield)	6	20	2,950
19 Apr.	England (at Halifax)	11	18	2,000
20 Apr.	Keighley	27	57	3,500
21 Apr.	Leigh	7	35	5,000

Played 7, won 0, lost 7, Pts for 109, against 291.

Back in Italy enthusiasm for Rugby League continued to grow and sides were established at Turin, Milan, Padua, Treviso and Venice. The British League Council officially recognised them and invested £16,000 in the venture during the late 1950s. British coaches visited Italy and, such was the rate of expansion, that the 21-club League had to be split into two sections, east and west. Australia gave the Italian League an air of respectability when its full Kangaroo touring team played two matches in Italy during 1959 on its way back from a tour of England and France.

But that was the high-point of the ill-fated scheme for, despite the high hopes and British investment, the code was destined to founder. Vital ingredients were missing in the attempt to establish the game in Italy—government approval and subsidies. Without them the game could not provide insurance cover for its players. Approval was not forthcoming and so ended a brave expansion attempt.

The game did not die quickly. It stumbled on for several years but, strangled by a shortage of players willing to risk playing without insurance cover, it dropped into obscurity. Today the game is not played in

| 15 Apr. 1951 | Italy | 17 | France | 29 | Cahors (France) |
| 22 May 1952 | Italy | 18 | France | 22 | Turin |

Italy on an organised basis.

Much could have been achieved if the Italian government approval had been given. The Italian League was used as a springboard for a brief attempt to establish the game in Yugoslavia and it is reported that the Italians played one game in Spain.

Two Italian players returned to play in Britain as professionals. " Toni Rossi "— he used an assumed name—led a tour of England by Padua in 1960 and they beat Wigan amateur team Triangle Valve at Central Park, Wigan. The professional side offered Rossi a contract and he played with them for a short while before moving on to Blackpool Borough. Another Italian, Ferdi Corsi, played with Rochdale Hornets.

The official name of the Italian League was " Comitato Italiano Rugby XIII " and its last president was Signor Angelo Gerardi of Venice.

Italians, however, still have some influence on the game. Several players are connected to French clubs and others, from ex-patriate Italian families, play in Australian competitions.

A number of amateur internationals were played by the Italians but the only recorded results were:

JOHN PLAYER COMPETITION

Nottingham-based tobacco giants John Player & Sons made their debut in Rugby League in 1967. For five seasons the company sponsored a Player of the Year award scheme. During the first three campaigns two award schemes were promoted, one decided by the votes of spectators, the other by official judges. In the two last years, only the judges' votes were invited.

The John Player Finals have been:

1972	Halifax	22	Wakefield Trinity	11	at Bradford
1973	Leeds	12	Salford	7	at Huddersfield
1974	Rochdale Hornets	16	Warrington	27	at Wigan
1975	Bradford Northern	3	Widnes	2	at Warrington
1976	Hull	13	Widnes	19	at Leeds
1977	Blackpool Borough	15	Castleford	25	at Salford
1978	Warrington	9	Widnes	4	at St Helens
1979	Widnes	16	Warrington	4	at St Helens
1980	Bradford Northern	6	Widnes	0	at Leeds

The John Player Man of the Match in the Final:

1972 Bruce Burton (Halifax)
1973 Keith Hepworth (Leeds)
1974 Kevin Ashcroft (Warrington)
1975 Barry Seabourne (Bradford Nor.)
1976 Reg Bowden (Widnes)
1977 Howard Allen (Blackpool Boro.) Gary Stephens (Castleford)
1978 Steve Hesford (Warrington)
1979 David Eckersley (Widnes)
1980 Len Casey (Bradford Northern)

Entry into the John Player Competition for the amateur representatives is obtained by reaching the National Cup Final. History was made in the 1977-78 tournament when Cawoods, of Hull, became the first amateur side to eliminate a professional club from the competition. Cawoods topped Halifax at Thrum Hall by 8-9, becoming the first "giant-killers" in a major Rugby League competition for 68 years.

Amateur clubs in the John Player Competition are:

Players No.6 Player of the Year Awards:
Judges' Awards
1968 Keith Hepworth (Castleford).
1969 Paul Charlton (Workington Town).
1970 Roger Millward (Hull Kingston Rovers).
1971 Stan Gittins (Batley).
1972 Bill Ashurst (Wigan).
Spectators' Awards
1968 Keith Hepworth (Castleford).
1969 Tommy Bishop (St Helens).
1970 Steve Nash (Featherstone Rovers).

In the 1971-72 season the John Player company suspended the annual awards and introduced a new knockout competition, entitled the Players No.6 Trophy, to be competed for in the first half of the season by the 30 professional clubs and two leading amateur sides. Prize money for the first competition totalled £9,500 rising to an agreed £40,000 for the 1980-81 tournament.

In the 1977-78 season, the tourney was renamed the John Player Competition.

1971-72	Ace Amateurs (Hull) and Thames Board Mills (Warrington)
1972-73	Dewsbury Celtic and Pilkington Recs. (St Helens)
1973-74	Dewsbury Celtic and Millom (Cumbria)
1974-75	Kippax White Swan (Castleford) and Lock Lane (Castleford)
1975-76	Mayfield (Rochdale) and Pilkington Recs. (St Helens)
1976-77	Ace Amateurs (Hull) and Ovenden (Halifax)
1977-78	Cawoods (Hull) and NDLB (Hull)
1978-79	Leigh Miners' Welfare and South Milford (Leeds)
1979-80	Pilkington Recs (St Helens) and West Hull

In the 1979-80 season, the John Player Amateur Sevens were introduced as curtain raisers to the John Player Trophy. The first final was:

1979-80: Waterhead (Oldham) 19
N.D.L.B. (Hull) 16

KANGAROOS

The nickname of the Australian Rugby League team, adopted from their native emblem, the Kangaroo.

See also AUSTRALIA

KEIGHLEY RLFC

Founded in 1876. Joined the Northern Union in 1900. Ground: Lawkholme Lane.

Colours: White jerseys, with scarlet red and emerald green " V ", white shorts.
Division Two Champions, 1902-03.
RL Cup Beaten Finalists, 1936-37.
Yorkshire Cup Beaten Finalists, 1943-44, 1951-52.
Club records:
  Attendance: 14,500 v Halifax (Rugby League Challenge Cup) 3rd March, 1951.
  Goals: 155 by B. Jefferson 1973-74.
  Tries: 30 by J. Sherburn 1934-35.
  Points: 331 by B. Jefferson 1973-74.

KIWIS

The nickname of the New Zealand Rugby League team, adopted from their native emblem, the Kiwi.

See also NEW ZEALAND

L

LANCASHIRE CUP

Season	Winners		Runners-up	
1905-06	Wigan	0	Leigh	0
(replay)	Wigan	8	Leigh	0
1906-07	Broughton R.	15	Warrington	6
1907-08	Oldham	16	Broughton R.	9
1908-09	Wigan	10	Oldham	9
1909-10	Wigan	22	Leigh	5
1910-11	Oldham	4	Swinton	3
1911-12	Rochdale H.	12	Oldham	5
1912-13	Wigan	21	Rochdale H.	5
1913-14	Oldham	5	Wigan	0
1914-15	Rochdale H.	3	Wigan	2
Wigan 2				
1915-16 to 1917-18	*Competition suspended*			
1918-19	Rochdale H.	22	Oldham	0
1919-20	Oldham	7	Rochdale H.	0
1920-21	Broughton R.	6	Leigh	3
1921-22	Warrington	7	Oldham	5
1922-23	Wigan	20	Leigh	2
1923-24	St Helens Recs.	17	Swinton	0
1924-25	Oldham	10	St Helens Recs.	0
1925-26	Swinton	15	Wigan	11
1926-27	St Helens	10	St Helens Recs.	2
1927-28	Swinton	5	Wigan	2
1928-29	Wigan	5	Widnes	4
1929-30	Warrington	15	Salford	2
1930-31	St Helens Recs.	18	Wigan	3
1931-32	Salford	10	Swinton	8
1932-33	Warrington	10	St Helens	9
1933-34	Oldham	12	St Helens Recs.	0
1934-35	Salford	21	Wigan	12
1935-36	Salford	15	Wigan	7
1936-37	Salford	5	Wigan	2
1937-38	Warrington	8	Barrow	4
1938-39	Wigan	10	Salford	7
1939-40*	Swinton	5	Widnes	4
	Swinton	16	Widnes	11
	Swinton won on aggregate 21-15			
1940-41 to 1944-45	*Competition suspended*			
1945-46	Widnes	7	Wigan	3
1946-47	Wigan	9	Belle Vue R.	3
1947-48	Wigan	10	Belle Vue R.	7
1948-49	Wigan	14	Warrington	8
1949-50	Wigan	20	Leigh	7

Season	Winners		Runners-up	
1950-51	Wigan	28	Warrington	5
1951-52	Wigan	14	Leigh	6
1952-53	Leigh	22	St Helens	5
1953-54	St Helens	16	Wigan	8
1954-55	Barrow	12	Oldham	2
1955-56	Leigh	26	Widnes	9
1956-57	Oldham	10	St Helens	3
1957-58	Oldham	13	Wigan	8
1958-59	Oldham	12	St Helens	2
1959-60	Warrington	5	St Helens	4
1960-61	St Helens	15	Swinton	9
1961-62	St Helens	25	Swinton	9
1962-63	St Helens	7	Swinton	4
1963-64	St Helens	15	Leigh	4
1964-65	St Helens	12	Swinton	4
1965-66	Warrington	16	Rochdale H.	5
1966-67	Wigan	16	Oldham	13
1967-68	St Helens	2	Warrington	2
(replay)	St Helens	13	Warrington	10
1968-69	St Helens	30	Oldham	2
1969-70	Swinton	11	Leigh	2
1970-71	Leigh	7	St Helens	4
1971-72	Wigan	15	Widnes	8
1972-73	Salford	25	Swinton	11
1973-74	Wigan	19	Salford	9
1974-75	Widnes	6	Salford	2
1975-76	Widnes	16	Salford	7
1976-77	Widnes	16	Workington T.	11
1977-78	Workington T.	16	Wigan	13
1978-79	Widnes	15	Workington T.	13
1979-80	Widnes	11	Workington T.	0

*Emergency Competition

See also FORSHAWS LANCASHIRE CUP.

LANCASHIRE LEAGUE CHAMPIONSHIP CUP

Year	Winners	Runners-up
1907-08	Oldham	Broughton R.
1908-09	Wigan	Oldham
1909-10	Oldham	Wigan
1910-11	Wigan	Oldham
1911-12	Wigan	Oldham
1912-13	Wigan	Broughton R.
1913-14	Wigan	Salford
1914-15	Wigan	Rochdale
1915-18	Competition Suspended	
1918-19	Rochdale H.	Leigh
1919-20	Widnes	Oldham
1920-21	Wigan	Warrington
1921-22	Oldham	Wigan
1922-23	Wigan	Swinton
1923-24	Wigan	Oldham
1924-25	Swinton	Wigan
1925-26	Wigan	Swinton
1926-27	St Helens R.	Swinton
1927-28	Swinton	St Helens R.
1928-29	Swinton	Wigan
1929-30	St Helens	Salford

Year	Winners	Runners-up
1930-31	Swinton	Wigan
1931-32	St Helens	Swinton
1932-33	Salford	Barrow
1933-34	Salford	Wigan
1934-35	Salford	Warrington
1935-36	Liverpool S.	Widnes
1936-37	Salford	Liverpool S.
1937-38	Warrington	Barrow
1938-39	Salford	Swinton
1939-40	Swinton	Salford
	(Emergency League Championship)	
1940-41	Wigan	Warrington
	(Emergency League Championship)	
1941-45	*Competition Suspended*	
1945-46	Wigan	Barrow
1946-47	Wigan	Widnes
1947-48	Warrington	Wigan
1948-49	Warrington	Wigan
1949-50	Wigan	Leigh
1950-51	Warrington	Workington Town
1951-52	Wigan	Warrington
1952-53	St Helens	Leigh
1953-54	Warrington	St Helens
1954-55	Warrington	Oldham
1955-56	Warrington	St Helens
1956-57	Oldham	Barrow
1957-58	Oldham	St Helens
1958-59	Wigan	St Helens
1959-60	St Helens	Wigan
1960-61	Swinton	St Helens
1961-62	Wigan	Workington Town
1962-63	Workington Town	Widnes (Western Division)
1963-64	St Helens	Swinton (Western Division)
1964-65	St Helens	Warrington
1965-66	St Helens	Swinton
1966-67	St Helens	Workington Town
1967-68	Warrington	St Helens
1968-69	St Helens	Wigan
1969-70	Wigan	Salford

LANCE TODD TROPHY

First awarded in 1946, the Lance Todd Trophy is Rugby League's most coveted individual award. The trophy is awarded to the Player-of-the-match in the Challenge Cup Final, the allocation of the prize being decided by the votes of members of the Rugby League Writers' Association reporting on the game's premier event.

The award is in memory of the famous Kiwi who first came to Britain with the 1907 New Zealand touring party. Todd made his name in Britain as a player with Wigan and Dewsbury, and as a manager with Salford. His untimely death in a road accident on the return journey from a game at Oldham was commemorated by the introduction of the Lance Todd Trophy.

The award was instituted by Australian-born Harry Sunderland, Warrington director Bob Anderton and John Bapty, of the *Yorkshire Evening Post*. Around 1950, the Red Devils' Association at Salford, comprising players and officials who had worked with Todd, raised sufficient funds to provide a trophy and replica for each winner.

In recent years the trophy had been sponsored by brewers Greenall Whitley.

The first man to receive the Lance Todd Trophy was Wakefield Trinity centre Billy Stott in the 1946 Final against Wigan. Gerry Helme is the only player to win the trophy twice, Len Killeen is the only winger to earn the award, and Ray Ashby and Brian Gabbitas the only players to share the honour.

Year	Winner	Team	Position
1946	Billy Stott	Wakefield Trinity (v. Wigan)	Centre
1947	Willie Davies	Bradford Northern (v. Wigan)	Halfback
1948	Frank Whitcombe	Bradford Northern (v. Wigan)	Forward
1949	Ernest Ward	Bradford Northern (v. Halifax)	Centre
1950	Gerry Helme	Warrington (v. Widnes)	Halfback
1951	Ces Mountford	Wigan (v. Barrow)	Halfback
1952	Billy Iveson	Workington Town (v. Featherstone R.)	Forward
1953	Peter Ramsden	Huddersfield (v. St Helens)	Halfback
1954	Gerry Helme	Warrington (v. Halifax)	Halfback
1955	Jack Grundy	Barrow (v. Workington Town)	Forward
1956	Alan Prescott	St Helens (v. Halifax)	Forward
1957	Jeff Stevenson	Leeds (v. Barrow)	Halfback
1958	Rees Thomas	Wigan (v. Workington Town)	Halfback
1959	Brian McTigue	Wigan (v. Hull)	Forward
1960	Tommy Harris	Hull (v. Wakefield Trinity)	Hooker
1961	Dick Huddart	St Helens (v. Wigan)	Forward
1962	Neil Fox	Wakefield Trinity (v. Huddersfield)	Centre
1963	Harold Poynton	Wakefield Trinity (v. Wigan)	Halfback
1964	Frank Collier	Widnes (v. Hull KR)	Forward
1965	Ray Ashby	Wigan	Fullback
	Brian Gabbitas	Hunslet	Halfback
1966	Len Killeen	St Helens (v. Wigan)	Wing-threequarter
1967	Carl Dooler	Featherstone Rovers (v. Barrow)	Halfback
1968	Don Fox	Wakefield Trinity (v. Leeds)	Forward
1969	Malcolm Reilly	Castleford (v. Salford)	Forward
1970	Bill Kirkbride	Castleford (v. Wigan)	Forward
1971	Alex Murphy	Leigh (v. Leeds)	Halfback
1972	Kel Coslett	St Helens (v. Leeds)	Forward
1973	Steve Nash	Featherstone Rovers (v. Bradford N.)	Halfback
1974	Derek Whitehead	Warrington (v. Featherstone Rovers)	Fullback
1975	Ray Dutton	Widnes (v. Warrington)	Fullback
1976	Geoff Pimblett	St Helens (v. Widnes)	Fullback
1977	Steve Pitchford	Leeds (v. Widnes)	Forward
1978	George Nicholls	St Helens (v. Leeds)	Forward
1979	David Topliss	Wakefield Trinity (v. Widnes)	Halfback
1980	Brian Lockwood	Hull KR (v. Hull)	Forward

LAWS OF THE GAME

SECTION 1
The Field of Play

The PLAN and markings thereon are part of these Laws. The metric equivalents (rounded off) of the distances shown in the PLAN are as follows:-

75 yds.	=	68m.
6 to 12 yds.	=	6 to 11 m.
10 yds.	=	10 m.
25 yds.	=	22m.
110 yds.	=	100 m.
18ft. 6in.	=	5.50 m.
10 ft.	=	3.5 m.
11 ft.	=	4 m.

SECTION 2
Glossary

The terms set out below shall have the meanings assigned to them:

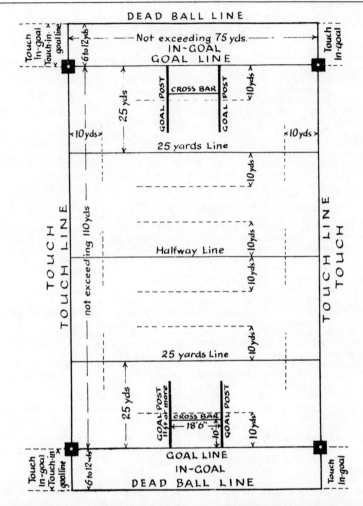

ADVANTAGE Allowing the advantage means allowing play to proceed if it is to the advantage of the side which has not committed an offence or infringement. The advantage must be allowed in all circumstances. (See Section 16).

ATTACKING TEAM is the team which at the time has a territorial advantage. If a scrum is to be formed on the half-way line the team which last touched the ball before it went out of play is the attacking team.

BACK as applied to a player means one who is not taking part in the scrum.

BALL BACK means to form a scrum where the ball was kicked after it has entered touch on the full.

BEHIND when applied to a player means, unless otherwise stated, that both feet are behind the position in question. Similarly "in front" implies "with both feet".

When applied to a position on the field-of-play, "behind" means nearer to one's own goal-line than the point in question. Similarly "in front of" means nearer to one's opponents' goal-line.

BLIND-SIDE means the side of the scrum or

of the play-the-ball nearer to touch (cf. open side).

CHARGING-DOWN is blocking the path of the ball with hands, arm or body as it rises from an opponent's kick.

CORNER POST is a post surmounted by a flag placed at the intersection of each touch-line and goal-line. The post shall be of non-rigid material and shall be not less than 4ft. (1.25m) high. The corner-posts are in touch-in-goal.

DEAD BALL means that the ball is out of play.

DEFENDING TEAM is the team opposing the attacking team (see above).

DIFFERENTIAL PENALTY see Section 13.

DROP-KICK is a kick whereby the ball is dropped from the hands (or hand) and is kicked immediately it rebounds from the ground.

DROP-OUT means a drop-kick from between the posts or from the centre of the " 25 " line when bringing the ball back into play.

DUMMY is the pretence of passing or otherwise releasing the ball while still retaining possession of it.

FIELD-OF-PLAY is the space bounded by, but not including, the touch-lines and goal-lines.

FORWARD means in a direction towards the opponents' goal-line. As applied to a player it means one who is at the time packing down in the scrum.

FORWARD PASS is a throw towards the opponents' dead-ball line (See Section 10).

FULL TIME means the end of the game. Also referred to as No-side.

GOAL see Section 6.

GROUNDING THE BALL means (a) placing the ball on the ground with hand or hands or (b) exerting a downward pressure on the ball with hand or arm, the ball itself being on the ground or (c) dropping on the ball and covering it with the part of the body above the waist and below the neck, the ball itself being on the ground.

HALF TIME means the end of the first half of the game.

HEEL is when a player propels the ball behind him with the sole or heel of his foot.

HOOK is the act of the hooker when he strikes for the ball in the scrum.

IN-GOAL see Plan (Section 1).

IN POSSESSION means to be holding or carrying the ball.

KICK means imparting motion to the ball with any part of the leg (except the heel) from knee to toe inclusive.

KICK OFF see Section 8.

KNOCK ON means to knock the ball towards the opponents' goal-line with hand or arm.

LOOSE ARM is an offence by the hooker if he packs with one arm loose in the scrum.

LOOSE BALL is when during play the ball is not held by a player and is not being scrummaged.

LOOSE HEAD refers to the front row forward in the scrum who is nearest to the referee.

MARK is the point at which a penalty kick is awarded.

OBSTRUCTION is the illegal act of impeding an opponent who does not have the ball.

OFF-SIDE as applied to a player means that he is temporarily out of play and may be penalised if he joins in the game (see Section 14).

ON-SIDE means that a player is not off-side.

OPEN SIDE means the side of the scrum or the play-the-ball further from touch (cf. Blind Side).

ON THE FULL means the ball is kicked over a given line without first bouncing.

PACK refers collectively to the forwards of any one team. To pack down means to form a scrum.

PASS is a throw of the ball from one player to another.

PENALISE is to award a penalty kick against an offending player.

PENALTY KICK see Section 13.

PLACE KICK is to kick the ball after it has been placed on the ground for that purpose.

PLAYING AREA is the space enclosed by the fence, or other such line of demarcation, which prevents the encroachment of spectators.

PLAY THE BALL is the act of bringing the ball into play after a tackle. (See Section 11).

PUNT is a kick whereby the ball is dropped from the hand or hands and is kicked before it touches the ground.

SCRUM or Scrummage or Scrimmage (See Section 12).

STRIKE as applied to the foot means to attempt to secure possession of the ball, usually by heeling it, in a scrum or at a play-the-ball.

TACKLE see Section 11.

TOUCH DOWN is the grounding of the ball by a defending player in his own in-goal.

TOUCH-IN-GOAL See Section 9.

UPRIGHT TACKLE is where the player in possession is effectively tackled without being brought to the ground (see Section 11).

Section 3
The Ball
Shape and Construction

1. The game shall be played with an oval air-inflated ball the outer casing of which shall be of leather or other approved materials and nothing shall be used in its construction which might prove dangerous to the players.

Size and weight

2. The dimensions of the ball shall be:

	Desired Dimensions	Permissible Min.	Permissible Max.
Length	11in.	10¾in.	11½in.
Longest circumference	29in.	28¾in.	29¾in.
Widest	23¼in.	23in.	24in.
Weight (clean and dry)	14½ozs.	13½ozs.	5-8cm

The metric equivalents of the dimensions relating to the ball are as follows:

	Desired Dimensions	Permissible Min.	Permissible Max.
Length	28cm	27cm	29cm
Longest circumference	74cm	73cm	76cm
Widest circumference	59cm	58cm	61cm
Weight (clean and dry)	410gms	380gms	440gms

Ball deflated

3. The Referee shall blow his whistle immediately he notices that the size and shape of the ball no longer comply with the Laws of the Game.

Section 4

The Players and Players' Equipment
13-a-side

1. The game shall be played by two teams each consisting of not more than thirteen players.

Substitutes

2. Each team may replace up to two players at any time provided that the names of the substitutes are made known to the referee before the commencement of the game.

   A replacement must be sanctioned by the referee and can only be effected when the ball is out of play or play is stopped because of injury.

Numbering and Naming of Players

3. The numbers displayed on the backs of the jerseys worn by the players shall normally indicate the positions occupied by the players as set out hereunder.

Backs.
No. 1. Full-back.
No. 2. Right Wing-threequarter.
No. 3. Right Centre-threequarter.
No. 4. Left Centre-threequarter.
No. 5. Left Wing-threequarter.
No. 6. Stand-off-half.
No. 7. Scrum-half.
Forwards.
No. 8. Front Row Prop Forward.
No. 9. Hooker.
No. 10. Front Row Forward.
No. 11 Second Row Forward.
No. 12. Second Row Forward.
No. 13. Loose Forward.
Substitutes.
No. 14. Reserve Back.
No. 15. Reserve Forward.

Players' Equipment

4. (a) A player shall not wear anything that might prove dangerous to other players.

   (b) A player's normal gear shall consist of a jersey of distinctive colour and/or pattern (preferably numbered—see para. 3 above), a pair of shorts, stockings of distinctive colour and/or pattern and studded boots or shoes.

   (c) Protective clothing may be worn provided it contains nothing of a rigid nature.

   #### Dangerous Equipment

   (d) The referee shall order a player to remove any part of his equipment which might be considered dangerous and shall not allow the player to take any further part in the game until the order is obeyed. The player shall retire from the field-of-play to remove the offending item if the start or re-start of the game would otherwise be delayed.

   #### Similar Colours

   (e) The colours of the jerseys worn by competing teams shall be easily distinguishable and, if, in the opinion of the Referee similarity between the jerseys might affect the proper conduct of the game he may, at his discretion, order either team to change jerseys in accordance with the Rules governing the competition in which the game is played.

Studs

(f) Studs on boots or shoes shall be no less than ⁵⁄₁₆in. (8mm.) diameter at the apex and, if made of metal, shall have rounded edges.

SECTION 5
Mode of Play
Object

1. The object of the game shall be to ground the ball in the opponents' in-goal to score tries (see Section 6) and to kick the ball over the opponents' cross-bar to score goals (see Section 6).

Start of Play

2. The captains of the two teams shall toss for choice of ends in the presence of the referee. The team of the captain losing the toss shall kick-off to start the game.

Mode of Play

3. Once play has started any player who is on-side or not out of play can run with the ball kick it in any direction and throw or knock it in any direction other than towards his opponents' goal-line. (See Section 10 for Knock-on and Forward Pass).

Tackling

4. A player who during play is holding the ball may be tackled by an opposing player in order to prevent him from running with the ball or from kicking or passing it to one of his own side (See Section 11 for Tackle).

Obstruction

5. A player who is not holding the ball shall not be tackled or obstructed. (See Section 15).

SECTION 6
Scoring—Tries and Goals
Value—Try and Goal

1. A Try shall count three points.
   A Goal shall count two points.
   A Drop Goal shall count one point.

Deciding winners

2. The game shall be won by the side scoring the greater number of points. If both sides score equal number of points, or if both sides fail to score, then the game shall be drawn.

Try—how scored

3. A try is scored when:
   (a) a player first grounds the ball in his opponents' in-goal provided that he is not in touch or touch-in-goal or on or over the dead-ball line.
   (b) opposing players simultaneously ground the ball in the in-goal area provided that the attacking player is not in touch or touch-in-goal or on or over the dead-ball line.

Sliding try

   (c) a tackled player's momentum carries him into the opponents' in-goal where he grounds the ball even if the ball has first touched the ground in the field-of-play but provided that when the ball crosses the goal-line the player is not in touch or touch-in-goal or on or over the dead-ball line.

Penalty try

   (d) the Referee awards a penalty try which he may do if, in his opinion, a try would have been scored but for the unfair play of the defending team. A penalty try is awarded between the goal-posts irrespective of where the offence occurred.

Touching Referee, etc.

   (e) an attacking player carrying the ball comes into contact with the Referee or a Touch-Judge or an encroaching spectator in the opponents' in-goal and play is thereby irregularly affected.

Position of Try

4. The Try is awarded:
   (a) where grounded if scored as in 3 (a) and 3 (b) above.
   (b) where it first crosses the goal-line if scored as in 3 (c) above.
   (c) between the posts if a penalty try.
   (d) where contact took place if scored as in 3 (e) above.

Referee—sole judge

5. Only the referee may award a try but he may take into consideration advice given by the touch-judges before arriving at his decision. He shall signal that a try has been scored by pointing to where the try has been allowed.

Goal—how scored

6. A goal is scored if the whole of the ball at any time during its flight passes over the opponents' cross-bar towards the dead-ball line after being kicked by a player (and not subsequently touching the ground or being touched in flight by any other player) in any of these circumstances:-
   (a) by a place-kick after a try has been scored.
   (b) by a place-kick or a drop-kick when a penalty kick has been awarded.
   (c) by a drop kick during play from any position in the field-of-play.

Where taken

7. A kick at goal after a try may be taken from any point on an imaginary line drawn parallel to the touch-line in the field-of-play and through the point where the try was awarded. A kick at goal from a penalty kick may be taken from the Mark or from any point on an imaginary line drawn from the Mark towards the kicker's own goal-line and parallel to the touch-line.

Players' positions

8. When a kick at goal is being taken following a try, the opposing players shall stand outside the field-of-play. Players of the kicker's side must be behind the ball. When a kick at goal is being taken from a penalty kick, the opponents retire to their goal-line or not less than ten yards from the Mark. (See Section 13).

Not to distract kicker

It is illegal to attempt to distract the attention of a player who is kicking at goal.

Goal-posts

9. For the purposes of judging a kick-at-goal, the goal-posts are assumed to extend indefinitely upwards.

Judging kicks at Goal

10. When a kick at goal is being taken, the Referee shall assign one Touch-Judge to each post. If a Touch-Judge is of the opinion that a goal has been scored he shall raise his flag above his head. If the kick is unsuccessful he shall wave his flag in front of him and below the waist. If there is no disagreement between the Touch-Judges their decision shall be accepted. In the event of disagreement, the Referee shall decide.

SECTION 7
Timekeeping
Length of game

1. The game shall normally be of eighty minutes duration.

Interval

At half-time there shall be an interval of five minutes but this may be extended or reduced by the referee.

Changing ends

2. A team shall defend one in-goal for the first half of the game and then change ends for the second half.

End of play

3. If time expires in either half when the ball is out of play or a player in possession is tackled, the referee shall immediately blow his whistle to terminate play. If the ball is in play when time expires, the referee shall terminate play when next the ball goes out of play or a player in possession is tackled but time shall be extended to allow a penalty kick or a kick at goal to be taken in which case the half is terminated when next the ball goes out of play or a tackle is effected.

Extra time

4. Extra time shall be added to each half to compensate for time wasted or lost from any cause. The referee shall be the sole judge of extra time. He shall inform the respective captains how much extra time is to be played and shall keep a written record of same except where these duties have been delegated to a timekeeper.

Recommencing play after injury

5. If the continuance of play endangers an injured player the referee may stop the game. If, when the game is stopped, a player is about to play-the-ball after a tackle, then the game shall be recommenced by that player playing-the-ball. If the injured player was in possession and is unable to resume playing or the ball is loose when play is stopped, then play is re-started with a scrum.

SECTION 8
The Kick-off and Drop-out
Kick-off

1. The kick-off is a place-kick from the centre of the half-way line. The team which loses the toss for choice of ends kicks-off to start the first half of the game and their opponents kick-off to start the second half.

When points have been scored, the team against which the points have been scored shall kick-off to re-start the game.

Re-starting play at "25"—with place kick

2. The game is re-started with a place-kick from the centre of the " 25 " line if:

   (a) an attacking player last touches the ball before it goes out of play over the dead-ball line or into touch in goal except after a penalty kick (see No. 3 below).

   (b) an attacking player infringes in the goal area.

   (c) an attacking player is tackled in the in-goal area before he grounds the ball. The ball may be kicked in any direction and is immediately in play. Opposing players shall retire ten yards from the " 25 " line and shall not advance until the ball has been kicked. Defending players shall not advance in front of the ball before it is kicked. Any deliberate offence by either side shall incur a penalty to be awarded at the centre of the " 25 " line.

—with drop-out after unsuccessful penalty

3. If the ball goes dead after an unsuccessful penalty kick at goal the game is re-started with a drop-out by a defending player from the centre of the " 25 " line.

Drop-out from Goal-line

4. The game is re-started with a drop-out by a defending player from the centre of his goal-line if:

   (a) a defending player last touches the ball before it goes over the dead-ball line or into touch-in-goal.

   (b) a defending player accidentally infringes in the in-goal area.

   (c) a defending player touches down in the in-goal area.

   (d) a defending player in possession is tackled in the in-goal area.

   (e) a defending player kicks the ball into touch on the full from his own in-goal.

   (f) the ball or a defending player carrying the ball touches the referee, a touch-judge, or an encroaching spectator in the in-goal area and play is thereby irregularly affected.

Offences incurring penalties—kicker

5. A player who kicks-off or drops-out shall be penalised if he:

   (a) advances in front of the appropriate line before kicking the ball.

   (b) kicks the ball on the full over the touch-line or over the dead-ball line.

   (c) kicks the ball so that it fails to travel at least ten yards forward in the field-of-play.

   (d) kicks the ball other than in the prescribed manner.

—other players

6. Any other player shall be penalised if he:

   (a) wilfully touches the ball after a kick-off or drop-out before it has travelled ten yards forward in the field-of-play.

   (b) runs in front of one of his own side who is kicking-off or dropping-out.

   (c) approaches nearer than ten yards to the line from which the kick is

being taken when an opponent is kicking-off or dropping-out.

SECTION 9
Touch and Touch-in-Goal
Ball in touch
Tackled player in touch on rising

1. The ball is in touch when it or a player in contact with it touches the touch-line or the ground beyond the touch-line or any object on or outside the touch-line except when a player, tackled in the field-of-play, steps into touch as he regains his feet, in which case he shall play-the-ball in the field-of-play.

Jumping player knocks ball back

The ball is in touch if a player jumps from touch and while off the ground touches the ball. The ball is not in touch if during flight it crosses the touch-line but is knocked back after jumping from the field-of-play.

Touch-in-goal

2. The ball is in touch-in-goal when it or a player in contact with it touches the touch-in-goal line, or any object on or outside the touch-in-goal lines.

Points of entry

3. When a ball has entered touch or touch-in-goal, the point of entry shall be taken as the point at which the ball first crossed the touch or touch-in-goal line.

Ball back

4. If the ball is kicked by or bounces off a player in a forward direction and it goes into touch on the full, a scrum is formed where contact with the ball was made (but not nearer than ten yards to the touch-line or five yards to the goal-line—(see Section 12).

Touch from Penalty

5. If the ball is kicked into touch from a penalty kick the game is re-started by placing the ball on the ground ten yards in field opposite the point of entry into touch and kicking it. (See Section 13).

Scrum on " 10 "

6. Other than as outlined in paras. 4 and 5 above, the game is re-started after the ball has gone into touch by forming a scrum ten yards in-field opposite the point of entry into touch but not nearer than five yards to the goal-line—(See Section 12).

SECTION 10
Knock-on and Forward Pass
Deliberate

1. A player shall be penalised if he deliberately knocks-on or passes forward.

Accidental

2. If, after knocking-on accidentally, the player knocking-on kicks the ball before it touches the ground, a goal-post or a cross-bar, then play shall be allowed to proceed. Otherwise play shall stop and a scrum shall be formed.

Charge-down

3. To charge-down a kick is permissible and is not a knock-on.

SECTION 11
The Tackle and Play-the-ball
Tackle player in possession

1. A player in possession may be tackled by an opposing player or players. It is illegal to tackle or obstruct a player who is not in possession.

When tackled. Grounded

2. A player in possession is tackled:
   (a) when he is held by one or more opposing players and the ball or the hand or arm holding the ball comes into contact with the ground.

   Upright tackle
   (b) when he is held by one or more opposing players in such a manner that he can make no further progress and cannot part with the ball.

   Succumbing to tackle
   (c) when, being held by an opponent, the tackled player makes it evident that he has succumbed to the tackle and wishes to be released in order to play-the-ball.

   Hand on player already grounded
   (d) when he is lying on the ground and an opponent places a hand on him.

   No moving of tackled player
3. Once a player in possession has been tackled it is illegal for any player to move or try to move him from the point where the tackle is effected.

Voluntary tackle

4. A player in possession shall not deliberately and unnecessarily allow himself to be tackled by voluntarily falling to the ground when not held by an opponent. If a player drops on a loose ball he shall not remain on the ground waiting to be tackled if he has time to regain his feet and continue play.

Sliding tackle

5. If a tackled player, because of his momentum slides along the ground, the tackle is deemed to have been effected where his slide ends. (See Section 6, 3(c)).

Verbal instructions to resolve doubt

6. If any doubt arises as to a tackle, the Referee should give a verbal instruction to " play on " or shout " held " as the case may be.

Scrum at sixth tackle

7. A team in possession shall be allowed five successive "play-the-balls" but if tackled a sixth time, the ball not having been touched by an opponent during this period, play shall be re-started with a scrum. The team which was not in possession shall out the ball into this scrum and shall have the loose head.

Losing possession—intentionally—accidentally

8. A tackled player shall not intentionally part with the ball other than by bringing it into play in the prescribed manner. If, after being tackled, he accidentally loses possession, a scrum shall be formed.

" Stealing " from tackled player

9. Once a tackle has been completed, no player shall take or attempt to take the ball from the tackled player.

10. The play-the-ball shall operate as follows:

    Release tackled player immediately
    (a) the tackled player shall be *immediately* released and shall not be touched until the ball is in play.

    Regain feet
    (b) the tackled player shall *without delay* regain his feet where he was tackled, lift the ball clear of the ground, face his opponents' goal-line and drop or place the ball on the ground in front of his foremost foot.

    Play with foot
    (c) when the ball touches the ground it may be kicked or heeled in any direction by the foot of any player after which it is in play.

    Player marking
    (d) one opponent may take up position immediately opposite the tackled player.

    Raising foot prematurely
    (e) neither the tackled player nor the player marking him shall raise a foot from the ground before the ball has been released.

    Acting half-back
    (f) a player of each side, to be known as the acting half-back, may stand immediately and directly behind his own player taking part in the play-the-ball.

Retire five yards
(g) players, other than the two taking part in the play-the-ball and the two acting half-backs, are out of play if they fail to retire five yards or more behind their own player taking part in the play-the-ball or to their own goal-line. Having retired five yards they may advance as soon as the ball has been dropped to the ground. A player who is out of play may again take part in the game when the advantage gained by not retiring has been lost.

Speed essential

11. The play-the-ball must be performed as quickly as possible. Any player who intentionally delays the bringing of the ball into play shall be penalised.

SECTION 12
The Scrum
When formed

1. A scrum is formed to re-start play whenever play is not being re-started with a kick-off, a drop-out (Section 8), a penalty kick (Section 13) or a play-the-ball (Section 11).

Formation of Scrum

2. To form a scrum not more than three forwards of either side shall interlock arms and heads and create a clear tunnel at right angles to the touch-line. The forward in the centre of a front row (i.e. the hooker) shall bind with his arms underneath those of the prop forwards. Not more than two second row forwards on each side shall pack behind their respective front rows by interlocking arms and placing their heads in the two spaces between the hooker and his prop forwards. The loose forward of each side shall pack behind his second row forwards by placing his head in the space between them. All forwards must pack square i.e. their bodies and legs must be at right angles to the tunnel. Once the ball has been put in the scrum no other player can lend his weight to it.

Number of backs and players in scrum

3. No more than six players on each side shall assist in the formation of a scrum and when the ball is in the scrum no more than seven players of each side shall act as backs.

No pushing

4. There shall be no pushing before the ball enters the scrummage (i.e. the scrummage must be stationary before the ball is fed).

Loose Head and Put-in

5. If a scrum is ordered after a side has been tackled six successive times the side which was not in possession of the ball shall have the advantages of the Loose Head and putting the ball into the scrum. In a scrum formed for any other reason, a player of the defending side shall put the ball into the scrum and the attacking side shall have the Loose Head.

Scrum-Half

6. (a) The ball shall from the Referee's side of the scrum be put into the centre of the tunnel formed by the opposing front row forwards. The scrum-half feeding the scrummage shall hold the ball horizontally (i.e. point to point) and shall propel it from a position between his knees and his ankles.

(b) The ball shall not be put in before the scrum has been correctly formed.

(c) There shall be no undue delay in putting the ball into the scrum.

(d) The player putting it in shall not hesitate or dummy and after putting it in he shall immediately retire behind his own pack of forwards.

(e) The scrum-half not putting the ball into the scrum shall reach forward with arm outstretched to place his hand on the rearmost forward in his pack and shall remain in that position until the ball has emerged correctly from the scrum.

Other Players outside

7. All players outside the scrum (other than the scrum-half putting the ball in) shall take up positions behind their own forwards and shall remain so until the ball has emerged correctly from the scrum.

Forwards in Scrum

8. When the ball is in the scrum it can only be played with the foot.

The front row forwards shall pack with the upper portions of their bodies parallel to the ground and shall not advance their feet into the tunnel or have one foot raised before the ball is put in or strike for the ball before the hookers.

A hooker may strike for the ball with either foot but not until it first contacts the ground in the centre of the tunnel. After the hookers have struck for the

My ball. George Nicholls, the St Helens and Great Britain second-row forward, is caught in possession during a match against Warrington.

(*Above*) Test action. Great Britain's Brogden about to pass to Smith during a 1932 Test match against Australia. Kangaroo Prigg tries to cut off the British advance.

(*Right*) Huddersfield's famous 1914 'team of All-Talents'. They won the Rugby League Championship, Challenge Cup, Yorkshire Cup and Yorkshire Senior Competition.

(*Left*) Harold Wagstaffe, nicknamed the 'Prince of Centres', was one of the 1914 Huddersfield all-conquering team.

Left—Wakefield Trinity's former Great Britain and Yorkshire halfback Jonty Parkin after a muddy match.

(*Right*) Another of Rugby League's Welsh converts Gus Risman established himself as an all-time great. Here he is pictured after leading Workington Town to victory over Featherstone Rovers in a Wembley Challenge Cup final.

ball the other forwards in the scrum may kick or heel the ball.

No player shall wilfully collapse a scrum or wilfully have any part of him other than his feet in contact with the ground. A player shall not wilfully delay the correct formation of a scrum.

Ball in Play

9. To be in play, the ball must emerge from between and behind the inner feet of the second row forwards.

   If the ball does not emerge correctly and the fault cannot be attributed to any one side then it should be put into the scrum once again.

Where formed

10. If a scrum is ordered it shall normally be formed where the breach of Laws occurs. If such breach is within ten yards of a touch-line or five yards of a goal-line the scrum shall be brought in ten yards from the touch-line and five yards from the goal-line.

Scrum wanders

11. If a penalty kick is awarded relating to a scrum offence and the scrum has wandered from its original position, the Mark is where the scrum was first formed.

Scrum wheels

12. If the ball emerges correctly from the scrum it is in play even though the scrum has wheeled. Any forward can detach himself from the scrum to gather or kick the ball. Any back can similarly play if provided he remained behind the scrum until the ball emerged.

Section 13
Penalty Kick
When awarded

1. A Penalty Kick shall be awarded against any player who is guilty of misconduct (Section 15) provided that this is not to the disadvantage of the non-offending side. Unless otherwise stated, the Mark is where the offence occurs. If misconduct occurs in touch the Mark shall be five yards from the touch-line in the field-of-play and opposite where the offence occurred or, in the case of obstruction, where the ball next bounces, in the field-of-play, or five yards opposite the point of entry if the ball enters touch on the full, or five yards from the goal-line if the ball crosses the goal-line on the full, whichever is to the greater advantage of the non-offending side. If the offence

is committed by a defender in his own in-goal the Mark is taken five yards into the field-of-play opposite where the offence occurred.

How taken

2. A player must take a Penalty Kick by punting, drop-kicking, or place-kicking the ball from any point on or behind the Mark and along the touch-line. The ball may be kicked in any direction, after which it is in play.

Position of Players

3. Players of the kicker's side must be behind the ball when it is kicked.

   Players of the side opposing the kicker shall retire to their own goal-line or ten yards or more from the Mark towards their own goal-line and shall not make any attempt to interfere with or distract the attention of the kicker. They may advance after the ball has been kicked.

Finding Touch

4. If the ball is kicked into touch without touching any other player the kicking side shall re-start play by placing the ball on the ground ten yards in-field opposite the point of entry into touch and kicking it. Opposing players shall retire ten yards from the point of entry into touch or to their own goal-line.

No delay

5. No player shall deliberately take any action which is likely to delay the taking of a Penalty Kick.

Kicker's side infringes

6. If the kick is not taken as stated or if a player of the kicker's side infringes, a scrum shall be formed at the Mark.

Opposing side infringes

7. If a player of the side opposing the kicker infringes, another Penalty Kick shall be awarded at the Mark or where the offence occurred, whichever is to the greater advantage to the non-offending side.

Explain why penalised

8. When the Referee penalises a player he must explain the nature of the offence.

Penalty kick Penalty in-goal offence— attacking team

9. Where a penalty would normally be awarded in the in-goal area for an offence by the attacking team play shall be re-started with a place kick from the centre of the " 25 " line as described in Section 8, paragraph 2.

—defending team

For an in-goal offence by the defending team which incurs a penalty the Mark is in the field-of-play five yards from the goal-line and opposite where the offence occurred except where foul play is committed on a player who scores a try in which case the Mark shall be the centre of the line ten yards from the goal line.

—extra kick at goal

This penalty kick shall take the form of a kick at goal only and shall be taken after the attempted conversion of the try.

Differential Penalty

10. The Differential Penalty will operate for technical offences at the scrum, the non-offending side being awarded a tap penalty to be taken at the Mark. The tap penalty is obligatory in this case: the non-offending side may *not* kick for goal or for touch.

SECTION 14
Offside
When offside

1. A player is offside except when he is in his own in-goal if the ball is kicked, touched or held by one of his own side behind him.

Out of play
Retire five yards

2. An offside player shall not take any part in the game or attempt in any way to influence the course of the game. He shall not encroach within five yards of an opponent who is waiting for the ball and shall immediately retire five yards from any opponent who first secures possession of the ball.

Placed onside

3. An offside player is placed onside if:
   (a) an opponent moves five yards or more with the ball.
   (b) an opponent touches the ball without retaining it.
   (c) one of his own side in possession of the ball runs in front of him.
   (d) one of his own side kicks the ball forward and takes up a position in front of him in the field-of-play.
   (e) if he retires behind the point where the ball was last touched by one of his own side.

SECTION 15
Player's Misconduct
Definition of misconduct

1. A player is guilty of misconduct if he:
   (a) deliberately trips, kicks or strikes another player.

(b) unnecessarily and viciously attacks the head of an opponent when effecting a tackle.
(c) drops knees first on to an opponent who is on the ground.
(d) uses any dangerous throw when effecting a tackle.
(e) deliberately breaks the Laws of the Game.
(f) uses foul or obscene language.
(g) disputes a decision of the Referee or Touch-Judge.
(h) re-enters the field-of-play without the permission of the Referee or a Touch-Judge having previously temporarily retired from the game.
(i) behaves in any way contrary to the true spirit of the game.
(j) deliberately obstructs an opponent who is not in possession. (See para. 2).

SECTION 16
Duties of Referees and Touch-Judges
One Referee Two Touch-Judges

1. In all matches a Referee and two Touch-Judges shall be appointed or mutually agreed upon by the contesting teams.

Enforce Laws

2. The Referee shall enforce the Laws of the Game and may impose penalties for any deliberate breach of the Laws. He shall be the sole judge on matters of fact except those relating to Touch and Touch-in-Goal (See para. 11 below).

Record scores

3. He shall record the tries and goals scored during the match.

Timekeeper

4. He shall be the sole time-keeper except where this duty has been delegated to another person (See Section 7).

Power to stop game

5. He may, at his discretion, temporarily suspend or prematurely terminate a match because of adverse weather, undue interference by spectators, misbehaviour by players, or any other cause which, in his opinion, interferes with his control of the game.

Permission to enter playing area

6. He shall not allow anyone apart from the players on to the playing area without his permission.

Power to dismiss

7. In the event of misconduct of a player, the Referee shall, at his discretion, caution or dismiss the offender. He shall dismiss any player who is guilty of

foul play and who has previously been cautioned.

Control of players

8. The players are under the control of the Referee from the time they enter the playing area until they leave it.

When to blow whistle

9. The Referee must carry a whistle which he shall blow to commence and terminate each half of the game. Except for these occasions the blowing of the whistle shall temporarily stop the play. The Referee shall blow the whistle:

(a) when a try or a goal has been scored.

(b) when the ball has gone out of play.

(c) when he detects a breach of the Laws of the Game, except when to stop the play would be to the disadvantage of the non-offending team.

(d) when play is irregularly affected by the ball or the player carrying the ball coming into contact with the Referee, a Touch-Judge, or with any person not taking part in the match or with any object which should not normally be on the field-of-play, a scrum shall be formed at the point of contact, the defending side to put the ball in, the attacking side to have the Loose Head.

(e) when any irregularity, not provided for in these Laws, occurs and one team unjustifiably gains an advantage.

(f) when a stoppage is necessary in order to enforce the Laws or for any other reason.

Changing decision

10. If the Referee judges on a matter of fact, he shall not subsequently alter that judgement but he may cancel any decision made if facts of which he had no prior knowledge are reported to him by a Touch-Judge.

Accept Touch-Judge decisions

11. The Referee shall accept the decision of a neutral Touch-Judge relating to touch and touch in-goal play and to kicks at goal.

Touch-Judge

12. Each Touch-Judge shall remain in touch, one on each side of, and near to, the playing area except:

(a) when judging kicks at goal (See Section 6) and

(b) when reporting a player's misconduct which has escaped the notice of the Referee.

Flag

13. Each Touch-Judge must carry a flag, triangular in shape, the longest sides being equal and not less than 12in. (30 cm) and the short side shall be not less than 9 in. (23 cm). The flag must be attached by the short side to a stick, the length of which shall be not less than 18 inches (45 cm).

Indicating Touch

14. A Touch-Judge shall indicate when and where the ball goes into touch by raising his flag and standing opposite the point of entry into touch except in the case of " ball back " (see Section 9 para. 4) when the Touch-Judge must indicate that no ground has been gained by waving his flag above his head accentuating the movement in the direction of the kicker's goal-line.

Indicating Touch-in-Goal

15. If the ball enters Touch-in-Goal the Touch-Judge shall wave his flag above his head and then point it towards the goal-posts if the ball last touched a defending player or towards the " 25 " line if it was last touched by an attacking player.

Judge kicks at goal

16. Touch-Judges shall assist the Referee in judging kicks at goal. (See Section 6 para. 10).

Indicating 10 yards

17. When a Penalty Kick is being taken, the nearer Touch-Judge shall take up a position near the touch-line ten yards beyond the Mark to act as a marker for the team which is required to retire. He shall wave his flag horizontally in front of him if any player fails to retire ten yards.

Official Inquiry

18. In cases where circumstances in connection with the match are likely to be made the subject of official investigation, the Referee and Touch-Judges shall report to the investigating authority only and shall refrain from expressing criticism or comment through other channels.

SECTION 17
Referee's Signals
Signal nature of offence

1. When the Referee is required to give a decision he shall whenever possible indicate the nature of his decision by making the appropriate signal.

Indicate how play re-starts

2. When he wishes to stop the game

temporarily, he shall, after blowing his whistle, point to the offending player, indicate the nature of the decision and then signal as to how the game is to be re-started.

3. The signals to be given by a Referee are set out below. Whenever possible the Referee should in addition point to the offending player.

Signals for Re-starting Play

Scrum. With bent arms, palms of hands facing each other at shoulder level, fingers together and slightly bent, bring the tips of the fingers together with a slight downward movement.

Penalty Kick. Face the non-offending team and extend the right arm forward with the hand slightly higher than the shoulder level and the palm of the hand at right angles to the ground.

Drop-out. Point to the place from which the drop-kick is to be taken.

Relating to scoring

Try. Point to where try is awarded. Instruct the Touch-Judge to stand on this point temporarily as a guide to the player who is to take the goal-kick.

Penalty Try. Point to mid-way between the posts and take up position temporarily on this point as a guide to the kicker.

Goal. Raise handkerchief above head.

Signals made when play is not necessarily stopped

Try disallowed. Wave hands, palms facing downwards across and in front of the body below the waist.

Play on. Wave the hands chest high palms facing away from the chest across and in front of the body.

Ball touched in Flight. Raise one hand above the head and tap the tips of the fingers with the fingers of the other hand.

Count of Tackles is cancelled. Raise clenched fist above head and wave from side to side.

Player "held" and to play-the-ball. Indicate that players not concerned with the play-the-ball must retire by making a signal chest-high, similar to the breaststroke in swimming.

Signals indicating infringements

1. *Knock-on.* With the hands in front of the body, below the waist, slightly apart, palms facing forward and fingers pointing towards the ground, make two or three forward movements of the hands.

2. *Forward Pass.* Make a forward movement with the straight arm indicating the line of flight of the ball.

Scrum

3. *Scrum half feeds "own feet".* With hands and arms mime the action of the scrum-half putting the ball into the scrum, but exaggerate the angle at which it was thrown.

4. *Scrum-half "dummies".* Mime the action of the Scrum-half but emphasise the backward motion of the hands.

5. *Scrum-half fails to retire.* Make a movement with the hand indicating the direction the Scrum-half should have taken.

6. *Scrum-half throws the ball upwards into the Scrum.* Mime the action of the Scrum-half exaggerating the upward movement of the hands.

7. *Hooker strikes prematurely.* Raise a foot from the ground in front of the body with the leg straight.

8. *Hooker packs a Loose Arm.* Raise one arm sideways with elbow bent so that the hand hangs downwards.

9. *Prop strikes for the ball.* Raise a foot from the ground by extending the leg sideways from the body.

10. *Handling in the Scrum.* Make a backward scooping action with the hand.

11. *Collapsing the Scrum.* Make a lifting motion with the hand.

12. *More than seven backs.* Point to one of the players who is detached from the Scrum and who normally is in the pack and then hold up seven fingers.

13. *More than six players pushing in the Scrum.* Point to the player who is pushing and who is not normally in the Scrum and then hold up six fingers.

Play-the-ball

14. *Tackled player delays regaining his feet.* Flick the hand in an upwards direction.

15. *Tackled player "dummies", when dropping the ball.* Mime the action of the offending player exaggerating the upward withdrawing movement of the hands.

16. *Tackled player fails to drop the ball correctly.* If the ball has been dropped between the player's legs, point backwards with one arm between the legs. If the ball has been dropped to the side point with one hand to the side.

17. *Tackled player does not lift the ball clear of ground.* Make a lifting movement with the hand.

18. *Tackled player does not face opponents' in-goal.* Stand at the angle

offending player adopted and then turn to face the opponents' in-goal.

19. *Tackled player passes when he should have played-the-ball.* Mime the gesture of playing-the-ball.

20. *Tackled player obstructs or butts with his head after playing the ball.* Mime his action.

21. *Voluntary tackle.* Make a lifting movement with hand.

22. *Player marking the tackled player kicks prematurely or dangerously.* Make a kicking movement with the foot.

23. *Player marking retains his hold on player playing-the-ball.* Make a decisive backwards movement with one hand. This signal applies to any interference by the player marking when the ball is actually being played other than kicking prematurely or dangerously (paragraph 22 above).

24. *Tackler delays releasing tackled player.* Make a downward movement with the hands in front of the body below the waist.

25. *Offside at the play-the-ball.* With a backward movement of the hand indicate that the player should be further back.

26. *Stealing the ball from the tackled player.* Mime the action in snatching the ball from the opponent.

27. *Dragging tackled player after tackle is effective.* Mime the action of dragging.

28. *Sixth tackle imminent.* Raise arm vertically above head with fingers and thumbs outstretched.

29. *Team is tackled six successive times.* Raise arm with fingers and thumb outstretched.

30. *Count of tackle is cancelled and start again.* Wave clenched fist from side to side above head.

Drop out or Penalty

31. *Kicker fails to bring foot into contact with the ball.* Tap the foot with one hand.

Other Infringements

32. *Offside.* Indicate player should have been further back (See No. 25).

33. *Player in possession touches official.* Point to the player in possession and tap the chest with one hand.

34. *Obstruction.* Mime the offending player's action.

35. *Tripping.* Extend one foot forward as if to trip.

36. *Stiff arm tackle.* Raise an arm in front of the body with fist clenched and as

the arm is moved forward tap the forearm with the other hand.

37. *Disputing decisions.* Place one hand on the mouth.

38. *Ball in Touch.* Point to appropriate Touch-Judge.

39. *Extra-Time.* Raise both arms vertically above head.

Touch-Judge Signals

40. The Touch-Judge cannot stop the play for any infringement but he may signal the nature of an infringement if the Referee is unsighted and seeks his guidance.

Signals which may be used by a Touch-Judge and which are not included in Para. 3 above are:

Touch. Flag raised above head at point of entry.

Ball Back. Flag waved above head accentuating backward movement.

Touch-in-Goal. Flag waved above head and then pointed to goal-posts or centre of "25" depending on how game is to be re-started (Section 16).

Successful Kick at Goal. Raise flag above head.

Unsuccessful Kick at Goal. Wave flag across and in front of the body below the waist. If the ball goes over the dead-ball line, tap the ground with the end of the flag-stick.

Players not retiring 10 yards when kick is being taken. Wave flag horizontally in front of body.

LEAGUE LEADERS TROPHY

Whenever Rugby League has staged a single division system, the league table has simply served to determine which clubs should take part in the end-of-season play-off to decide the Champions.

After a two-year trial with two divisions, the single-tier league was re-introduced in the 1964-65 season, with a new top sixteen play-off replacing the traditional top four format. With the exception of the 1966-67 season when the top four formula was briefly reinstated, the top sixteen play-off was staged until the two division fixture plan was brought back for a third time in 1973-74.

To cater for a demand from clubs that the team at the top of the 30-club league should be rewarded for its consistency, a League Leaders Trophy was introduced in the 1964-65, the holders being:

1964-65	St Helens
1965-66	St Helens
1966-67	Leeds

1967-68   Leeds
1968-69   Leeds
1969-70   Leeds
1970-71   Wigan
1971-72   Leeds
1972-73   Warrington

From the 1973-74 season, the title of Rugby League Champions is bestowed on the leaders of the First Division, who receive the Championship Trophy. The team at top of the Second Division is termed the Second Division Champions, being presented with the Second Division Championship Bowl.

LEEDS RLFC

Founded in 1890. Founder member of the Northern Union. Ground: Headingley. Colours: Blue and amber jerseys, white shorts.
RL Championship Winners, 1960-61, 1968-69, 1971-72.
  Beaten Finalists, 1914-15, 1928-29, 1929-30, 1930-31.
League Leaders Trophy Winners, 1966-67, 1967-68, 1968-69, 1969-70, 1971-72.
RL Cup Winners, 1909-10, 1922-23, 1931-32, 1935-36, 1940-41, 1941-42, 1956-57, 1967-68, 1976-77, 1977-78.
  Beaten Finalists, 1942-43, 1946-47, 1970-71, 1971-72.
Yorkshire League Winners, 1927-28, 1930-31, 1933-34, 1934-35, 1936-37, 1937-38, 1950-51, 1954-55, 1956-57, 1960-61, 1966-67, 1967-68, 1968-69, 1969-70.
Yorkshire Cup Winners, 1921-22, 1928-29, 1930-31, 1932-33, 1934-35, 1935-36, 1937-38, 1958-59, 1968-69, 1970-71, 1972-73, 1973-74, 1975-76, 1976-77, 1979-80.
  Beaten Finalists, 1919-20, 1947-48, 1961-62, 1964-65.
BBC2 Floodlit Trophy Winners, 1970-71.
Player's No. 6 Trophy Winners, 1972-73.
Premiership Winners, 1974-75, 1979-80.
Club Records:
  Attendance: 40,175 v. Bradford N. (League) 21 May 1947.
  Goals: 166 by L. Jones, 1956-57.
  Tries: 63 by E. Harris, 1935-36.
  Points: 431 by L. Jones, 1956-57.

LEIGH RLFC

Founded in 1877. Founder member of the Northern Union. Ground: Hilton Park. Colours: Cherry and white jerseys, white shorts.
RL Championship Winners, 1905-06.

Division Two Champions, 1977-78.
RL Cup Winners, 1920-21, 1970-71.
Lancashire Cup Winners, 1952-53, 1955-56, 1970-71.
  Beaten Finalists, 1905-06, 1909-10, 1920-21, 1922-23, 1949-50, 1951-52, 1963-64, 1969-70.
BBC2 Trophy Winners, 1969-70, 1973-73.
  Beaten Finalists, 1967-68, 1976-77.
Club Records:
  Attendance: 31,324 v. St Helens (RL Cup) 14 Mar. 1953.
  Goals: 166 by S. Ferguson, 1970-71.
  Tries: 35 by W. Kindon, 1956-57.
  Points: 356 by S. Ferguson, 1970-71.

LEVY FUND

The introduction of the two-division League structure gave rise to fears that First Division clubs would become wealthier at the expense of Second Division clubs. In a bid to distribute the extra revenue generated by the more attractive and lucrative First Division fixtures, the Northern Rugby Football League introduced a Levy Fund.

Fifteen per cent of gross receipts for all First Division matches are paid into the Levy Fund within a fortnight of the matches being played. At the end of each League season, the money in the Levy Fund is divided equally between all the clubs, both First and Second Division.

LIMITED TACKLES

Until the mid-1960s, Rugby League laws allowed a team to keep possession of the ball as long as it was able to. Season 1967-68 heralded the introduction of the limited tackle rule, after an eight-month trial period, in a bid to produce faster, more attractive play. If a team in possession succumbed to four successive tackles, a scrum was formed.

The four-tackle limit increased the pace of the game, but also led to more kicking and instances of erratic play.

At the start of the 1972-73 season, the limit was extended to six tackles in a successful attempt to allow teams extra time to build up sustained attacks. Four years later, after a period of five-tackle limit, the International rule was also extended to a uniform six-tackle limit.

See also PLAY THE BALL

LITERATURE

The earliest magazine devoted to the break-away sport was the *Northern Union*

News, published from 1910 to 1914 and used by many clubs as part of their official programme.

Subsequent journals have been *Rugby League Review*, edited by S. Chadwick, first published in 1946; *Rugby League Gazette*, N. Berry, 1948; *Rugby League Record*, T. Webb, 1962; *Rugby League Magazine*, A. N. Gaulton, 1963. The *Rugby Leaguer*, a weekly newspaper, first appeared in 1949 and is published by South Lancashire Newspapers.

A number of hardback books appeared in the 1950s and 1960s, written by leading journalists and players, but this was followed by a dearth of publications as attendances fell dramatically.

On the weekly newspaper front, *Pro-Ball* was launched in Jan. 1973, becoming the official organ of the Rugby Football League before ceasing publication in May 1973. *Touchdown*, produced for the Rugby Football League by an agency, lasted only four editions in early 1977.

A new annual was produced for the 1976-77 season called *Rugby League Review*, going on to become an established publication. *Rugby League Annual*, designed for the young reader, appeared in the 1977-78 season.

A periodical for international supporters was launched by editor and publisher Harry Edgar in 1976, called *Open Rugby*.

The *John Player Yearbook*, Rugby League's most extensive publication, was first published in 1973-74 but ceased publication after the 1976-77 edition because of rising costs and company policy. The first edition of this encyclopaedia was compiled by A. N. Gaulton and published in 1968.

A compilation of profiles of stars of the 1970s called *Who's Who* and sponsored by Shopacheck was published in 1980.

LOCAL RADIO

The advent of local BBC and Independent radio in the early 1970s brought a new dimension to Rugby League media coverage.

Highlighted by intensive match results and reviews service on a Sunday, local radio coverage also featured match commentaries, personality interviews and a focus on the amateur game.

BBC stations include Radio Carlisle, Humberside, Leeds, Manchester and Merseyside. Independent stations serving the Rugby League populus feature Radio City (Merseyside), Pennine (Bradford) and Piccadilly (Manchester).

LOSING RUNS

In 1906-07 Liverpool City played 30 League matches and lost them all. This is the only time a team playing more than a dozen League matches has failed to win one. They conceded 1,398 points.

Liverpool also lost their two Cup-ties that season. This particular Liverpool club played only that one season before disbanding.

Between Nov. 1975 and Apr. 1977 Doncaster had a losing run of 40 Division Two matches. Their only win in this period was a Cup-tie, preceding a run of 37 Cup and League defeats.

MACKESON CONTESTS

Spanning nearly a decade, the Mackeson Contests took four forms before coming to an end in 1970.

Phase one was a pilot scheme in 1961, when gold watches were awarded to members of the team scoring most points against the New Zealand Tourists.

This concept of rewarding points scorers was widened in the 1962-63 season to cover League football. The Mackeson Trophy and a cash prize was presented to the team with the best scoring average over the season. Also, the season was divided into five periods of six weeks each, with the top scoring team in each period receiving the Mackeson flag and a cash prize.

This continued until the 1968-69 season, when the Mackeson Golden Ball was introduced. The ball started the season in the possession of Warrington. Whenever the holder of the Golden Ball was defeated, the ball was passed to the victor.

The fourth phase was entered in the following season 1969-70, heralding the Mackeson Merit Table, positions being decided by the difference in points scored for and against a club. Once again, there was a season's winner and four period winners.

Mackeson Contest

	Main Contest	*Period Contest*
1962-63	St Helens 18.30	Workington Town
		Workington Town
		Wigan
		Wakefield Trinity
		St Helens
1963-64	Wigan 18.88	Oldham
		Wigan
		Leigh
		Castleford
		Workington Town
1964-65	Halifax 18.66	St Helens
		St Helens
		Featherstone Rovers
		Leeds
		Halifax
1965-66	Wigan 17.61	Hull Kingston Rovers
		Wigan
		Wakefield Trinity
		Wigan
		Halifax
1966-67	Hull Kingston Rovers 20.18	Leeds
		Hull Kingston Rovers
		Castleford
		Wakefield Trinity
		Wakefield Trinity
1967-68	Leeds 20.86	Bradford Northern
		Leeds
		Leeds
		Leeds
		Hull

Mackeson Golden Ball
1968-69   Wigan 11 matches, Salford and Warrington 8, Leeds and Huyton 3,
                 Leigh, Oldham, Swinton and Workington Town 1.

Mackeson Merit Table

	Main Contest	*Period Contest*
1969-70	St Helens 410 points	St Helens 162 points
		Leeds 117 points
		Leeds 87 points
		Wigan 78 points

NEW ZEALAND

The sequence of events which led to the birth of Rugby League in the Southern Hemisphere began on the New Zealand Rugby Union tour of England in 1905. A member of that touring party, winger George W. Smith, a famous New Zealand athlete, met several Northern Union officials and players during the trip and was very impressed with what he saw. He agreed to consider a suggestion from the Northern Union that he should assemble a party of New Zealand Rugby players and return to England to undertake a tour against the Northern Union as "paid men".

When Smith arrived back in New Zealand, he discussed the project with a 24-year-old Post Office clerk, Albert Henry Baskerville. It was to be an historic meeting for Rugby League because Baskerville, who was a forward with Wellington's Oriental Rugby Union club, entered the new enterprise with missionary zeal. Their scheme caused uproar in New Zealand sporting circles to whom professionalism was virtually a dirty word. But the two pioneers were not easily discouraged and they managed to find enough players to tour England in the 1907-8 season.

While arrangements were being made cloak-and-dagger style for the tour, the organisers received a cable from some disgruntled Australian Rugby enthusiasts (see AUSTRALIA) and the New Zealanders agreed to play three matches across the Tasman Sea *en route* for England. The matches, played under 15-a-side Rugby Union laws because nobody had seen Northern Union laws "down under" were played at Sydney Showground and the New Zealanders won them 12-8, 19-5 and 5-3.

The tourists received a £500 guarantee for the three matches and a portion of that money was allocated to adding brilliant Australian player H. H. ("Dally") Messenger to the touring party. The All Golds, the nickname they acquired because they played for money, set sail for England and the party was:- A. H. Baskerville, G. W. Smith, H. R. Wright (capt.), C. Byrne, T. Cross, A. Callum, C. Dunning, D. G. Fraser, D. Gilchrist, J. Gleeson, W. Johnson, A. F. Kelly, J. Lavery, A. Lyle, W. Mackrell, D. McGregor, H. H. Messenger, C. J. Pearce, H. F. Rowe, W. Trevarthen, H. S. Turtill, W. T. Tyler, H. Tyne, E. Watkins, E. Wrigley, R. Wynyard, W. T. Wynyard; managers Baskerville and H. J. Palmer.

The tourists landed at Folkestone on 30 Sept. 1907 facing a formidable task. They were scheduled to play 35 games and only pioneer Smith knew anything about Northern Union laws. Feeling was still running very high in New Zealand against the tourists and the Agent General in London expressed the opinion that the All Golds would bring no credit to their country. How wrong can people be!

They started their tour with an agreement from the Northern Union that they should take 70 per cent of the gate receipts, and receive guarantees of £50 for mid-week games and £100 for Saturday games. In Nov. 1907 the New Zealand Rugby Union declared the All Golds professionals and suspended them. In spite of this predictable decision, the tourists completed their tour winning 19 matches losing 14, scoring 414 points and conceding 294 points.

A welcome lift for Rugby League "down under" was the All Gold's 2-1 win in the first ever Northern Union or Rugby League Test series. The thirteen-a-side's first trans-globe international was staged in Leeds on 25 Jan. 1908 and England won 14-6. But the New Zealanders had the last laugh, taking the next two Tests 18-6 at Stamford Bridge, Chelsea (London), and 8-5 at Cheltenham.

Several of the tourists signed for English clubs, notably Smith, who joined Oldham, Edgar Wrigley who helped create Huddersfield's immortal "team of all talents", and the best known of them all, Lance Todd, who played for Wigan and went on to manage Salford.

The All Golds returned South of the Equator, but instead of going straight back to New Zealand they called in at Australia to play their first ever Test series against the Australians. And to complete the double the New Zealanders won that series, winning two of the matches and drawing the other.

Tragedy struck the triumphant tourists before they could return home when Baskerville died after an attack of pneumonia in Brisbane. His body was returned to New Zealand and he was buried in his home town of Wellington. The inscription on his grave stone reads: "In Loving memory of Albert Henry Baskiville* who died in Brisbane while on tour with the New Zealand football team 20th May 1908, Age 25."

Before they disbanded after their tenmonth, two-day tour, the All Golds played a benefit match for Baskerville's mother at Athletic Park, which ironically is now the home of Wellington Rugby Union club. It was the first Northern Union match to be played in New Zealand and a crowd of 6,000 turned up to watch the match, Blacks v. Reds, which the Blacks won 55-20.

Fortunately for Rugby League that was not the end of the story in New Zealand. The All Gold success had established a following for the game and in 1908 the native Maoris, who had adapted well to the new code, sent a touring team to Australia and that was followed by a visit by a New Zealand team to Australia in 1909. New South Wales sent teams to New Zealand in 1912 and 1913 and they both returned with 100 per cent records.

The First World War put an end to touring until 1919 when the Kiwis again crossed the Tasman Sea. The countries established another Rugby League first in 1922 when New Zealand received a visit from the Australian Universities team. The game is still well established at University level in both countries.

Consolidation continued until the Second World War. The outbreak of hostilities in Sept. 1939 cost the New Zealand League £8,000 the price of sending a touring side to Britain to play just two games before war was declared on Hitler's Germany. The return of peace in 1945 and 1946 saw Rugby League resume its programme in New Zealand and in 1952 the Kiwis gained one of their greatest triumphs, winning a three Test series in Australia. In 1965 the New Zealanders faced the Australians in another Test series and it was notable for the debut of centre Roy Christian, one of New Zealand's greatest ever players. A descendant of Fletcher Christian, of

Mutiny-on-the-*Bounty* fame, he led New Zealand as captain against Australia, France and Great Britain, including the Test series win in Britain in 1971, and was awarded an MBE for his services to the game.

Because the New Zealand game, even at senior level, is run on an amateur basis some of their best players have pursued their careers in Australia and Great Britain. British clubs have attracted such players as Brian Nordgren and Ces Mountford, both to Wigan, while the rich pickings across the Tasman in Sydney have claimed players like Henry Tatana, one of the best ever prop forwards to play the game. This has, of course, affected the strength of their international team. Some, like the 1952 and 1971 teams, were outstanding Rugby League sides but that constant drain of good players has made it difficult for New Zealand to maintain that kind of success. They could well be one of the nations to benefit most from the International Board's decision in 1977 to introduce a four-year international transfer ban.

The game is controlled in New Zealand by a 12-man Rugby League Council. Although the game is spread throughout the North and South islands of New Zealand, the real power base for the code is in Auckland, North Island, where the game is most popular. It seems very strange that the New Zealand All Gold pioneers were pilloried for their professionalism, but that the all-amateur modern Rugby League is probably less "professional" today than their more popular Rugby Union counterparts!

During the last ten years Rugby League has expanded dramatically in New Zealand. The startling progress was touched off when the New Zealand Universities started to play the game in 1969. The student game has expanded to such an extent that five of the country's six universities are playing the game, both in their own and outside competitions, and they have made a tour of Australia.

In the same year the game was introduced to the North Island central region based at Tokaroa.

By 1974 two new Leagues had been formed, Hawkes Bay and Marlborough. The Marlborough League was centred on Blenheim and it was so successful that in 1976 it expanded to take in the Tasmanian Bay area. The next new recruit in 1976 was the Gisborne—East Coast Bays League and this was a particularly welcome addi-

*There is still confusion about the spelling of his surname, but most historians accept Baskerville as being correct.

tion for it was an area where Rugby League had not been played before. The 13-a-side code was also re-introduced to Invercargill in South Island and at Wanganui on the West Coast of North Island.

The major Leagues in New Zealand are at Auckland, Waikaito (South Island), Bay of Plenty (Central North Island), Wellington and Canterbury.

The following list, demonstrates the spread and strength of the Leagues and their member clubs.

Auckland League: Blockhouse Bay, City-Newtown, East Coast Bay, Ellersie, Glenfield, Glenora, Howick, Manakau, Mangere, East Manurewa, Marist, Mount Albert, Mount Roskill, North Shore, Northcote Otahuhu, Otar, Papakura, Pakuranga, Papatoetoe, Ponsonby, Port, Chevalier, Richmond, Te Atatu, Waitemata.

Canterbury League: Addington, Eastern Suburbs, Hornby, Kaiapoi, Linwood, Marist, Papanui, Sydenham.

Gisborne-East Coast Bays League: Country, Kati, Marist, Mazda, Midway.

Hamilton League: Chartwell, Church College OB, City Tigers, Fairfield, Frankton Albion, Hillcrest Hornets.

Hawkes Bay League: Cook Islands, Flaxmere Hornets, Heretaunga, Loons, Napier Hawks, Pania, Tamoana, Waipukurau.

Midlands Bay of Plenty League: Cenral, City, Marist, Murupara, Nga lwi, Ngongotaka, Pacific, Taupo, Turangi, Tokoroa, United.

Manawatu League: Aotea, Criterion Lions, Dannevirke, Feilding, Kia Ora, Levin, Marton, Massey, Suburbs, Tarako.

Northland League: Kaitaia, Moerewa, Portland Parrots, Takahiwai, West End Jumbos.

Otago-Southland League: Celtic, City, Kia Toa, Leopards Blue, Leopards Red University.

Marlborough League: Nelson, Blenheim City, Motueka, Woodbourne.

Taranaki League: Fitzroy, Hawera. Inglewood, Marist, Midhurst, Nganu Tu, Waitara.

Waikato League: Albions, Church College, City Tigers, Fairfield, Hillcrest, Huntly South, Ngaruawahia, Tainui, Taniwharau, Turangawaewae, United.

West Coast League: Cobden-Kohinoor, Marist, Runanga, Suburbs, Waro-Rakau.

Wellington League: Eastern Suburbs, Gold Coast, Korodale, Marist, Miramar, Petone, Porirua City, Randwick, St George, Upper Hutt, Wainuiomata, Waterside.

Rothman's Championship

The championship is the leading inter-provincial competition in New Zealand. The competition is run on a knock-out basis and the games are played on the grounds of the higher-ranked Leagues. The Leagues play in three regional qualifying Leagues which are:

North Region: Auckland, Waikato, Northland, Hamilton, Bay of Plenty, Gisborne-East Coast Bays.

Central Region: Wellington, Taranaki, Midlands, Hawkes Bay, Manawatu.

Southern Region: Canterbury, West Coast, Marlborough, Otago-Sutherland.

Winners

Auckland: 1965, 66, 67, 68, 69, 71, 72, 73, 74, 76, 77, 78.

Canterbury: 1975

Wellington: 1970

The New Zealand roll of honour is:

North Island v. South Island

Winners

North Island: 1925, 26, 27, 28, 31, 32, 34, 36, 39, 44, 47, 49, 51, 52, 54, 55, 56, 59, 60, 63, 65.

South Island: 1929, 30, 46, 48, 50, 53, 58, 62, 64.

No matches were staged in 1933, 35, 37, 38, 40, 41, 42, 43, 45, 57, 61. In 1966 the competition was changed into inter-zone matches with Wellington joining the South Island zone for the sake of the competition.

Winners since 1966 have been:

Northern Zone: 1966, 67, 68. Southern Zone: 1969, 73.

No contests were staged in 1970, 71, 72, 74, 75, 76, 77.

Rugby League Cup

Until 1969 it was known as the Northern Union Cup. It is an inter-provincial competition played on a challenge basis. In 1956 the trophy was at stake every time the holder played in all but Rothman Cup games.

Winners

1913 to 1921	Auckland
1922	South Auckland
1923	South Auckland
1924 to 1929	Auckland
1930	South Auckland
1931	North Auckland
1932	South Auckland
1933 to 1946	West Coast
1947 to 1949	Wellington
1950 to 1961	Auckland
1962 to 1963	Canterbury
1964 to 1967	Auckland

1968	Canterbury
1969	West Coast
1970	Canterbury
1971 to 1973	West Coast
1974	Canterbury
1975 to 1976	Waikato
1977	Taranaki

Player of the Year Award

1961	Gary Phillips (Auckland)
1962	Mel Cooke (Canterbury)
1963	Graham Kennedy (West Coast)
1964	Don Hammond (Auckland)
1965	Bill Deacon (Waikato)
1966	Roy Christian (Auckland)
1967	Bobby Irvine (Canterbury)
1968	Ernie Wiggs (Auckland)
1969	Colin O'Neill (Wellington)
1970	Roy Christian (Auckland)
1971	Roy Christian (Auckland)
1972	John Whittaker (Wellington)
1973	John Hibbs (West Coast)
1974	Ken Stirling (Auckland)
1975	Ken Stirling (Auckland)
1976	Tony Coll (West Coast)
1977	John Smith (Auckland)

Auckland Club Championship—Fox Memorial

City: 1910, 11, 16, 21, 22, 23, 25, 44.
Devonport: 1928, 32, 33.
Eastern: 1961, 63.
Ellerslie: 1957, 74.
Grafton 1915.
Manakau: 1936, 42, 43.
Marist: 1924, 31, 38, 48, 65, 66.
Maritime: 1920.
Mount Albert: 1939, 47, 50, 68, 69.
Mount Wellington: 1976.
Newtown: 1912, 27.
North Shore: 1913, 14, 41.
Otahuhu: 1945, 64, 70, 71, 75, 77.
Ponsonby: 1917, 18, 19, 26, 29, 30, 52, 54, 58, 67, 72, 73.
Port Chevalier: 1953.
Richmond: 1934, 35, 37, 40, 46, 49, 55, 56.
    Championship shared 1951 Richmond and Mount Albert; 1960 Eastern and Western; 1962 Eastern and Glenora.

Canterbury Club Championship—Smith Trophy

Addington: 1923, 29, 31, 35, 37, 39, 44.
Christchurch: 1948.
Federal: 1920, 21.
Hornby: 1926, 27, 30, 34, 36, 52, 58, 62, 64, 65, 66, 67, 69.
Linwood: 1932, 38, 51, 61, 63, 68, 70.
Marist: 1924, 25, 28.
Papanui: 1957, 59, 71, 72, 73, 74, 76, 77.

Prebbleton: 1949.
Rakaia: 1946.
Sydenham: 1913, 14, 15, 17, 18, 19, 22, 40, 41, 45, 47, 50, 53, 54, 55, 56.
Christchurch—Eastern Suburbs: 1975.
No competition 1916 and 1933.
Championship shared
1942
Hornby-Rakai-Riccarton: 1942.
Sydenham-Rakai: 1943.
Linwood-Papanui: 1960.

Wellington Club Championship—Appleton Shield

Celtic: 1929-33
Central: 1959
City: 1915
Hutt: 1921, 23, 24, 25, 27, 28
Korodale: 1954, 60, 61
Marist: 1948, 49, 59, 65, 71
Miramar: 1941, 42, 51, 52, 62, 64
Petone: 1913, 19, 20, 22, 26, 37, 38, 43, 72, 73, 74
Randwick: 1944, 46, 56, 68, 69, 70, 76
St George: 1934, 35, 36, 40, 53, 55, 57, 58, 77
Suburbs: 1914
Waterside: 1945, 50, 67, 75
Competition suspended 1916
No competition: 1930
Championship shared
Marist and Randwick: 1947
Korodale and Marist: 1963
Miramar and Waterside: 1966

All Blacks

Whichever brand of Rugby takes your fancy the All Blacks, the New Zealand Rugby Union national side, must command respect. Their unsmiling faces and tough rugby is world famous and nine of them have switched to Rugby League since the last war: 1946 Jimmy Haig (Otago), who went to play 53 times for the Kiwis; 1949-50 Peter Henderson (Wanganui) moved to play for Huddersfield in England; 1951 Tom Lynch (Canterbury) also moved to England; 1955 Tom Katene (club not known); 1964 Dennis Cameron (mid-Canterbury); 1965 Vic Yates (North Auckland); 1968 Owen Stephens (Wellington); 1972-73 Graeme Whiting (King Country) and 1976 Joe Karam (Auckland).

Maori teams to tour Australia

1908: Played 12, won 6, lost 6, pts for 197, pts against 180.
1909: Played 10, won 5, lost 5, pts for 161, pts against 166.
1956: Played 14, won 6, lost 8, pts for 296, pts against 257.

New Zealand teams to tour Great Britain and France

1907-08

H. R. Wright (capt.), G. W. Smith (vice-capt.), A. H. Baskerville, C. Byrne, T. Cross, A. Callam, C. Dunning, D. G. Frater, D. Gilchrist, J. G. Gleeson, W. Johnston, A. F. Kelly, J. A. Lavery, A. Lisle, W. Mackrell, D. McGregor, H. H. Messenger, C. J. Pearce, H. F. Rowe, L. B. Todd, W. Trevarthen, H. S. Turtill, W. T. Tyler, H. Tyne, E. Watkins, E. Wrigley, R. Wynyard, W. T. Wynyard.

Managers: A. H. Baskerville and H. J. Palmer.

Played 35, won 19, lost 14, drawn 2, pts for 414, pts against 294.

1926-27

H. Avery (capt.), N. Mouat (vice-capt.), H. Brisbane, L. Brown, A. Carroll, H. Cole, B. Davidson, F. Delgrosso, W. L. Desmond, W. Devine, C. Dufty, G. Gardiner, E. C. Gregory, A. W. Hall, F. Henry, E. Herring, J. Kirwan, L. Mason, A. B. Menzies, J. Parkes, L. Petersen, J. Sanders, A. Singe, H. Thomas, C. Webb, J. Wright.

Managers: E. H. Mair (coach) and G. H. Ponder (Financial).

Played 34, won 17, lost 17, pts for 562, pts against 554.

1939-40

R. K. King (capt.), J. R. Banham (vice-capt.), G. W. Beadle, G. R. Bellaney, L. Brown, J. J. Campbell, T. H. Chase, J. Clark, J. G. Cootes, C. H. Davidson, J. Hemi, R. D. Jones, A. G. Kay, B. Leatherbarrow, A. J. McInnarney, H. Mataira, H. M. Milliken, L. D. Mills, G. G. Mitchell, G. A. Orman, P. Ririnui, V. J. Scott, J. Smith, D. Solomon, I. Sterling, W. H. Tittleton.

Managers: J. A. Redwood and R. Doble.

Played 2, won 2, pts for 41, pts against 13.*

1947-48

P. A. Smith (capt.), A. H. Graham (vice-capt.), H. D. Anderson, D. Aynsley, D. A. Barchard, R. J. Clark, S. W. Clarke, R. Cunningham, W. G. Davidson, J. A. Forrest, A. E. C. Gillman, J. S. Haig, C. C. Hancox, T. H. Hardwick, J. J. Johnson, L. R. Jordan, C. McBride, R. G. McGregor, A. J. McInnarney, A. W. McKenzie, K. Mountford, J. Newton, R. Nuttall, L. R. Pye, M. W. Robertson.

Managers: J. A. Redwood and L. Hunter.

*Tour was abandoned following outbreak of World War Two in September 1939 after playing 2 games.

Played 35, won 20, lost 13, drawn 2, pts for 509, pts against 344.

1951-52

M. W. Robertson (capt.), J. S. Haig (vice-capt.), A. J. Atkinson, D. A. Barchard, T. O. Baxter, A. Berryman, D. L. Blanchard, G. J. Burgoyne, R. J. Cranch, J. J. Curtain, W. G. Davidson, J. F. Dodd, C. A. Eastlake, J. R. Edwards, K. English, J. A. Forrest, B. K. Hough, C. R. Johnson, C. McBride, W. R. McLennan, G. Menzies, F. G. Mulcare, D. Richards-Jolley, B. E. Robertson, W. Sorenson, D. H. White.

Managers: D. A. Wilkie, and T. F. McKenzie.

Played 40, won 25, lost 14, drawn 1, pts for 663, pts against 441.

1955-56

T. O. Baxter (capt.), W. R. McLennan (vice-capt.), A. Atkinson, V. A. N. Bakalich, D. L. Blanchard, J. E. Bond, S. E. Belsham, J. R. Butterfield, P. J. Creedy, N. L. Denton, I. N. Grey, R. Haggie, R. P. Hawes, T. T. Kilkelly, H. D. Maxwell, G. S. MacDonald, R. J. McKay, L. J. McNichol, G. Menzies, R. L. Moore, R. W. Percy, J. Riddell, N. K. Roberts, B. E. Robertson, W. Sorenson, J. E. Yates.

Managers: H. Tetlow and C. Siddle.

Played 38, won 19, lost 16, drawn 3, pts for 640, and pts against 610.

1960–World Cup

C. Johnson (capt.), G. Menzies (vice-capt.), R. C. Ackland, J. R. Butterfield, M. L. Cooke, R. S. Cooke, N. L. Denton, C. A. Eastlake, R. K. Griffiths, B. T. Hadfield, T. T. Kilkelly, H. T. Maxwell, L. J. Olliff, G. R. Phillips, T. Reid, N. K. Roberts, W. Sorenson, G. P. Turner.

Played 4, won 2, lost 2, pts for 50, pts against 56.

1961-62

R. D. Hammond (capt.), M. L. Cooke (vice-capt.), G. R. Bailey, R. W. Bailey, A. N. Amer, J. A. Bond, J. R. Butterfield, B. E. Castle, R. S. Cooke, R. H. G. Duffy, S. K. Edwards, H. R. Emery, J. E. Fagan, G. S. Farrar, J. P. Ford, B. T. Hadfield, R. W. Harrison, W. R. Harrison, R. G. Hart, G. M. Kennedy, B. S. Lee, K. R. McCracken, J. G. Patterson, B. T. Reidy, W. L. Snowden, N. T. Tiller.

Managers: C. Siddle. Coach: W. (Snowy) Telford.

Played 29, won 14, lost 13, drawn 2, pts for 470, pts against 385.

1965-66

W. L. Snowden (capt.), G. M. Kennedy (vice-capt.), R. W. Bailey, L. Brown, R. Christian, W. Deacon, K. Dixon, S.

Edwards, H. R. Emery, J. E. Fagan, D. R. Hammond, R. Irvine, B. Langton, G. Mattson, E. Moore, C. O'Neill, R. I. Orchard, B. T. Reidy, R. Scholefield, P. Schultz, W. T. Schultz, R. Strong, R. Tait, J. Walsche, J. L. White, P. M. White.

Managers: W. O'Callaghan and T. Wellsmore. Coach: W. Telford.

Played 31, won 16, lost 13, drawn 2, pts for 343, pts against 341.

1970 World Cup

F. R. Christian (capt.), M. P. Brereton, W. J. Burgoyne, E. Carson, C. R. Cooksley, W. Deacon, D. J. Gailey, L. Graham, J. Greengrass, E. Heatley, E. Kereopa, A. P. Kriletch, D. Ladner, B. R. Lowther, R. C. McGuinn, C. O'Neil, G. M. Smith, J. A. Whittaker, G. J. Wollard.

Manager M. C. Montford. Coach Mr L. Blanchard.

Played 3, won 1, lost 2, pts for 44, pts against 89.

1971-72

F. R. Christian (capt.), M. P. Brereton, W. J. Burgoyne, G. R. Cooksley, W. G. Deacon, D. S. Dowsett, M. K. Eade, J. H. Fisher, D. Gailey, J. Greengrass, A. P. Kriletch, B. R. Lowther, M. J. McLennan, R. C. McGuinn, D. K. Mann, P. C. Orchard, R. I. Orchard, J. C. O'Sullivan, G. M. Smith, D. Sorenson, K. L. Stirling, H. Tatana, J. A. Whittaker, D. A. Williams, R. F. Williams, G. J. Wollard.

Managers: Mr W. O.'Callaghan and Mr J. Williams.

Played 20, won 10, lost 10, pts for 319, pts against 300.

1975–World Cup (European Section)

K. Stirling (capt.), W. Collicoat, P. Orchard, J. Smith, D. Williams, B. Dickison, R. Jarvis, L. Proctor, T. Conroy, J. Greengrass, R. Baxendale, T. Coll, M. Eade, T. Gordon, P. Gurnick, F. A. Kuoi, D. Sorenson, K. Sorenson, L. Beehre.

Managers:

Played: 5, won 2, lost 2, drawn 1, pts for 92, pts against 72.

NICKNAMES

The vast majority of professional clubs have acquired nicknames.

Barrow:	Shipbuilders
Batley:	Gallant Youths
Blackpool Borough:	Seasiders
Bradford Northern:	Northern
Bramley:	Villagers
Castleford:	Glassblowers
Doncaster:	Dons
Featherstone Rovers:	Colliers
Halifax:	Thrum Hallers
Huddersfield:	Fartowners
Hull:	Airlie Birds
Hull Kingston Rovers:	The Robins
Huyton	Ton
Keighley:	Lawkholmers
Leeds:	Loiners
Oldham:	Roughyeds
Rochdale Hornets:	Nets
St Helens:	Saints
Salford:	Red Devils
Swinton:	Lions
Wakefield Trinity:	Dreadnoughts
Warrington:	Wires
Whitehaven:	Haven
Widnes:	Chemics
Wigan:	Riversiders
Workington Town:	Town
York:	Wasps

NORTHERN RUGBY FOOTBALL LEAGUE

Not to be confused with the Rugby Football League, the Northern Rugby Football League is specifically responsible for the organisation of a league format for its member clubs and any end-of-season competition based on the final league positions.

The Northern Rugby Football League is administered by an Executive Committee, consisting of the Chairman and Vice-Chairman of the Rugby League Council and eight other Council members, four from Yorkshire clubs and four from Lancashire and Cumbrian clubs.

NORTHERN RUGBY FOOTBALL UNION

The great split in the Rugby Union world which saw 22 of the northern clubs breaking away and forming the Northern Rugby Football Union came in 1895. The name was altered to Rugby Football League at the Annual Meeting in June 1922.

The disagreement over the question of payment for Broken Time (i.e., whether amateur players should be compensated for loss of wages sustained as a result of their participation in the game) had aroused a great deal of controversy in the years preceding 1895. At a meeting held in London on 20 Sept. 1893, two Yorkshire representatives of the English Rugby Football Union (M. N. Newsome and J. A. Millar) proposed that " Players be allowed compensation for *bona-fide* loss of time." The meeting declined to sanction the motion by 282 votes to 136, but the northern clubs were far from satisfied.

Several of them were suspended for paying their players for loss of wages, and the apparent lack of understanding on the part of the Rugby Union authorities who did not appreciate that men in the northern industrial areas could ill afford to lose money in order to play rugby brought matters to a head.

At a meeting at the George Hotel, Huddersfield, the northern clubs took their irrevocable step on 29 Aug 1895. The chairman of the meeting was H. H. Waller (Brighouse) and 21 clubs were represented. Of these, only one—Dewsbury—did not agree to join the new Northern Rugby Football Union. The 20 clubs who boldly took the plunge were:

Lancashire:
Broughton Rangers, Leigh, Oldham, Rochdale Hornets, St Helens, Tyldesley, Warrington, Widnes, Wigan.

Yorkshire:
Batley, Bradford, Brighouse Rangers, Halifax, Huddersfield, Hull, Hunslet, Leeds, Liversedge, Manningham, Wakefield Trinity.

At a later meeting Runcorn and Stockport were admitted to membership, making a total of 22 clubs for the first season. Dewsbury soon realised they had made a mistake in not joining and they applied for and were given membership at the Annual Meeting in June 1898.

The new League was popularly known as the Northern Union, and after all these years the term is still part and parcel of the northern dialect. The saying "t' best in t' Northern Union" became an everyday one and is still in use in Lancashire and Yorkshire. They even used it in the 'Coronation Street' television programme.

The first N.U. games were played on 7 Sept. 1895. Professionalism was declared illegal and the rate of 6s. a day was fixed as the maximum payable for broken time. The first season ended with Runcorn winning the Lancashire Senior Competition and Manningham (who played at Valley Parade, Bradford) winning the Yorkshire Senior Competition. There were many prophecies of doom for the Northern Union, but despite a lot of teething troubles the infant proved to be a lusty one. Improvements were continually sought and in season 1896-97 the N.U. Challenge Cup Competition was launched. This created a great deal of interest which has been maintained over the years and which now builds up to a tremendous climax with the Wembley Finals.

In 1897 changes were made in the rules to improve play from the spectator's viewpoint. Scoring values were altered so that a goal, however kicked, would only count two points. The line-out was abolished in favour of a kick-in from touch, and clubs were warned that they would be fined if they did not start their matches on time.

The number of clubs had now grown to 80 and the code was prospering despite its many problems. One of the latter was that as players began to appreciate their value as crowd-pullers the demands for a higher rate of broken time payment became more insistent. In 1898 professionalism was adopted, but the Northern Union authorities were still adamant that no one should make his living out of the game. A "working clause" was introduced whereby players had to have legitimate employment in a full-time job.

Several well-known Rugby Union players became attracted by the prospects of financial reward in the Northern Union game and the bitter feelings towards the new code continued, particularly in Wales. Many talented footballers left the Welsh Valleys then and in the years that were to follow, but in fairness to the professional clubs it should be said that the first approach did not always come from them.

Rule changes were made in almost each of the early seasons in an effort to increase the game's spectacular appeal, for some clubs ran into difficulties and had to disband in the early 1900s. One important change, made in 1906, was the reduction of the number of players in a team from 15 to 13. This was yet another step away from Rugby Union ideas.

The introduction of the NU code to Australia and New Zealand in 1907 and the establishing of overseas Tours was destined to start an era of prosperity which ended with the closing down of competitive football during the Great War. Since then, despite industrial recessions, another World War, and many minor internal problems, the game has prospered. Many deplore the present financial dependence on outside sources such as pools, but all clubs have a solid core of through-thick-and-thin supporters, whose ranks are considerably added to when a team enjoys a run of success.

Rugby League Football is part of their way of life to a very great number of people in the North of England.

OLDEST PLAYER

While there have been instances of players making the odd appearance after their 45th birthday the oldest regular first team player is believed to have been Gus Risman who played within three months of his 44th birthday.

Risman, born at Cardiff on 21 Mar. 1911, played his first match for Salford on 31 Aug. 1929. He joined Workington Town in 1946 and stayed until a brief spell with Batley for whom he played his last match on 27 Dec. 1954.

Risman captained a victorious Workington at Wembley in 1952 when he was 41.

OLDHAM RLFC

Founded in 1876. Founder member of the Northern Union. Ground: Watersheddings. Colours: Red and white hooped jerseys, navy shorts.

RL Championship Winners, 1909-10, 1910-11, 1956-57.

Beaten Finalists, 1906-07, 1907-08, 1908-09, 1921-22, 1954-55.

Division One Champions, 1904-05.

Division Two Champions, 1963-64.

RL Cup Winners, 1898-99, 1924-25, 1926-27.

Beaten Finalists, 1906-07, 1911-12, 1923-24, 1925-26.

Lancashire League Winners, 1907-08, 1909-10, 1921-22, 1956-57, 1957-58.

Lancashire Cup Winners, 1907-08, 1910-11, 1913-14, 1919-20, 1924-25, 1933-34, 1956-57, 1957-58, 1958-59.

Beaten Finalists, 1908-09, 1911-12, 1918-19, 1921-22, 1954-55, 1966-67, 1968-69.

Club Records:

Attendance: 28,000 v. Huddersfield (League) 24 Feb. 1912.

Goals: 200 by B. Ganley, 1957-58.

Tries: 49 by R. Farrar, 1921-22.

Points: 412 by B. Ganley, 1957-58.

PACIFIC CUP

This competition is one of the major newcomers on the international Rugby League scene. The Pacific Cup is staged bi-annually and in 1977 it was contested by Australian State sides Western Australia, Northern Territory and Victoria, twice-winners New Zealand Maoris and Papua-New Guinea.

The idea for the competition was inspired by a desire to take international Rugby League round the Pacific basin and to encourage the growth of amateur Rugby League in that area. Mooted in 1972, the competition, which is run on a round-robin qualifying rounds and grand final basis, was first held in Port Moresby, Papua-New Guinea in 1975.

The New Zealand Maoris, who exclude full New Zealand internationals from their team, went through the tournament unbeaten. Western Australia and Victoria played in the first competition and Northern Territory were admitted in time for the second series in New Zealand in 1977.

Rarotonga made a late attempt to gain admission for the 1977 series, but they could not be accommodated. It was hoped that they would be included in 1979 round when it was to be staged in Western Australia. Interest in the competition has also been expressed by the Cook Islands and Norfolk Islands.

The Maoris repeated their winning feat in 1977 beating Western Australia 35-12 in the grand final at Auckland.

The New Zealand round was notable because it was the first time a team from Papua-New Guinea had been seen outside their own country and one of their players, loose-forward John Wagambi, was voted player of the series. The competition is run by Australian coaching expert Keith Gittoes, a player with Hull in the 1950s, with the official title of co-ordinator.

Reports during 1978 suggested that the competition was experiencing financial problems and that it was hoped to make it more viable by inviting the British and French amateur teams to take part. No further developments have been reported.

PAPUA—NEW GUINEA

After its success in Australia and, to a lesser extent, in New Zealand, it was natural that Rugby League should spread to the Pacific region and the sport is now powerfully established in the emerging nation of Papua-New Guinea.

The game was first played in Papua-New Guinea by servicemen during the Second World War and now it is virtually recognised as their national sport, despite pressure from Australian Rules football, baseball and soccer. In a survey completed in 1977, it was revealed that the Papua-New Guinea Rugby Football League controlled approximately 300 clubs and their growing strength was recognised by the rest of the League world in 1978 when they were formally admitted as a full member of the international board after several years as an associate member.

International board secretary Mr W. Fallowfield reports that the last member to give their assent was Papua's nearest neighbours, Australia.

The headquarters of the Papua-New Guinea League are in Port Moresby, but the actual day-to-day administration of club activities are delegated to four area zones, the Highlands, the Islands, Northern and Southern. Although the sport was progressing at a satisfactory rate in Papua-New Guinea before 1975 it was from that point that the country started to emerge as an international force. Their only previous experience of representative football was an annual exchange of schoolboy teams with Australia, but that changed dramatically.

They entered the first Pacific Cup competition which was played at Port Moresby and then England played a match in the country on their way home from the Southern hemisphere rounds of the ill-fated international championship.

In 1977 Papua's international representative team left their shores for the first time to compete in the second Pacific Cup competition in New Zealand and, in May, they entertained the French team who were on their way to play in the revived World Cup competition in Australia. The Papuans won that historic encounter against the

French 37-6 before an ecstatic crowd of 14,500 in Port Moresby.

During 1978 the Papuans played hosts to two more touring teams, the British amateurs and the full New Zealand international team who were returning from a tour of Australia.

As this volume was being prepared provisional plans were being prepared for the Papuans to tour France during 1979. International League enthusiasts are hoping for a similar reaction that the Fijians brought to Rugby Union because the Papuans play the same brand of exciting, flowing rugby.

PATRONS

Her Majesty Queen Elizabeth II is a patron of the Rugby Football League.

His Royal Highness Prince Philip, Duke of Edinburgh, KG, KT, is a patron of the Australian Rugby Football League.

See also ROYALTY

PERSONALITY GIRL

As a part of a new publicity campaign, the Rugby Football League introduced the appointment of a Personality Girl in 1977. Holding the office for a year, the role of the Personality Girl is to undertake promotional and photographic work. The title holders have been:

1977: Miss Linda Taylor of Huddersfield.
1978: Miss Tina Wilson of Bradford.
1979: Miss Teresa Lockwood of Huddersfield.
1980: Miss Debbie Windass of Hull

PLAYER

A player is either amateur or professional. A professional is a player who agrees with his club to receive money for playing. Such agreement is in writing and signed by a responsible club official and by the player, or parent or guardian if the player is under eighteen years of age.

The agreement provides for the payment of match fees only and it is illegal to sign or attempt to sign a player under-17.

When a player relinquishes his amateur status to turn professional, he can receive a signing-on fee, which could include the payment of further money if he gains representative honours. After 10 years continuous service for the same club, a player is eligible for a benefit.

A player registered with a professional club is not allowed to turn out for an amateur side without his club's permission. A current professional player cannot serve on a club's committee or board of directors.

PLAY-OFFS

Whenever the Rugby Football League has organised a single league competition, the Championship title has been determined by a play-off.

From 1907 to 1962 the Championship was decided by a top four play-off. The top club played the fourth placed, the second club meeting the third placed, with the leading two clubs having ground advantage. The Championship final was staged at a neutral venue, with the winners receiving the Championship Trophy.

After a two-year break for a two division set-up, the Championship play-off returned in 1964-65 season as a top sixteen play-off and for the 1973-74 season was restructured as the Club Championship.

Two-division football was reintroduced again in the 1974-75 season, making the Championship play-off unnecessary.

The play-offs were by their nature very appealing to spectators and at various times soccer grounds have been hired to accommodate the large crowds, examples of which are listed below:

83,190	Wigan v. Wakefield T. at Odsal, Bradford, 1960.
75,194	Huddersfield v. Warrington at Maine Road, Manchester, 1949.
69,504	Salford v. Castleford at Maine Road, Manchester, 1939.
69,143	Warrington v. Bradford N. at Maine Road, Manchester, 1948.
67,136	Wigan v. Huddersfield at Maine Road, Manchester, 1946.
65,065	Wigan v. Huddersfield at Maine Road, Manchester, 1950.
62,199	Oldham v. Hull at Odsal, Bradford, 1957.
61,618	Workington T. v. Warrington at Maine Road, Manchester, 1951.
58,149	Hull v. Workington T. at Odsal, Bradford, 1958.
54,112	Hunslet v. Leeds at Elland Road, Leeds, 1938.

CHAMPIONSHIP ROLL OF HONOUR

Season	Winners		Runners-up		Venue	Attendance
1906-07	Halifax	18	Oldham	3	Huddersfield	13,200
1907-08	Hunslet	7	Oldham	7	Salford	14,000
Replay	Hunslet	12	Oldham	2	Wakefield	14,054
1908-09	Wigan	7	Oldham	3	Salford	12,000
1909-10	Oldham	13	Wigan	7	Broughton	14,000
1910-11	Oldham	20	Wigan	7	Broughton	20,000
1911-12	Huddersfield	13	Wigan	5	Halifax	12,000
1912-13	Huddersfield	29	Wigan	2	Wakefield	17,000
1913-14	Salford	5	Huddersfield	3	Leeds	8,091
1914-15	Huddersfield	35	Leeds	2	Wakefield	14,000
1915-19	*Competition suspended*					
1919-20	Hull	5	Huddersfield	2	Leeds	12,513
1920-21	Hull	16	Hull KR	14	Leeds	10,000
1921-22	Wigan	13	Oldham	2	Broughton	26,000
1922-23	Hull KR	15	Huddersfield	5	Leeds	15,000
1923-24	Batley	13	Wigan	7	Broughton	15,000
1924-25	Hull KR	9	Swinton	5	Rochdale	21,580
1925-26	Wigan	22	Warrington	10	St Helens	22,000
1926-27	Swinton	13	St Helens Rec.	8	Warrington	24,432
1927-28	Swinton	11	Featherstone R.	0	Oldham	15,451
1928-29	Huddersfield	2	Leeds	0	Halifax	25,604
1929-30	Huddersfield	2	Leeds	2	Wakefield	30,350
Replay	Huddersfield	10	Leeds	0	Halifax	18,563
1930-31	Swinton	14	Leeds	7	Wigan	31,000
1931-32	St Helens	9	Huddersfield	5	Wakefield	19,386
1932-33	Salford	15	Swinton	5	Wigan	18,000
1933-34	Wigan	15	Salford	3	Warrington	31,565
1934-35	Swinton	14	Warrington	3	Wigan	27,000
1935-36	Hull	21	Widnes	2	Huddersfield	17,276
1936-37	Salford	13	Warrington	11	Wigan	32,000
1937-38	Hunslet	8	Leeds	2	Leeds	54,112
1938-39	Salford	8	Castleford	6	Manchester	69,000
1939-45	*Competition suspended*					
1945-46	Wigan	13	Huddersfield	4	Manchester	67,136
1946-47	Wigan	13	Dewsbury	4	Manchester	40,921
1947-48	Warrington	15	Bradford N.	5	Manchester	69,341
1948-49	Huddersfield	13	Warrington	12	Manchester	75,194
1949-50	Wigan	20	Huddersfield	2	Manchester	65,500
1950-51	Workington T.	26	Warrington	11	Manchester	61,618
1951-52	Wigan	13	Bradford N.	6	Huddersfield	48,656
1952-53	St Helens	24	Halifax	14	Manchester	51,083
1953-54	Warrington	8	Halifax	7	Manchester	36,500
1954-55	Warrington	7	Oldham	3	Manchester	49,434
1955-56	Hull	10	Halifax	9	Manchester	36,678
1956-57	Oldham	15	Hull	14	Bradford	62,217
1957-58	Hull	20	Workington T.	3	Bradford	58,149
1958-59	St Helens	44	Hunslet	22	Bradford	65,000
1959-60	Wigan	27	Wakefield Trinity	3	Bradford	82,067
1960-61	Leeds	11	Warrington	4	Bradford	60,000
1961-62	Huddersfield	14	Wakefield Trinity	5	Bradford	37,407
1962-63⎫ 1963-64⎭	*No play-offs, Two-Division Championship*					
1964-65	Halifax	15	St Helens	7	Swinton	20,776
1965-66	St Helens	35	Halifax	12	Swinton	30,165
1966-67	Wakefield Trinity	7	St Helens	7	Leeds	20,024
Replay	Wakefield	21	St Helens	9	Swinton	33,537
1967-68	Wakefield Trinity	17	Hull KR	10	Leeds	22,000

Season	Winners		Runners-up		Venue	Attendance
1968-69	Leeds	16	Castleford	14	Bradford	28,442
1969-70	St Helens	24	Leeds	12	Bradford	28,447
1970-71	St Helens	16	Wigan	12	Swinton	21,700
1971-72	Leeds	9	St Helens	5	Swinton	24,055
1972-73	Dewsbury	22	Leeds	13	Bradford	18,889

PLAY-THE-BALL

One of Rugby League's most controversial aspects, the play-the-ball, is the method employed to bring the ball back into play after a tackle. The current mode of play-the-ball is described in Section 11, paragraph 10 of the rules as outlined under LAWS OF THE GAME

Several alternative operations have been tested. Two experimental games were staged at Odsal Stadium, Bradford, on 8 Oct. 1956. Leigh beat Oldham 26-12 using the Rugby Union method of releasing the ball in the tackle, while Bradford Northern beat Huddersfield 14-6 operating a rule where the ball was played forward after the tackle. Spectators were asked to express their preference on voting slips, but the experiment proved without value as only 1,084 attended.

Critics of the play-the-ball argued that the team in possession had an unfair advantage, being able to retain possession for long periods. In October 1966, the limited tackle principle was introduced, where after four consecutive tackles a scrum was formed. This was later extended to six tackles.

See also LIMITED TACKLES

POINTS

Most points by one team in a season: 1,220 by Leeds in 1972-73. The total was amassed as follows:

34 League matches	810
6 Player's No 6	158
4 Yorkshire Cup	117
4 Top 16 Play-off	95
2 BBC Floodlit Trophy	18
1 RL Challenge Cup	11
1 v New Zealand	11
Total 52	1,220

Most League points by one team in a season: 1,005 by St Helens in 38 matches in 1958-59.

Most Points by one team in a match: 119 by Huddersfield v. Swinton Park 2 (RL Challenge Cup, 28 Feb. 1914).

Most Points by a player in a match: 53 by George West (Hull KR) v. Brookland Rovers (RL Challenge Cup, 4 Mar. 1905) 11 tries, 10 goals).

Most points in a career

Neil Fox is the most prolific points scorer of all time. His total after 1979-80 was 6,220. Fox made his debut for Wakefield on 10 Apr. 1956, a month short of his 17th birthday. He had 19 seasons with Wakefield, but also had spells with Bradford Northern, Hull Kingston Rovers, York, Bramley and Huddersfield.

His season-by-season details are:

Season	Goals	Tries	Pts
1955-56	6	0	12
1956-57	54	10	138
1957-58	124	32	344
1958-59	148	28	380
1959-60	171	37	453
1960-61	94	20	248
1961-62	183	30	456
1962 Tour			
(Australasia)	85	19	227
(South Africa)	19	4	50
1962-63	125	14	292
1963-64	125	21	313
1964-65	121	13	281
1965-66	98	11	229
1966-67	144	16	336
1967-68	98	18	250
1968-69	95	9	217
1969-70	17	5	49
1970-71	110	12	256
1971-72	84	6	186
1972-73	138	8	300
1973-74	62	8	148
1974-75	146(1)	14	333
1975-76	102(1)	4	215
1976-77	79(1)	6	175
1977-78	95(1)	9	216
1978-79	50	4	112
1979-80	2	—	4
Total	2575(4)	358	6220

Figures in parenthesis are dropped goals included in main total.

Most in a season by a player: 496 (194 goals and 36 tries) by Lewis Jones (Leeds) in 1956-57.

For Leeds:

1956					
17 Aug.	Halifax (h)		3	0	6
22	Bradford N (a)		11	3	31
25	Wigan (a)		4	0	8
27	Featherstone R (h)		4	1	11
1 Sept.	Wakefield T (a) YC	3	1	9
8	Dewsbury (a)		6	0	12

15	Warrington (h)	7	0	14
22	Huddersfield (a)	3	0	6
29	York (h)	6	0	12
6 Oct.	Batley (a)	4	2	14
13	Australia (h)	Did not play		
20	Hull KR (a)	Did not play		
27	Wigan (h)	2	0	4
3 Nov.	Hunslet (a)	1	0	2
10	Barrow (h)	3	2	12
17	Halifax (a)	4	0	8
24	Keighley (h)	3	3	15
1 Dec.	Barrow (a)	4	0	8
8	Bramley (a)	5	0	10
15	Doncaster (h)	1	2	8
22	Bradford N (h) abandoned	1	1	5
25	Batley (h)	8	1	19
29	Keighley (a)	3	0	6

1957				
5 Jan.	Hull (h)	5	2	16
12	Warrington (a)	0	3	9
19	St Helens (h)	5	1	13
26	Doncaster (a)	Did not play		
2 Feb.	Huddersfield (h)	6	0	12
9	Wigan (h) RL Cup	2	1	7
16	York (a)	7	1	17
23	Workington (h) RL Cup	5	1	13
27	Castleford (h)	4	1	11
9 Mar.	Halifax (a) RL Cup	5	0	10
16	Wakefield T (h)	5	1	13
20	Bradford N (h)	5	1	13
23	Hull (a)	2	0	4
30	Whitehaven (Odsal RL Cup SF)	1	0	2
3 Apr.	Wakefield T (a)	3	0	6
6	St Helens (a)	0	0	0
12	Hull KR (h)	Did not play		
13	Dewsbury (h)	6	2	18
19	Hunslet (h)	5	2	16
20	Featherstone R (h)	2	0	4
22	Castleford (a)	2	0	4
23	Bramley (h)	7	1	17
4 May	Oldham (a) Play Off	3	0	6
11	Barrow (Wembley RL Cup Final)	0	0	0

Representative matches.
For Great Britain:

26 Jan.	France (at Leeds)	9	1	21
3 Mar.	France (at Toulouse)	5	1	13
10 Apl.	France (at St Helens)	7	1	17

For Rest:

| 3 Oct. | Great Britain XIII (at Odsal) | 4 | 0 | 8 |

For RL XIII:

| 29 Oct. | Australia (at Leigh) | 3 | 0 | 6 |

POSTPONEMENTS

Snow and ice have repeatedly affected Rugby League fixture programmes. The first complete wipe-out of a weekend programme was on 16 Feb. 1929 due to frozen grounds.

Frost, snow and ice played havoc with war-time Emergency League fixtures during January and February of 1940 and there were postponements on nine successive Saturdays.

During the 1946-47 season, blizzards decimated the February fixture list and the campaign had to be extended, causing the Championship Final to be delayed until 21 June.

The famous winter of 1962-63 became the big freeze-up, only one game being played during January, braziers de-icing the Castleford pitch, and only six during February. At the start of March there were 156 postponed matches to be arranged and the last game of the season was not played until 1 June.

Snow and ice decimated the 1978-79 programme, disrupting the League, the John Player Competition, the State Express Challenge Cup and the European Championship. Seven consecutive weekends were wiped out or severely curtailed by the arctic weather starting with 10 postponements on 30 Dec. through until 18 Feb. when nine matches were called off. About 140 matches were postponed due to the weather, causing the League programme, due to end on 22 Apr. to be extended to 13 May for the First Division and 20 May for the Second Division, with the Premiership Final closing the season on 27 May, a week later than planned.

See also SUMMER RUGBY; UNDERSOIL HEATING

PREMIERSHIP TROPHY

A regrettable latter-day trend has been constantly to revise the end-of-season Championship formula. The traditional top-four format was replaced by a top-sixteen play-off and a Club Championship, mainly due to bids to stop the decline in attendances and to cater for the third period of two-division football.

In 1974-75, the end of season competition was retitled the 1975 Premiership, with the winners receiving the newly instated Premiership Trophy. The tournament, decided by a draw, was contested by the top 12 clubs in the First Division table and the top four clubs in the Second Division.

The following season it was decided to establish the Premiership and the new format of a top-eight play-off between the leading clubs in the First Division was launched, the pairings being decided on merit basis i.e. 1 v. 8, 2 v. 7 etc. The semi-finals are staged on a two-legged basis, with the final on a neutral venue.

From the 1979-80 season, the tournament was retitled the Slalom Lager Premiership under a new three-year sponsorship with brewers Matthew Brown, of Blackburn.

Premiership Trophy holders are:

1975:	Leeds
1976:	St Helens
1977:	St Helens
1978:	Bradford Northern
1979:	Leeds
1980:	Widnes

See also SLALOM LAGER.

PRESIDENT

The President of the Rugby Football League is the Rt Hon. the Earl of Derby, M.C. He accepted the office in April 1948, succeeding his grandfather, the seventeenth Earl of Derby, President since 1911 and who died on 4 Feb. 1948 at the age of 82.

PROGRAMMES

Every club in membership with the Rugby Football League has to publish an official programme for home fixtures. The standard of club programmes has dramatically improved in recent years, graduating from printed advertisement sheets before the 1945 war.

For the premier matches, including Internationals and Test matches, special souvenir programmes are issued by the Rugby Football League and in recent years these have been labelled the "Big Match" series.

The official programme for the Challenge Cup is published by the Wembley authorities.

The collecting of Rugby League programmes is a popular pastime and there are even agencies dealing in old programmes.

PUBLIC RELATIONS

The first staff appointment of a Public Relations Officer by the Rugby Football League was made in 1974, when Hull-born David Howes took up office on 28 Oct.

At the age of 23, the former *Hull Daily Mail* journalist took responsibility for publicity and promotions at a time when Rugby League was bidding to create a new image.

New policies played a major part in the rapid improvement in attendances, publicity and sponsorship.

One of the innovations was the design of the official RL symbol, now the trademark of Rugby League and the basis of a thriving commercial department.

The concept of a Public Relations Officer was introduced by Mr Brian Snape at the start of his two-year reign of office as Chairman of the Rugby Football League in 1974.

Previously, the Council had commissioned John Caine Associated (Consultants) Ltd. to prepare a marketing report on Rugby League, their contract running from April 1971 to April 1972.

RECORD KEEPERS' CLUB

Before 1970 there was no universally accepted method of compiling Rugby League records. Published records would include or exclude friendly and charity games depending on the whim of the compiler and this caused a great deal of confusion. In 1970 the Northern Rugby League agreed to issue a directive that would set out guide lines for the future. It read " Charity and friendly matches should not count towards players try and goal scoring records, but all competitive games at first team level and representative games or any special challenge matches sanctioned by the League should count."

In order to sort out the anomalies that existed in the previous 75 years records the NRL also agreed to sponsor the Rugby League Record Keepers' Club. This is organised by Irvin Saxton and is an association of Rugby League supporters keenly interested in the statistics and records of the game. A complete check is being carried out by the club on a season by season basis commencing in 1895, and by the summer of 1979 this was up to 1930.

Two publications are issued by the club. *Rugby League Football–A Statistical Review* is a straightforward listing of league tables, play-offs, cup-tie results, and all cup final and representative game details. *Rugby League Records* is concerned with the records of competition, clubs, players and representative games.

The major scoring records of Brian Bevan, Neil Fox and Jim Sullivan as shown in this encyclopaedia have been completely revised by club members. Further details of the club are available from the organiser at 17 Katrina Grove, Purston, Pontefract, West Yorkshire WF7 5LW.

REFEREES

Before the breakaway movement of 1895, Rugby Football rules were declared by the opposing captains prior to the kick-off of each match. Eventually two umpires were elected for each match, one from each side.

Since both these systems were open to partiality, the authorities decided in 1885 to appoint a third arbitrator, the fore-runner of the modern referee. His role was to adjudicate when the two match umpires failed to agree. He was provided with a whistle, but it was not until 1893 that he could blow without being called on to give a decision by the two umpires.

This power to blow at any time gave him virtual control and the two umpires became secondary decision makers, a role similar to the touch-judges of today.

Referees are given a grading after passing the Rugby Football League's annual examination. Promotion to Grade Two status permits match officials to be appointed for senior games, with representative honours being awarded to Grade One referees.

In 1976, the League appointed former top referee Sam Shepherd to the new post of Referees Assessor. His role is to assess the potential of a small number of Grade Five officials who have been earmarked as possible senior referees. The up-and-coming whistlers undertake a probationary year, at the end of which the decision to upgrade or not is taken.

Senior referees receive match fees and expenses, the rates being fixed by the League's Executive Committee.

ROCHDALE HORNETS RLFC

Founded 1871. Founder member of the Northern Union. Ground: Athletic Grounds. Colours: White jerseys, with blue and red band, white shorts.
RL Cup Winners, 1921-22.
Lancashire League Winners, 1918-19.
Lancashire Cup Winners, 1911-12, 1914-15, 1918-19.
 Beaten Finalists, 1912-13, 1919-20, 1965-66.
Player's No. 6 Trophy, Beaten Finalists, 1973-74.
BBC2 Floodlit Trophy, Beaten Finalists, 1971-72.
Club Records:
 Attendance: 41,831 Wigan v. Oldham (RL Cup Final) 12 Apr. 1924.
 Goals: 109 by W. Gowers, 1933-34.
 Tries: 30 by J. Williams, 1934-35.
 Points: 235 G. Starkey, 1966-67.

ROYALTY

It was announced on 15 Apr. 1911 that His Majesty King George V had "graciously consented" to become patron of the Northern Rugby Football Union, although he never actually watched a match.

His son, HRH the Prince of Wales, was the first member of the Royal Family to view a game when he visited Wigan on 23 Nov. 1932 and watched a boys match

refereed by the legendary Jim Sullivan at Central Park.

The first Royal Wembley was on 6 May 1933 when the Prince of Wales, later to become the Duke of Windsor, attended the Empire Stadium.

Her Majesty Queen Elizabeth II is the current Patron of the Rugby Football League.

Year	Trophy presented by	Winning Captain
1933	HRH The Prince of Wales	L. C. Bowkett (Huddersfield)
1947	HRH The Duke of Gloucester	E. Ward (Bradford N.)
1948	HM King George VI	J. Egan (Wigan)
1949	HRH The Duke of Edinburgh	E. Ward (Bradford N.)
1951	HRH The Duke of Gloucester	C. Mountford (Wigan)
1955	HRH The Duke of Edinburgh	W. Horne (Barrow)
1959	HRH The Princess Royal	E. Ashton (Wigan)
1960	HM Queen Elizabeth II	D. Turner (Wakefield T.)
1965	HRH Princess Alexandra	E. Ashton (Wigan)
1967	HM Queen Elizabeth II	M. Dixon (Featherstone R.)
1968	HRH The Duke of Kent	M. Clark (Leeds)
1975	HRH Princess Alexandra	D. Laughton (Widnes)
1980	HRH The Queen Mother	R. Millward (Hull KR)

See also PATRONS.

RUGBY LEAGUE COUNCIL

The Rugby Football League is governed by the Council, consisting of one representative from each professional club. The objects of the Council are "to foster, develop, extend and govern Rugby League Football".

The Council elects five main committees:
  Consultative Committee
  Disciplinary Committee
  Finance and General Purposes
    Committee
  International, Cup, and Rules
    Revision Committee
  Selection Committee.

The Council elects a Chairman. Until 1970, the Chairman served for one year, but since then the appointment has been for two years.

Past Chairmen of the Council

1895-97	H. H. Waller, Brighouse Rangers
1897-98	J. E. Warren, Warrington
1898-99	D. F. Burnley, Batley
1899-1900	J. H. Smith, Widnes
1900-01	H. Hutchinson, Wakefield Trinity
1901-02	J. H. Houghton, St Helens
1902-03	J. Clifford, Huddersfield
1903-04	R. Collinge, Rochdale Hornets
1904-05	F. Lister, Bradford
1905-06	J. H. Smith, Widnes
1906-07	J. B. Cooke, Wakefield Trinity
1907-08	H. Ashton, Warrington
1908-09	J. Nicholl, Halifax
1909-10	J. H. Houghton, St Helens
1910-11	J. W. Wood, Leeds
1911-12	G. Taylor, Wigan
1912-13	W. D. Lyon, Hull
1913-20	J. H. Smith, Widnes
1920-22	W. Fillan, Huddersfield
1922-23	J. Counsell, Wigan
1923-24	J. H. Dannatt, Hull
1924-25	R. Gale, Leigh
1925-26	J. F. Whitaker, Batley
1926-27	E. Osborne, Warrington
1927-28	C. Preston, Dewsbury
1928-29	F. Kennedy, Broughton Rangers
1929-30	W. J. Lingard, Halifax
1930-31	F. Mattinson, Salford
1931-32	E. Brown, Millom (Cumberland)
1932-33	W. Popplewell, Bramley
1933-34	W. M. Gabbatt, Barrow
1934-35	J. Lewthwaite, Hunslet
1935-36	T. Ashcroft, St Helens Recs.
1936-38	A. A. Bonner, Wakefield Trinity
1938-40	G. F. Hutchins, Oldham
1940-42	A. Townend, Leeds
1942-45	R. F. Anderton, Warrington
1945-46	R. Lockwood, Huddersfield
1946-47	W. H. Hughes, Salford

1947-48	W. A. Crockford, Hull Kingston Rovers
1948-49	T. Brown, Liverpool Stanley
1949-50	H. Hornby, Bradford Northern
1950-51	A. Widdeseson, Representative
1951-52	Sir Edwin Airey, Leeds
1952-53	B. Manson, Swinton
1953-54	C. W. Robinson, York
1954-55	J. Hilton, Leigh
1955-56	G. Oldroyd, Dewsbury
1956-57	H. E. Rawson, Hunslet
1957-58	C. E. Horsfall, Halifax
1958-59	F. Ridgeway, Oldham
1959-60	W. Cunningham, Huddersfield
1960-61	J. S. Barritt, Bradford Northern
1961-62	T. Mitchell, Workington Town
1962-63	W. Spaven, Hull Kingston Rovers
1963-64	Dr H. Roebuck, Liverpool City
1964-65	A. Walker, Rochdale Hornets
1965-66	A. B. Sharman, Leeds
1966-67	J. B. Harding, Leigh
1967-68	J. N. Smallwood, Keighley
1968-69	J. Jepson, Featherstone Rovers
1969-70	J. J. Davies, Widnes
1970-72	H. Lockwood, Huddersfield
1972-74	R. Simpson, Castleford
1974-76	G. B. Snape, Salford
1976-78	H. Womersley, Bradford Northern
1978-80	S. Baxendale, Wigan
1980-81	J. Myerscough, Leeds

RUGBY LEAGUE WRITERS' ASSOCIATION

Formed in 1960, the Association caters for journalists who regularly cover Rugby League affairs. Its main objects are to establish a good working relationship with the Rugby Football League, the British Amateur Rugby League Association, all national controlling bodies and all clubs: and to assist overseas Rugby League journalists who are visiting Britain.

The Association's major social function of the year is its annual dinner which has the reputation for being one of the best of its kind in Rugby League Football. In recent years the Association instituted various social functions to entertain British touring teams before their departure down-under.

Most leading Rugby League journalists are involved in the running of the Association. A leading light for many years was Joe Humphreys (*Daily Mirror*), who, before his retirement in 1977, had spent many years as secretary and chairman. The present Association committee is chairman: Tom Bergin (*Salford City Reporter*); secretary: Paul Harrison (*The Sun*); assistant secretary: John Huxley (*Sunday Mirror*); treasurer: Alan Tweedale (*Rochdale Observer*); committee; David Hodgkinson (*Rugby Leaguer*), John Robinson (*Sunday People*), Stan Townsend (*Rochdale Observer*), Brian Smith (*Bradford Telegraph and Argus*), Derek Crabtree (Bradford freelance), Cyril Briggs (Warrington freelance).

Similar organisations also exist in Australia and New Zealand.

ST HELENS RLFC

Founded in 1875. Founder member of the Northern Union. Ground: Knowsley Road. Colours: White jerseys with red " V ", white shorts.
RL Championship Winners, 1931-32, 1952-53, 1958-59, 1965-66, 1969-70, 1970-71.
  Beaten Finalists, 1964-65, 1966-67, 1971-72.
Division One Champions, 1974-75.
League Leaders Trophy Winners, 1964-65, 1965-66.
Club Championship (Merit Table) Beaten finalists, 1973-74.
RL Cup Winners, 1955-56, 1960-61, 1965-66, 1971-72, 1975-76.
  Beaten Finalists, 1896-97, 1914-15, 1929-30, 1952-53, 1977-78.
Lancashire Cup Winners, 1926-27, 1953-54, 1960-61, 1961-62, 1962-63, 1963-64, 1964-65, 1967-68, 1968-69.
  Beaten Finalists, 1932-33, 1952-53, 1956-57, 1958-59, 1959-60, 1970-71.
Lancashire League Winners, 1929-30, 1931-32, 1952-53, 1959-60, 1964-65, 1965-66, 1966-67, 1968-69.
Premiership Winners, 1975-76, 1976-77.
  Beaten Finalists, 1974-75.
Western Division Championship Winners, 1963-64.
BBC2 Trophy Winners, 1971-72, 1975-76.
  Beaten Finalists, 1965-66, 1968-69, 1970-71, 1977-78, 1978-79.
Club Records:
  Attendance: 35,695 v. Wigan (League) 26 Dec. 1949.
  Goals: 214 by K. Coslett, 1971-72.
  Tries: 62 by T. Van Vollenhoven, 1958-59.
  Points: 452 by K. Coslett, 1971-72.

SALFORD RLFC

Founded in 1879. Joined the Northern Union in 1896. Ground: The Willows.
Colours: Red jerseys, white shorts.
RL Championship Winners, 1913-14, 1932-33, 1936-37, 1938-39.
  Beaten Finalists, 1933-34.
Division One Champions, 1973-74, 1975-76.
RL Cup Winners, 1937-38.
  Beaten Finalists, 1899-00, 1901-02, 1902-03, 1905-06, 1938-39, 1968-69.
Lancashire League Winners, 1932-33, 1933-34, 1934-35, 1936-37, 1938-39.
Lancashire Cup Winners, 1931-32, 1934-35, 1935-36, 1936-37, 1972-73.
  Beaten Finalists, 1929-30, 1938-39, 1973-74, 1974-75, 1975-76.
Premiership Beaten Finalists, 1975-76.
Player's No. 6 Trophy Beaten Finalists, 1972-73.
BBC2 Trophy Winners, 1974-75.
Club Records:
  Attendance: 26,470 v. Warrington (RL Cup) 13 Feb. 1937.
  Goals: 221 by D. Watkins, 1972-73.
  Tries: 46 by K. Fielding, 1973-74.
  Points: 493 by D. Watkins, 1972-73.

SCHOOLBOY RUGBY LEAGUE

One of Rugby League's greatest strengths in Britain has been its presence in Northern schools alongside Soccer, Rugby Union and other sports. It is there that so many players get their first taste of the game and its value to the game, not only in Britain, is immeasurable.

Amazingly, for a sport which is in sight of its centenary, a national schools organisation did not arrive on the scene until relatively modern times. The English Schools Rugby League was not born until 1965, and they are now a well-organised, progressive body.

The county schools organisations were in existence long before the ESRL. The Lancashire League was founded in 1913, and it was around then that the ESRL was built. The smallest administration unit in the ESRL is the local association which consists of schools from within a town area. Each association has representatives on the two regional bodies and six representatives from the regions serve on the ESRL executive.

Since local government reorganisation in 1974, the three original county organisations have been superseded and, as far as the ESRL is concerned, their counties are now based on local education authority boundaries. For the sake of clarity a dividing line from north to south was made down the middle of the country and two regions, North-West Counties and East of Pennines were created. These now provide the two teams for the inter-county championship.

Members of the ESRL are: Barrow, Bolton, Bradford, Castleford, Dewsbury and Batley, Huddersfield, Humberside, Hunslet, Leeds, Leigh, London, Morley, Oldham, Salford, St Helens, Wakefield, Warrington, Warrington Junior Schools, Whitehaven, Widnes, Wigan and York.

The ESRL run five competitions:

1. English Schools RL Trophy—a knock-out competition for Under 16 age group players at inter-association level.
2. English Schools RL Division I—a league of eight teams at Under 16 level on an inter-association basis. Four teams from each region are nominated at the start of each season.
3. English Schools RL Division II—a league for those associations not involved in Division I.
4. English Schools RL Intermediate League—an Under 13 level competition which is sub-divided into two divisions " A " and " B " with the same make-up pattern as the Under 16 competition. There is a play-off between the top two in each division to decide the overall championship.
5. National Under 13 seven-a-side tournament which starts at school level, the champion school association goes forward to the finals.

In 1978-79 the National League Division I teams were: Wigan, St Helens, Leigh, Oldham (NW Counties), Hull, Leeds, Hunslet and Castleford (east of Pennines). Division II members were Barrow, Whitehaven, Salford, Warrington, Bradford, York, Dewsbury and Batley, Wakefield and Bolton.

The only major difference between Under-16 and Under-13 was that Huddersfield fielded just an Under-13 team in Division " B ".

As with any other voluntary sporting organisation there have been highpoints and setbacks over the last few years. Their biggest triumph was the Rugby Football League's decision to allow schoolboys to play a curtain-raiser before the Challenge Cup Final at Wembley as from 1975. It is now a highly popular part of Rugby League's big day in London.

Competition with Rugby Union, which has grown in popularity in the North of England in recent years, is fierce and one depressing feature of schools Rugby League development has been the loss of Widnes high schools. They have switched the Saturday morning allegiance to Rugby Union leaving Sunday, a less popular choice, to Rugby League. There is, however, still great hopes for the Cheshire town as their junior schools league is still thriving.

In 1973 the European schools game took a big step forward when the French schools toured England. The following year an English team returned the visit and since then tours have been swapped on an alternate year cycle. The usual pattern of tours is three regional games and an international.

The ESRL is now responsible for finding and training its own referees. They run their own referees' examination system with two grades, qualified and advanced.

English Schools RL Roll of Honour

English Schools Trophy

1967	Wigan	1973	Leigh
1968	Castleford	1974	St Helens
1969	Wigan	1975	Hull
1970	Hull	1976	St Helens
1971	Leeds	1977	Hunslet
1972	Leeds	1978	Hull

English Schools Division I

1975	St Helens	1977	Hunslet
1976	Castleford	1978	Hull

English Schools Division II

1975	Hull	1977	Hunslet
1976	Whitehaven	1978	Hull

English Schools Intermediate Championship

1976	Leigh	1978	Wigan
1977	Wigan		

English Schools Intermediate Seven-a-Side

1972	Cardinal Newman, Wigan
1972	Thomas à Beckett, Wakefield
1974	Castleford Central High School
1975	Arthur Greenwood School, Hunslet
1976	St John Fisher, Dewsbury
1977	Campion, St Helens
1978	Thomas More, Wigan

Wembley curtain-raiser team

1975	Widnes and Wigan
1976	Hull and Leeds
1977	Oldham and Hull
1978	York and Leigh
1979	St Helens and Wakefield
1980	Hunslet and Warrington

Tours

One of the biggest influences on the development of today's British schools game was the Australian Combined High Schools tour of England in 1972. They played 12 matches in Britain and returned undefeated.

But that was not what impressed the British authorities so much, it was the manner of their triumph. They scored 402 points and conceded just 17. They scored 108 tries and conceded just one—in the last match of the tour.

The English Schools were supposed to make a return visit in 1974 but the plan came to nothing because of the enormous travelling costs involved.

The Australian tour record was:

Australia	30	East Lancashire	4	at Oldham
Australia	18	South Lancashire	2	at Warrington
Australia	28	Lancashire	2	at St Helens
Australia	26	Cumberland	2	at Whitehaven
Australia	56	Barrow	0	at Barrow
Australia	40	Cumbria	0	at Millom
Australia	37	Castleford	2	at Castleford
Australia	28	Yorkshire	0	at Hull
Australia	36	Comb Leeds and Hull XIII	4	at Bramley

Australia v. West Yorkshire—cancelled

Test series

Australia	27	England	2	at Wigan
Australia	30	England	0	at Wakefield
Australia	46	England	3	at Hayes, Middlesex

The quality of the Australian players who were, on average nine months older than the British boys because of the differences in school leaving ages, can be judged by the fact that two of them, winger Ian Schubert and prop Craig Young, have become full professional internationals and toured Great Britain and France in 1978. Schubert, in fact, was a star in the 1975 International Championships although he was not such a success on his second appearance in Britain in 1978.

The first New Zealand schoolboy team to tour was in 1962 when they crossed the Tasman Sea to play in New South Wales. Their full record was played 7, won 5, lost 2, pts for 121, against 54.

See also BRITISH AMATEUR RUGBY LEAGUE ASSOCIATION; WEMBLEY STADIUM.

SECRETARIES

The Council of the Rugby Football League has been served by only four secretaries since formation in 1895.

Joseph Platt was an honorary official of the Northern Union until his resignation in June 1920, when he was made a life member. An Oldham solicitor, he steered the code through the pioneering decades. He died on 23 Sept. 1930, aged 72.

John Wilson was in Australia as co-manager of the 1920 Great Britain Tourists when he was appointed full-time secretary in succession to Platt. Resigning as a director of Hull Kingston Rovers, he served the League for 26 years, retiring in May 1946, later becoming a director of Leeds RLFC. During his reign of office, he played a major part in the bold decision to stage the Challenge Cup Final at Wembley, and also helped pioneer the 13-a-side code in France. He died on 24 Nov. 1957, aged 81.

William Fallowfield, OBE, MA, succeeded Wilson, having served at Rugby League Headquarters since December 1945. A former Rugby Union forward with Northampton and East Midlands and a war-time English RU International, he came from a Barrow Rugby League orientated family and played at amateur level. He retired in July 1974. His term of office was highlighted by a redrafting of the laws of the game, the introduction of official coaching courses, managership of International teams and touring parties, television commentating and services on the International front. After retirement from the League, he continued to serve as Secretary of the International Board.

David Oxley MA became the fourth supremo of British Rugby League in July 1974, taking the title of Secretary-General. After National Service, this native of Hull took an honours degree in English Literature at Oxford and during the same period was a member of the Old Hymerians, Hull,

Rugby Union side which won the Yorkshire Cup in 1959. Having studied a further year for a Diploma of Education, Mr Oxley's career as a public schoolmaster involved appointments in Middlesex, Oxford, York and Dover. In his short current reign, he has succeeded in revitalising enthusiasm and interest in the game of Rugby League, with subsequent increase in attendances and sponsorship.

SEREENA COACH OF THE MONTH AWARDS

Introduced in the 1978-79 season, the Sereena Sportswear scheme provides awards for the Division One and Two coaches of the month throughout the season. The winners receive an inscribed statuette and a cash prize.

The Sereena roll of honour is:

1978-79
Division One

Sept.	Eric Ashton MBE (St Helens)
Oct.	Doug Laughton (Widnes)
Nov.	Billy Benyon (Warrington)
Dec.	Roger Millward (Hull KR)
Feb.	Doug Laughton (Widnes)
Mar.	Frank Foster (Barrow)
Apr.	Tom Grainey (Leigh)
May	Syd Hynes (Leeds)

Division Two

Sept.	Maurice Bamford (Halifax)
Oct.	Arthur Bunting (Hull)
Nov.	Albert Fearnley (Blackpool Bor.)
	Bak Diabira
Dec.	Don Robinson (Bramley)
Feb.	Arthur Bunting (Hull)
Mar.	Bill Ramsey (New Hunslet)
Apr.	Paul Daley (York)
May	Arthur Bunting (Hull)

1979-80
Division One

Sept.	Sol Roper (Workington Town)
	Eric Bell
Oct.	Alex Murphy (Salford)
Nov.	Syd Hynes (Leeds)
Dec.	Arthur Bunting (Hull)
Jan.	Peter Fox (Bradford N.)
Feb.	Doug Laughton (Widnes)
Mar.	Arthur Bunting (Hull)
Apr.	Tom Grainey (Leigh)

Division Two

Sept.	Maurice Bamford (Halifax)
Oct.	Tommy Smales (Batley)

Nov.	Paul Daley (Featherstone R.)
Dec.	Graham Starkey (Oldham)
	Bill Francis
Jan.	Phil Kitchin (Whitehaven)
Feb.	Maurice Bamford (Halifax)
Mar.	Frank Myler (Swinton)
Apr.	Geoff Fletcher (Huyton)

SEVEN-A-SIDES

Seven-a-side Rugby League is an abbreviated form of the game, usually staged in the close season as a summer attraction. A sevens team is made up of three forwards and four backs. Qualifying matches are of 15 minutes duration, with the final being extended to 20 minutes. Extra time is played if the scores are level at the end of normal play, the winners being the side to score first.

Traditional Rugby League rules apply, except that play stops immediately the timekeeper sounds the hooter.

Several sevens tournaments have been staged, the first annual competition being held at Odsal Stadium, Bradford in the 1930s, during which time Huddersfield were acknowledged as sevens champions. In August 1965, the Rugby League staged a seven-a-side tournament at London's Crystal Palace as part of the International Sports Festival, Wigan beating Workington Town 14-13 in the final.

In recent years Leeds and Wigan have established annual seven-a-side tournaments, both attracting sponsorship and television coverage. Swinton recently launched the Jeff Whiteside Sevens in memory of the young Lions winger who died from injuries sustained in an A-team match.

The roll of honour in the Leeds and Wigan Sevens is:

Year	Leeds	Wigan
1923		Wigan
1949		Salford
1959		Wigan
1960		Wigan
1961		Wigan
1962		Wigan
1963		Wigan
1964	Bradford N.	Wigan
1965	St Helens	Warrington
1966	Bradford N.	Oldham
1967	Huddersfield	Halifax
1968	Salford	Salford
1969	Salford	Salford
1970	Salford	Wigan
1971	Wakefield T.	Wigan

1972	Halifax	—
1973	Leeds	Wigan
1974	Salford	Leeds
1975	Wigan	Leeds
1976	Castleford	Wigan
1977	—	Wigan
1978	Widnes	Workington T.

SLALOM LAGER

In a £215,000 three-year deal, the League and the Premiership were to be sponsored from 1980 to 1983 by brewers Matthew Brown, of Blackburn, who adopted the title of Slalom Lager to the competitions.

A feature of the deal was the brewery's acceptance of lucrative secondary sponsorship at club level.

See also PREMIERSHIP TROPHY TWO DIVISIONS.

SOCCER GROUNDS

During the early years of this century many Northern Union representative and exhibition matches were played on Association Football clubs' grounds in various parts of the country in the hopes of spreading interest in the new code. These efforts failed in their desired object, and in the majority of cases the games would have proved far more profitable financially had they been played in Lancashire or Yorkshire.

In later years Rugby League turned to soccer grounds again when interest in the RL Championship Finals had reached such a pitch that no Rugby League ground with the exception of Odsal Stadium could accommodate the expected crowds.

When two Leeds clubs reached the Championship Final in 1938 the game was played on the Leeds United AFC ground at Elland Road where a record attendance up to that time (54,112) was established. There were also large attendances during the post-war years when the Championship Finals were played at the Maine Road ground of Manchester City.

Australian Touring teams have trained on Arsenal's ground at Highbury when they have been in London, and the 1951-52 New Zealanders met a British Empire RL team at Stamford Bridge, Chelsea, on 23 Jan. 1952. The Kiwis lost 2—26 and the attendance was 6,286.

In recent years the practice of soccer grounds being available for hire to Rugby League authorities has been stopped.

See also PLAY-OFFS

FULHAM RLFC

SOUTH AFRICA

Rugby League's attempt to gain world-wide recognition alongside Rugby Union has been a constant problem since the birth of the 13-a-side code in 1895. In Australia, France, Great Britain and New Zealand, the two codes exist in a mood of reluctant tolerance, but in South Africa the situation was completely different. Quite a number of South African Rugby Union players have been persuaded to turn professional with varying degrees of success but Rugby League has never been able to establish a permanent toe-hold in the country because of the intense pressure from the powerful Rugby Union lobby.

The first move of any significance to establish a Rugby League presence in South Africa was in 1957. A promoter, Mr Ludwig Japhet, had talks with British League secretary Bill Fallowfield and as a result the British and French teams played three games in South Africa on their way home from the 1957 World Cup competition in Australia. The games were played at Benoni, Durban and East London. Britain won all three 61-41, 32-13 and 69-11. The South African rugby public, however, did not appreciate the " exhibition " type game and the first move to promote the game in the country failed.

It was 1961 before the next serious attempts were made and that was the formation of two organisations, one called Rugby League South Africa and the other the National League. The two did not amalgamate and that certainly hit Rugby League's chances of success in South Africa.

In 1962 the National League invited Wakefield Trinity out for a six-match tour. The English team won all their matches scoring 281 points and conceding 66. The Trinity club, in addition to their own South African players, included several " guest " South Africans from other clubs.

A month later, in August 1962, the Great Britain team, which was returning from an Australian tour, played three matches against teams representing Rugby League South Africa in Pretoria, Durban and Johannesburg. Defensive tactics were clearly ignored as the British cruised to three victories: 49-30, 39-33, 45-23.

A contribution from Australia to the South African venture was to send out a former Kangaroo captain Dave Brown to help coach new recruits.

Establishing the League code in what was, and still is, prime Rugby Union territory proved very difficult and one of the new game's major problems was finding suitable grounds on which to stage their games. Despite these problems a Springbok international team was raised in 1963 and they made a tour of Australia and New Zealand. The touring party was managed by Irwin Benson and Harry Kelley, captained by Dawie Ackerman and included players with British club experience, Alan Skene, Aipa Coetzer and Colin Greenwood (Wakefield Trinity), Johnny Gaydon (Widnes), and Fred Griffiths (Wigan). Fortified by this core of experience the Springboks won two of their nine Australian matches, but they found Australia too experienced in the two international encounters as they lost 34-6 in Brisbane and 54-21 in Sydney.

Then they moved on to New Zealand

and the experience they had gained in Australia started to bear fruit. They won two of their four matches including the historic International Match, the only one ever played between the two countries at Rugby League at Carlaw Park, Auckland on 10 Aug. 1963. In the muddy conditions they emerged with a 4-3 advantage. The game, however, is not accepted as an official international by New Zealand because the Springbok included some guest players from Australia.

The Tour details were:

In Australia
Australia v. South Africa
First Test: Australia 34, South Africa 6, at Brisbane on the 20 July 1963, attendance 12,000.
Second Test: Australia 54, South Africa 21, at Sydney on the 27 July 1963.

Australian Programme Results:

Date	Opponents	Points for and against	Venue and attendance
7 July	v. Northern New South Wales	20-40	Tamworth 5,750
10 July	v. Monaro	41-2	Canberra, 3,500
13 July	v. Sydney	5-49	Sydney, 18,219
16 July	v. Queensland	16-32	Brisbane, 6,742
20 July	v. Australia, First Test	6-34	Brisbane, 10,210
24 July	v. South Queensland	21-30	Brisbane, 2,187
27 July	v. Australia, Second Test	21-54	Sydney, 16, 995
28 July	v. Newcastle	17-27	Newcastle, 7,634
30 July	v. Parramatta	18-39	Parramatta, 5,372

Played 9, Won 2, Lost 7, pts for 165, pts against 277.

In New Zealand

Opponents	Points for and against
v. Wellington	21-12
v. South Island	8-12
v. Auckland	4-10
v. New Zealand	4-3

Played 4, won 2, lost 2, pts for 37, pts against 37.

The total record for the tour was played 13, won 4, lost 9, pts for 202, pts against 314.

The leading South African scorers were:

	P. Tests	Tries	Gls.	Pts.
G Smit	10	1	2	23	52
F. Griffiths	5	1	2	17	40
J. De Waal	6	–	6	–	18
J. Pieterse	11	2	4	–	12
M. Pelser	4	–	3	–	9
A. Skene	7	1	3	–	9
C. Greenwood	7	1	3	–	9
F. Gericke	8	–	1	3	9

The other tourists were K. Pelser, O. Oosthizen, B. Erasmus, B. Oberholzer, W. Vermass, O. Odendaal, R. Peacock, G. van Zyl, N. Rens, D. Ackermann (capt.) J. Verwey, G. Coetzer, H. Bennett, G. Wilson and F. Anderson.

Their international success against New Zealand, however, was not enough to ensure a future for the code in South Africa. An amnesty was granted by the South African Rugby Union for players who had switched codes and that, together, with the crippling ground shortage was the death-knell for South African Rugby League.

Individually converts from South Africa Rugby Union have made interesting contributions to Rugby League lore. Their impact on the British game has been erratic because of difficulties in adjusting to the winter weather conditions, but there have been notable exceptions. Without doubt

The big little man. Great Britain's scrum-half Steve Nash (with ball) is set to do battle with his main rival of the seventies, Australian counterpart Tommy Raudonikis, during the first Test of the 1978 series.

Phil Hogan, once the world's most expensive player—he cost Hull Kingston Rovers £35,000 from Barrow in 1979—strides out in fine style for Great Britain.

Eyes down. Roger Millward, the Hull Kingston Rovers player-coach and legend during his own career, kicks for ground in a Test match against Australia.

(*Right*) Billy Batten, one of Hull's most famous players, pictured with the Yorkshire League Championship Trophy.

(*Below*) David Watkins, the former Newport, Wales and British Lions Rugby Union stand off half, was an important capture for Salford in 1967. He became a record-breaking performer for his club and coached Great Britain in 1977.

the most successful convert was former Springbok RU winger Tom Van Vollenhoven, who became a living legend within his own playing career with St Helens, between 1957-1968. He scored 392 tries for St Helens and topped the League try-scoring list three times. Wigan had a successful excursion into the South African market for full-back Fred Griffiths. Griffiths kicked 702 goals, topping the League's goal list in 1958-59, and scored 48 tries before moving on to Australia. Other South African names that will be fondly remembered by British enthusiasts were Jan Prinsloo (St Helens), and Wilf Rosenburg (Leeds).

The only South Africans playing for British clubs at the time of writing were coloured wingers Green Vigo (Wigan) and David Barends (Bradford Northern). They might not be alone for much longer, however, for reports have filtered through of that enterprising Leeds area club New Hunslet having tried to recruit from that troubled African country.

STATE EXPRESS

State Express of London, the tobacco company, became the first sponsors of the Rugby League Challenge Cup in 1979.

The illustrious Challenge Cup became a major feature of the State Express Challenge scheme in a £220,000 three-year deal.

Prize money for the 1979 Cup campaign totalled £55,000, with £12,555 being presented to the winner. The sponsorship deal also featured the issue of three challenges:

£500 each time an individual kicked five goals or more in a Cup tie.

£5,000 each time an individual player scored five tries or more in a Cup tie.

£5,000 each time a team scored 55 points or more in a Cup tie.

The challenge rewards were received by the League, who gained permission to donate 20 per cent to the club involved in the scoring achievement. As part of the deal, the competition was retitled The State Express Challenge Cup.

See also CHALLENGE CUP.

SUBSTITUTES

First introduced in the 1964-65 season, the principle of substitutes is based on the theory that the paying public is entitled to see two numerically equal teams in contest. The initial ruling allowed for up to two injured players to be replaced during the first half of play.

Following complaints that the rule was being abused, the insistence on the player being replaced having to be injured was relaxed and substitutions became tactical ploys. The rule was gradually extended, and today the two substitutes can be brought on once at any stage of the match, with the players they replace being allowed to return to the field as substitutes, but once only.

Towards the end of the 1976 season, substitute boards were introduced to speed up the practical substitution. A club official standing on the touchline with the substitute, displays the board bearing the number of the player to be replaced. As the replaced player leaves the field, the new man comes on.

SUMMER RUGBY

A demand for a March-November season inevitably follows a severe winter, with the resultant postponement of matches and fixture backlog. As early as the 1930s the legendary Lance Todd was putting forward a summer-based season. A proposal by St Helens in 1969 narrowly failed to secure the necessary majority, although the move was made against a backcloth of falling attendances.

After the wipe-out of fixtures in early 1979 by snow and ice, Bradford Northern canvassed support for a new bid to restructure the season.

SUNDAY FOOTBALL

From being completely forbidden, Sunday has taken over as the main match day on the Rugby League calendar. There was for many years a Rugby Football League bye-law which read: " Professional Football shall not be played on Sundays in Great Britain."

British players' first taste of Sunday football came when France staged Internationals. The move to stage first-team matches on a Sunday gained momentum in the 1967-68 season.

Previously an exhibition game had been staged at Leeds on 6 Nov. 1966, but the first professional Sunday matches were played on 17 Dec. 1967. League encounters between Bradford Northern-York and Leigh-Dewsbury took place on that Sunday. Other clubs followed the pioneering example and the general consensus was that attendances were higher than would have been anticipated for a Saturday fixture.

In the early days of Sunday football, opposition was mounted by a Sunday Observance Laws lobby and prosecutions were threatened. Under the 1780 Sunday Observance Act, clubs had to provide a "free" gate, although the practice was not strictly adhered to.

For the 1977-78 season, the Rugby League amended a bye-law to declare that the official match day is Sunday, not the Saturday as had always been the tradition. See also POSTPONEMENTS.

SUPPORTERS' CLUBS

The first Rugby League supporters' club was formed at Huddersfield in June 1921. The object of the new body was to "secure and support suitable members to serve on the various committees and sub-committees of the premier club, and also to use its influence in the general interest of the Huddersfield club".

By March 1923 there were nine Yorkshire teams with supporters' clubs and a meeting in Leeds witnessed the formation of the Yorkshire Federation of Rugby League Supporters' Clubs. After a gap of 24 years, the National Federation was formed in 1947, with member clubs from Cumbria, Lancashire and Yorkshire, plus Welsh representation.

The basic aim of both federations was to foster friendship among the fans of individual clubs, while exchanging views and ideas related to supporting the parent clubs financially. Travelling problems caused the discontinuation of the National Federation in 1961.

After a brief launching period, the Lancashire Federation was reformed in 1976.

The following Rugby League clubs have official Supporters' Clubs: Barrow, Blackpool Borough, Leigh, Oldham, St. Helens, Salford, Swinton, Widnes, Wigan, and Workington, all members of the Lancashire Federation;

Batley, Bradford Northern, Bramley, Castleford, Dewsbury, Doncaster, Featherstone Rovers, Halifax, Huddersfield, Hull, Hull Kingston Rovers, Keighley, Leeds, New Hunslet, Wakefield Trinity and York, all members of the Yorkshire Federation.

SWINTON RLFC

Founded in 1867. Joined the Northern Union in 1896. Ground: Station Road. Colours: Blue jerseys with white "V" white shorts.

RL Championship Winners, 1926-27, 1927-28, 1930-31, 1934-35.

Beaten Finalists, 1924-25, 1932-33.

War League Beaten Finalists, 1939-40.

Division One Champions, 1962-63, 1963-64.

RL Cup Winners, 1899-00, 1925-26, 1927-28.

Beaten Finalists, 1926-27, 1931-32.

Lancashire League Winners, 1924-25, 1927-28, 1928-29, 1930-31, 1960-61.

Lancashire War League Winners, 1939-40.

Lancashire Cup Winners, 1925-26, 1927-28, 1939-40, 1969-70.

Beaten Finalists, 1910-11, 1923-24, 1931-32, 1960-61, 1961-62, 1962-63, 1964-65, 1972-73.

Western Division Championship Beaten Finalists, 1963-64.

Club Records:

Attendance: 44,621 Wigan v. Leigh (Lancashire Cup Final), 27 Oct. 1951.

Goals: 128 by A. Blan, 1960-61.

Tries: 42 by J. Stopford, 1963-64.

Points: 283 by A. Blan, 1960-61.

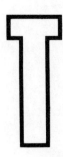

TELEVISION

Despite the fact that Rugby League has been televised for the past 28 years, television still remains one of the most controversial subjects in the game.

The first Test match to be screened was Great Britain v. New Zealand at Swinton on 10 Nov. 1951. The inaugural televised League match was Wigan v. Wakefield Trinity on 12 Jan. 1952. Wembley first attracted the cameras for the Featherstone Rovers v. Workington Town clash on 19 April 1952.

Anti-television lobbies are repeatedly staged and in April 1966 Wigan were fined £500 and withdrawn from the television fee share out for refusing to play a cup tie at Odsal Stadium in front of the television cameras.

The regular BBC Television commentator has been Eddie Waring, while Independent Television screened a series of Sunday afternoon amateur inter-town matches in the early 1960s with commentary by the then League Secretary Bill Fallowfield.

The first " live " Sunday afternoon television match featuring professional Rugby League was the Forward Chemicals Second Test between Great Britain and Australia at Odsal Stadium, Bradford, on 5 Nov. 1978.

Traditionally, the BBC contract has allowed for up to 36 matches to be screened in a season, including 24 on Saturday afternoon " Grandstand " and the remaining 12 on the BBC2 Floodlit Trophy series.

This tally of matches was reduced to about 20 when the contract was renegotiated in 1980, with the scrapping of the traditional BBC2 Floodlit Trophy format.

See also BBC2 FLOODLIT TROPHY; ENTERTAINMENT.

TESTS

The first Northern Union Test match was played at Headingley, Leeds on 25 Jan. 1908 when England beat New Zealand 14-6 and ever since then the very mention of " Test " matches has sent Rugby League enthusiasts' hearts racing.

The most prestigious Test series in the League world is Great Britain v. Australia. The first Test match between the two countries was played at Stamford Bridge, London 12 Dec. 1908 and they have been battling for supremacy ever since.

Until 1954 France had been afforded only international status, but, after their successful staging of the first World Championship, they were elevated to Test status.

The following record of Test matches refers to the British team as England (see Great Britain) until their name was changed to Great Britain in 1948.

Great Britain v. Australia

Date					
12 Dec. 1908	England	22	Australia	22	London
23 Jan. 1909	England	15	Australia	5	Newcastle-upon-Tyne
10 Feb. 1909	England	6	Australia	5	Birmingham
18 Jun. 1910	England	27	Australia	20	Sydney
2 July 1910	England	22	Australia	17	Brisbane
8 Nov. 1911	England	10	Australia	19	Newcastle
18 Dec. 1911	England	11	Australia	11	Edinburgh
1 Jan. 1912	England	8	Australia	33	Birmingham
27 Jun. 1914	England	23	Australia	5	Sydney
29 Jun. 1914	England	7	Australia	12	Sydney
4 Jul. 1914	England	14	Australia	6	Sydney
26 Jun. 1920	England	4	Australia	8	Brisbane
3 Jul. 1920	England	8	Australia	21	Sydney
10 Jul. 1920	England	23	Australia	13	Sydney
1 Oct. 1921	England	6	Australia	5	Leeds
5 Nov. 1921	England	2	Australia	16	Hull
14 Jan. 1922	England	6	Australia	0	Salford

23 Jun. 1924	England	22	Australia	3	Sydney
28 Jun. 1924	England	5	Australia	3	Sydney
12 Jul. 1924	England	11	Australia	21	Brisbane
23 Jun. 1928	England	15	Australia	12	Brisbane
14 Jul. 1928	England	8	Australia	0	Sydney
21 Jul. 1928	England	14	Australia	21	Sydney
5 Oct. 1929	England	8	Australia	31	Hull
9 Nov. 1929	England	9	Australia	3	Leeds
4 Jan. 1930	England	0	Australia	0	Swinton
15 Jan. 1930	England	3	Australia	0	Rochdale
6 Jun. 1932	England	8	Australia	6	Sydney
18 Jun. 1932	England	6	Australia	15	Brisbane
16 Jul. 1932	England	18	Australia	13	Sydney
7 Oct. 1933	England	4	Australia	0	Manchester
11 Nov. 1933	England	7	Australia	5	Leeds
16 Dec. 1933	England	19	Australia	16	Swinton
29 Jun. 1936	England	8	Australia	24	Sydney
4 Jul. 1936	England	12	Australia	7	Brisbane
18 Jul. 1936	England	12	Australia	7	Sydney
16 Oct. 1937	England	5	Australia	4	Leeds
13 Nov. 1937	England	13	Australia	3	Swinton
18 Dec. 1937	England	3	Australia	13	Huddersfield
17 Jun. 1946	England	8	Australia	8	Sydney
6 Jul. 1946	England	14	Australia	5	Brisbane
20 Jul. 1946	England	20	Australia	7	Sydney
9 Oct. 1948	Great Britain	23	Australia	21	Leeds
6 Nov. 1948	Great Britain	16	Australia	7	Swinton
29 Jan. 1949	Great Britain	23	Australia	9	Bradford
12 Jun. 1950	Great Britain	6	Australia	4	Sydney
1 Jul. 1950	Great Britain	3	Australia	15	Brisbane
22 Jul. 1950	Great Britain	2	Australia	5	Sydney
4 Oct. 1952	Great Britain	19	Australia	6	Leeds
8 Nov. 1952	Great Britain	21	Australia	5	Swinton
13 Dec. 1952	Great Britain	7	Australia	27	Bradford
12 Jun. 1954	Great Britain	12	Australia	37	Sydney
3 Jul. 1954	Great Britain	38	Australia	21	Brisbane
17 Jul. 1954	Great Britain	16	Australia	20	Sydney
17 Nov. 1956	Great Britain	21	Australia	10	Wigan
1 Dec. 1956	Great Britain	9	Australia	22	Bradford
15 Dec. 1956	Great Britain	19	Australia	0	Swinton
14 Jun. 1958	Great Britain	8	Australia	25	Sydney
5 Jul. 1958	Great Britain	25	Australia	18	Brisbane
19 Jul. 1958	Great Britain	40	Australia	17	Sydney
17 Oct. 1959	Great Britain	14	Australia	22	Swinton
21 Nov. 1959	Great Britain	11	Australia	10	Leeds
12 Dec. 1959	Great Britain	18	Australia	12	Wigan
9 Jun. 1962	Great Britain	31	Australia	12	Sydney
30 Jun. 1962	Great Britain	17	Australia	10	Brisbane
14 Jul. 1962	Great Britain	17	Australia	18	Sydney
16 Oct. 1963	Great Britain	2	Australia	28	Wembley, London
9 Nov. 1963	Great Britain	12	Australia	50	Swinton
30 Nov. 1963	Great Britain	16	Australia	5	Leeds
25 Jun. 1966	Great Britain	17	Australia	13	Sydney
16 Jul. 1966	Great Britain	4	Australia	6	Brisbane
23 Jul. 1966	Great Britain	14	Australia	19	Sydney
21 Oct. 1967	Great Britain	16	Australia	11	Leeds
3 Nov. 1967	Great Britain	11	Australia	17	London
9 Dec. 1967	Great Britain	3	Australia	11	Swinton
6 Jun. 1970	Great Britain	15	Australia	37	Brisbane
20 Jun. 1970	Great Britain	28	Australia	7	Sydney

4 Jul. 1970	Great Britain	21	Australia	17	Sydney
3 Nov. 1973	Great Britain	21	Australia	12	Wembley, London
24 Nov. 1973	Great Britain	6	Australia	14	Leeds
1 Dec. 1973	Great Britain	5	Australia	15	Warrington
15 Jun. 1974	Great Britain	6	Australia	12	Brisbane
6 Jul. 1974	Great Britain	16	Australia	11	Sydney
20 Jul. 1974	Great Britain	18	Australia	22	Sydney
21 Oct. 1978	Great Britain	6	Australia	15	Wigan
5 Nov. 1978	Great Britain	18	Australia	14	Bradford
18 Nov. 1978	Great Britain	6	Australia	24	Leeds
16 Jun. 1979	Great Britain	0	Australia	35	Brisbane
30 Jun. 1979	Great Britain	16	Australia	24	Sydney
14 July 1979	Great Britain	2	Australia	28	Sydney

	Played	Won	Lost	Drawn	Tries	Goals	D/Goal	Pts for
Great Britain	90	49	37	4	232	233	2	1164
Australia	90	37	49	4	235	266	4	1244

Records

Highest score for Great Britain: 40—Third Test, Sydney 19 July 1958
Highest score for Australia: 50—Second Test, Swinton 9 Nov. 1963
Record attendance in GB: 42,000—Third Test, Bradford 29 Jan. 1949
Record attendance in Australia: 70,204—First Test, Sydney 6 Jun. 1932
Record receipts in GB: £34,800—Third

Test, Leeds 18 Nov. 1978
Record receipts in Australia: $91,225—Third Test, Sydney 20 Jul. 1974
Tries in a match: 4 J. Leytham (Wigan) Second Test, Brisbane 2 July 1910
Goals in a match: 10 L. Jones (Leeds)—Second Test, Brisbane 3 July 1954
Points in a match: 20 L. Jones (Leeds)—Second Test, Brisbane 3 July 1954.

Great Britain v. New Zealand

25 Jan. 1908	England	14	New Zealand	6	Leeds
8 Feb. 1908	England	6	New Zealand	18	Stamford Bridge
15 Feb. 1908	England	5	New Zealand	8	Cheltenham
30 Jul. 1910	England	52	New Zealand	20	Auckland
1 Aug. 1914	England	16	New Zealand	13	Auckland
31 Jul. 1920	England	31	New Zealand	7	Auckland
7 Aug. 1920	England	19	New Zealand	3	Christchurch
14 Aug. 1920	England	11	New Zealand	10	Wellington
2 Aug. 1924	England	8	New Zealand	16	Auckland
6 Aug. 1924	England	11	New Zealand	13	Wellington
9 Aug. 1924	England	31	New Zealand	18	Dunedin
2 Oct. 1926	England	28	New Zealand	20	Wigan
13 Nov. 1926	England	21	New Zealand	11	Hull
15 Jan. 1927	England	32	New Zealand	17	Leeds
4 Aug. 1928	England	13	New Zealand	17	Auckland
18 Aug. 1928	England	13	New Zealand	5	Dunedin
25 Aug. 1928	England	6	New Zealand	5	Christchurch
30 Jul. 1932	England	24	New Zealand	9	Auckland
13 Aug. 1932	England	25	New Zealand	14	Christchurch
20 Aug. 1932	England	20	New Zealand	18	Auckland
8 Aug. 1936	England	10	New Zealand	8	Auckland
15 Aug. 1936	England	23	New Zealand	11	Auckland
10 Aug. 1946	England	8	New Zealand	13	Auckland
4 Oct. 1947	England	11	New Zealand	10	Leeds
8 Nov. 1947	England	7	New Zealand	10	Swinton
20 Dec. 1947	England	25	New Zealand	9	Bradford
29 Jul. 1950	Great Britain	10	New Zealand	16	Christchurch
12 Aug. 1950	Great Britain	13	New Zealand	20	Auckland
6 Oct. 1951	Great Britain	21	New Zealand	15	Bradford

10 Nov. 1951	Great Britain	20	New Zealand	19	Swinton
15 Dec. 1951	Great Britain	16	New Zealand	12	Leeds
24 Jul. 1954	Great Britain	27	New Zealand	7	Auckland
31 Jul. 1954	Great Britain	14	New Zealand	20	Greymouth
14 Aug. 1954	Great Britain	12	New Zealand	6	Auckland
8 Oct. 1955	Great Britain	25	New Zealand	6	Swinton
12 Nov. 1955	Great Britain	27	New Zealand	12	Bradford
17 Dec. 1955	Great Britain	13	New Zealand	28	Leeds
26 Jul. 1958	Great Britain	10	New Zealand	15	Auckland
9 Aug. 1958	Great Britain	32	New Zealand	15	Auckland
30 Sept. 1961	Great Britain	11	New Zealand	29	Leeds
21 Oct. 1961	Great Britain	23	New Zealand	10	Bradford
4 Nov. 1961	Great Britain	35	New Zealand	19	Swinton
28 Jul. 1962	Great Britain	0	New Zealand	19	Auckland
11 Aug. 1962	Great Britain	8	New Zealand	27	Auckland
25 Sept. 1965	Great Britain	7	New Zealand	2	Swinton
23 Oct. 1965	Great Britain	15	New Zealand	9	Bradford
6 Nov. 1965	Great Britain	9	New Zealand	9	Wigan
6 Aug. 1966	Great Britain	25	New Zealand	8	Auckland
20 Aug. 1966	Great Britain	22	New Zealand	14	Auckland
11 Jul. 1970	Great Britain	19	New Zealand	15	Auckland
19 Jul. 1970	Great Britain	23	New Zealand	9	Christchurch
25 Jul. 1970	Great Britain	33	New Zealand	16	Auckland
25 Sept. 1971	Great Britain	13	New Zealand	18	Salford
16 Oct. 1971	Great Britain	14	New Zealand	17	Castleford
6 Nov. 1971	Great Britain	12	New Zealand	3	Leeds
27 Jul. 1974	Great Britain	8	New Zealand	13	Auckland
4 Aug. 1974	Great Britain	17	New Zealand	8	Christchurch
10 Aug. 1974	Great Britain	20	New Zealand	0	Auckland
21 Jul. 1979	Great Britain	16	New Zealand	8	Auckland
5 Aug. 1979	Great Britain	22	New Zealand	7	Christchurch
11 Aug. 1979	Great Britain	11	New Zealand	18	Auckland

	Played	Won	Lost	Drawn	Tries	Goals	D/Goal	Pts for
Great Britain	61	41	19	1	239	178	2	1073
New Zealand	61	19	41	1	140	179	0	778

Records

Highest score for Great Britain: 52—First Test, Wellington 30 July 1910

Highest score for New Zealand: 29 First Test, Leeds 30 Sept. 1961

Record attendance in New Zealand: 34,000 First Test, Auckland 30 July 1920

Record attendance in Great Britain: 42,680 Third Test, Bradford, 20 Dec. 1947

Record receipts in New Zealand: $37,455

Third Test, Auckland 10 Aug. 1974

Record receipts in Great Britain: Not Available

Tries in a match: 4 W. J. Boston (Wigan) First Test, Auckland 24 July 1954

Goals in a match: 7 N. Fox (Wakefield Trinity) Third Test, Swinton 4 Nov. 1961

Points in a match: 15 J. Lomas (Salford) First Test, Auckland 30 July 1910

Great Britain v. France

26 Jan. 1957	Great Britain	45	France	12	Leeds
3 Mar. 1957	Great Britain	19	France	19	Toulouse
10 Apr. 1957	Great Britain	29	France	14	St Helens
3 Nov. 1957	Great Britain	25	France	14	Toulouse
23 Nov. 1957	Great Britain	44	France	15	Wigan
2 Mar. 1958	Great Britain	23	France	9	Grenoble
19 Mar. 1959	Great Britain	50	France	15	Leeds
5 Apr. 1959	Great Britain	15	France	24	Grenoble
6 Mar. 1960	Great Britain	18	France	20	Toulouse
26 Mar. 1960	Great Britain	17	France	17	St Helens
11 Dec. 1960	Great Britain	21	France	10	Bordeaux

28 Jan. 1961	Great Britain	27	France	8	St Helens
17 Feb. 1962	Great Britain	15	France	20	Wigan
11 Mar. 1962	Great Britain	13	France	23	Perpignan
2 Dec. 1962	Great Britain	12	France	17	Perpignan
3 Apr. 1963	Great Britain	42	France	4	Wigan
8 Mar. 1964	Great Britain	11	France	5	Perpignan
18 Mar. 1964	Great Britain	39	France	0	Leigh
6 Dec. 1964	Great Britain	8	France	18	Perpignan
23 Jan. 1965	Great Britain	17	France	7	France
16 Jan. 1966	Great Britain	13	France	18	Perpignan
5 Mar. 1966	Great Britain	4	France	8	Wigan
22 Jan. 1967	Great Britain	16	France	13	Carcassonne
4 Mar. 1967	Great Britain	13	France	23	Wigan
11 Feb. 1968	Great Britain	22	France	13	Paris
2 Mar. 1968	Great Britain	19	France	8	Bradford
11 Oct. 1968	Great Britain	34	France	10	St Helens
2 Feb. 1969	Great Britain	9	France	13	Toulouse
2 Feb. 1971	Great Britain	8	France	16	Toulouse
17 Mar. 1971	Great Britain	24	France	2	St Helens
6 Feb. 1972	Great Britain	10	France	9	Toulouse
12 Mar. 1972	Great Britain	45	France	10	Bradford
20 Jan. 1974	Great Britain	24	France	5	Grenoble
17 Feb. 1974	Great Britain	29	France	0	Wigan

	Played	Won	Lost	Drawn	Tries	Goals	D/Goal	Pts for
Great Britain	34	21	11	2	158	143	0	760
France	34	11	21	2	71	102	2	419

Records

Highest score for Great Britain: 50 Wigan, 14 Mar. 1959

Highest score for France: 24 at Grenoble, 5 Apr. 1959

Record attendance in France: 20,000 Grenoble, 3 Mar. 1958

Record attendance in Great Britain: 23,250 St Helens, 10 Apr. 1957

Record Receipts in France: 167,537F Toulouse, 7 Feb. 1971

Record Receipts in Great Britain: £3,207 Bradford, 2 Mar. 1968

Tries in a match: 4 A. J. Murphy (St Helens) Leeds, 14 Mar. 1959

Goals in a match: 10 W. B. Ganley (Oldham) Wigan, 23 Nov. 1957

Points in a match: 21 N. Fox (Wakefield Trinity) Wigan, 3 Apr. 1963

21 N. Fox (Wakefield Trinity) Leigh, 18 Mar. 1964

Australia v. New Zealand

9 May 1908	Australia	10	New Zealand	11	Sydney
30 May 1908	Australia	12	New Zealand	24	Brisbane
6 Jun. 1908	Australia	14	New Zealand	9	Sydney
12 Jun. 1909	Australia	11	New Zealand	19	Sydney
26 Jul. 1909	Australia	10	New Zealand	5	Brisbane
— 1909	Australia	25	New Zealand	5	Sydney
6 Jun. 1910	Australia	13	New Zealand	10	Brisbane
23 Aug. 1919	Australia	44	New Zealand	21	Wellington
30 Aug. 1919	Australia	10	New Zealand	26	Christchurch
6 Sept. 1919	Australia	34	New Zealand	23	Auckland
19 Sept. 1919	Australia	32	New Zealand	2	Auckland
28 Sept. 1935	Australia	14	New Zealand	22	Auckland
2 Oct. 1935	Australia	29	New Zealand	8	Auckland
5 Oct. 1935	Australia	31	New Zealand	8	Auckland
7 Aug. 1937	Australia	12	New Zealand	8	Auckland
14 Aug. 1937	Australia	15	New Zealand	16	Auckland
29 May 1948	Australia	19	New Zealand	21	Sydney
12 Jun. 1948	Australia	13	New Zealand	4	Brisbane
17 Sept. 1949	Australia	21	New Zealand	26	Wellington

8 Oct. 1949	Australia	13	New Zealand	10	Auckland
9 Jun. 1952	Australia	25	New Zealand	13	Sydney
28 Jun. 1952	Australia	25	New Zealand	49	Brisbane
2 Jul. 1952	Australia	9	New Zealand	19	Sydney
27 Jun. 1953	Australia	5	New Zealand	25	Christchurch
4 Jul. 1953	Australia	11	New Zealand	12	Wellington
18 Jul. 1953	Australia	18	New Zealand	16	Auckland
9 Jun. 1956	Australia	12	New Zealand	9	Sydney
23 Jun. 1956	Australia	8	New Zealand	2	Brisbane
30 Jun. 1956	Australia	31	New Zealand	14	Sydney
13 Jun. 1959	Australia	9	New Zealand	8	Sydney
27 Jun. 1959	Australia	38	New Zealand	10	Brisbane
4 Jul. 1959	Australia	12	New Zealand	38	Sydney
1 Jul. 1961	Australia	10	New Zealand	12	Auckland
8 Jul. 1961	Australia	10	New Zealand	8	Auckland
8 Jun. 1963	Australia	7	New Zealand	3	Sydney
22 Jun. 1963	Australia	13	New Zealand	16	Brisbane
29 Jun. 1963	Australia	14	New Zealand	0	Sydney
19 Jun. 1965	Australia	13	New Zealand	8	Auckland
26 Jun. 1965	Australia	5	New Zealand	7	Auckland
10 Jun. 1967	Australia	22	New Zealand	13	Sydney
1 Jul. 1967	Australia	35	New Zealand	22	Brisbane
8 Jul. 1967	Australia	13	New Zealand	9	Sydney
1 Jun. 1969	Australia	20	New Zealand	10	Auckland
7 Jun. 1969	Australia	14	New Zealand	18	Auckland
26 Jun. 1971	Australia	3	New Zealand	24	Auckland
8 Jul. 1972	Australia	36	New Zealand	11	Sydney
15 Jul. 1972	Australia	31	New Zealand	7	Brisbane
24 Jun. 1978	Australia	24	New Zealand	2	Sydney
15 Jul. 1978	Australia	38	New Zealand	7	Brisbane
22 Jul. 1978	Australia	33	New Zealand	16	Sydney

Australia v. France

2 Jan. 1938	Australia	35	France	6	Paris
16 Jan. 1938	Australia	16	France	11	Marseilles
9 Jan. 1949	Australia	29	France	10	Marseilles
23 Jan. 1949	Australia	10	France	10	Bordeaux
11 Jun. 1951	Australia	15	France	26	Sydney
30 Jun. 1951	Australia	23	France	11	Brisbane
21 Jul. 1951	Australia	14	France	35	Sydney
27 Dec. 1952	Australia	16	France	12	Paris
11 Jan. 1953	Australia	0	France	5	Bordeaux
25 Jan. 1953	Australia	5	France	13	Lyons
11 Jun. 1955	Australia	20	France	8	Sydney
2 Jul. 1955	Australia	28	France	29	Brisbane
23 Jul. 1955	Australia	5	France	8	Sydney
1 Jan. 1956	Australia	15	France	8	Paris
12 Dec. 1956	Australia	10	France	6	Bordeaux
3 Jan. 1957	Australia	26	France	21	Lyons
31 Oct. 1959	Australia	20	France	19	Paris
20 Dec. 1959	Australia	17	France	2	Bordeaux
20 Jan. 1960	Australia	16	France	8	Roanne
11 Jun. 1960	Australia	8	France	8	Sydney
2 Jul. 1960	Australia	56	France	6	Brisbane
16 Jul. 1960	Australia	5	France	7	Sydney
8 Dec. 1963	Australia	5	France	8	Bordeaux
22 Dec. 1963	Australia	21	France	9	Toulouse
18 Jan. 1964	Australia	16	France	8	Paris
13 Jun. 1964	Australia	20	France	7	Sydney
4 Jul. 1964	Australia	27	France	2	Brisbane

18 Jul. 1964	Australia	35	France	9	Sydney
—	Australia	7	France	7	Marseilles
—	Australia	3	France	10	Carcassonne
—	Australia	13	France	16	Toulouse
9 Dec. 1973	Australia	21	France	9	Perpignan
16 Dec. 1973	Australia	14	France	3	Toulouse
26 Nov. 1977	Australia	10	France	13	Carcassonne
12 Dec. 1978	Australia	10	France	11	Toulouse

New Zealand v. France

1947-48	New Zealand	11	France	7	Paris
	New Zealand	7	France	25	Bordeaux
1951	New Zealand	16	France	15	Auckland
1951-52	New Zealand	3	France	8	Paris
	New Zealand	7	France	17	Bordeaux
1955	New Zealand	9	France	19	Auckland
	New Zealand	11	France	6	Auckland
1955-56	New Zealand	7	France	24	Toulouse
	New Zealand	31	France	22	Lyons
	New Zealand	3	France	24	Paris
1960	New Zealand	9	France	2	Auckland
	New Zealand	9	France	3	Auckland
1960-61	New Zealand	11	France	22	Paris
	New Zealand	6	France	6	Bordeaux
	New Zealand	5	France	5	Saint-Ouen
1964	New Zealand	24	France	16	Auckland
	New Zealand	18	France	8	Christchurch
	New Zealand	10	France	2	Auckland
1965	New Zealand	3	France	14	Marseilles
	New Zealand	2	France	6	Perpignan
	New Zealand	5	France	28	Toulouse
1970	New Zealand	2	France	16	Carcassonne(*)
1971	New Zealand	27	France	11	Perpignan
	New Zealand	24	France	2	Carcassonne
	New Zealand	3	France	3	Toulouse.

*denotes unofficial international games.

TIMEKEEPING

Traditionally, the duration of a Rugby League match is under the sole control of the referee. This principle still applies except at first team and International levels where independent timekeepers are employed. The Australian practice was first adopted by the English League in the mid-1960s for televised amateur matches and was extended to feature in two Internationals.

A meeting of the League's Executive Committee on 23 Jun. 1972 decided that all professional clubs would employ a timekeeper, one for each team, and each supplied with stop watches to determine that the match contained a full 80 minutes of play. Each club was ordered to obtain a horn to signal half-time and full time, although the varying standards of hooter systems has repeatedly led to controversy.

A stoppage in play is signalled by the referee to the timekeepers to ensure that the match takes place in its entirety.

TRANSFERS

In 1901 Jim Lomas was transferred from Bramley to Salford for £100. Shortly after returning as the captain of the first touring side to Australasia in 1910 he moved on to Oldham for £300. Both fees were considered extremely high even for a centre of his class, but they were soon overtaken by a deal that staggered the Northern Union. Within a few days of Billy Batten, Hunslet's Test centre, asking for a move Hull stepped in to sign him for £600 in 1913. Hull had their critics who felt no player was worth that amount but such was Batten's crowd-pulling power that after his first three matches at the Boulevard gate receipts had totalled more than £600.

Eight years later Hunslet were again involved in a notable transfer deal when Harold Buck, a winger, moved to Leeds for £1,000—the first four-figure transfer.

There were unconfirmed reports that another Hunslet player moved with Buck to Leeds which throws doubts about it being the first £1,000 transfer. Since then there have been other deals in which one player has moved in exchange for another plus cash. When this happens it is anybody's guess about the true value of the transfer.

Hunslet, yet again, transferred loose forward Brian Shaw to Leeds in 1961 for a reported record of £13,250. In fact, they received £9,500 plus Bernard Prior (valued £3,500) and Norman Burton (£250).

When Colin Dixon left Halifax for Salford in 1968 it was claimed to be for a record £15,000. In fact, Salford gave Halifax £12,000 plus a player valued at £3,000.

More recently, Steve Norton (on Castleford's transfer list at £25,000) joined Hull in 1978. In exchange Castleford received £10,000 plus Jimmy Crampton (on Hull's transfer list at £15,000). Norton's transfer was reported as a record at the time, but no one could put an accurate figure on his value.

With several clubs making huge profits from lotteries, 1978 was a boom year for transfers and in addition to the Norton move the record for a straight cash deal was broken three times. It reached a peak when Hull Kingston Rovers paid Barrow £35,000 for Test loose forward Phil Hogan.

All the aforementioned records refer to deals between English clubs, but it is also worth noting a trend in the early 1970s which saw top players lured to Australia. Penrith were the biggest spenders in that field, signing Mick Stephenson from Dewsbury for £20,000 in 1973 and the same year paying Wigan £15,000 for Bill Ashurst.

Several other Test players joined Australian clubs before the introduction in 1977 of a ban on inter-country transfers. This was done primarily to stop the draining off of England's best players to Australia.

About 25 years earlier a similar ban had halted English clubs buying the top talent in Australia and New Zealand.

The growth of transfer fees involving English clubs only in straight cash deals is shown in the following table:

1901-02	Jim Lomas (Bramley to Salford)	£100
1910-11	Jim Lomas (Salford to Oldham)	£300
1912-13	Billy Batten (Hunslet to Hull)	£600
1921-22	Harold Buck (Hunslet to Leeds)	£1,000
1929-30	Stanley Smith (Wakefield to Leeds)	£1,075
1933-34	Stanley Brogden (Huddersfield to Leeds)	£1,200
1937-38	Billy Belshaw (Liverpool S. to Warrington)	£1,450
1946-47	Willie Davies (Huddersfield to Dewsbury)	£1,650
1947-48	Bill Hudson (Batley to Wigan)	£2,000
1947-48	Jim Ledgard (Dewsbury to Leigh)	£2,650
1948-49	Ike Owens (Leeds to Castleford)	£2,750
1948-49	Ike Owens (Castleford to Huddersfield)	£2,750
1948-49	Stan McCormick (Belle Vue R. to St Helens)	£4,000
1949-50	Albert Naughton (Widnes to Warrington)	£4,600
1950-51	Bruce Ryan (Hull to Leeds)	£4,750
1950-51	Joe Egan (Wigan to Leigh)	£5,000
1950-51	Harry Street (Dewsbury to Wigan)	£5,000
1957-58	Mick Sullivan (Huddersfield to Wigan)	£9,500
1958-59	Ike Southward (Workington to Oldham)	£10,650
1960-61	Mick Sullivan (Wigan to St Helens)	£11,000
1960-61	Ike Southward (Oldham to Workington)	£11,002 10s
1968-69	Colin Dixon (Halifax to Salford)	£12,000
1969-70	Paul Charlton (Workington to Salford)	£12,500
1972-73	Eric Prescott (St Helens to Salford)	£13,500
1975-76	Steve Nash (Featherstone to Salford)	£15,000
1977-78	Bill Ashurst (Wigan to Wakefield)	£18,000
1978-79	Clive Pickerill (Castleford to Hull)	£20,000
1978-79	Phil Hogan (Barrow to Hull K.R.)	£35,000
1979-80	Len Casey (Bradford N. to Hull K.R.)	£38,000
1980-81	Trevor Skerrett (Wakefield T. to Hull)	£40,000

TRIES

Most tries in a career

Brian Bevan was a try-scoring phenomenon. His total of 796 tries is far ahead of his nearest challenger. An Australian, he signed for Warrington in 1946 and became one of the greatest wingers the game has known. He stayed with Warrington until the end of the 1961-62 season and finished his career with Blackpool Borough. Bevan scored 740 tries for Warrington, 17 for Blackpool and 39 in representative matches. His season-by-season record was:

1946-47	48
1947-48	57
1948-49	56
1949-50	33
1950-51	68
1951-52	51
1952-53	72
1953-54	67
1954-55	63
1955-56	57
1956-57	17
1957-58	46
1958-59	54
1959-60	40
1960-61	35
1961-62	15
1962-63	10
1963-64	7

In addition, Bevan kicked 34 goals in his first season.

Most Tries in a Match

11 by George "Tich" West (Hull Kingston Rovers) v. Brookland Rovers (RL Cup, 4 Mar. 1905).

Most Tries in a Season

80 by A. A. Rosenfield (Huddersfield) in 1913-14 in 42 matches.
The tries were scored as follows:

1913	Against		Tries
6 Sept.	York	(a)	4
8	Warrington	(h)	2
13	Leeds	(h)	5
20	Halifax	(a)	2
4 Oct.	Oldham	(h)	2
18	Bramley (Y.C.)	(h)	2
25	Dewsbury	(a)	4
1 Nov.	Halifax (Y.C.)	(a)	2
8	Wigan	(a)	1
15	Dewsbury (Y.C.)	(h)	3
19	Bradford	(h)	3
22	Leeds	(a)	3
29	Bradford (Y.C.F.)	Hfx.	1
3 Dec.	Halifax	(h)	3
6	Hunslet	(a)	2

13	Rochdale Hornets	(h)	3
20	Hull K.R.	(a)	2
26	Wakefield T.	(h)	3
1914			
10 Jan.	York	(h)	3
17	Keighley	(a)	2
24	Dewsbury	(h)	1
14 Feb.	Bramley	(h)	5
21	Wigan	(h)	3
28	Swinton P'k Cup	(h)	7
7 Mar.	Wakefield T.	(a)	2
14	Hull K.R. (Cup)	(a)	2
18	Bramley	(a)	3
25	Keighley	(h)	3
28	Hull K.R.	(h)	1
30	Bradford N.	(a)	1
			<u>80</u>

Albert Rosenfield, one of the original Australian RL "pioneers" who played in the three games against Baskerville's New Zealand team at Sydney in 1907, came to England with the first Australian Tour Team in 1908 and signed for Huddersfield towards the end of the Tour.

TROPHIES

In addition to the three clubs who achieved the traditional "All Four Cups" feat, St Helens, Warrington and Widnes have each won four trophies in a season.

In 1965-66 St Helens won the Championship, the RL Challenge Cup, the Lancashire League Cup and the League Leaders Trophy.

In 1973-74 Warrington won the RL Challenge Cup, the Player's No. 6 Trophy, the Capt. Morgan Trophy and the Club Championship. The latter two competitions lasted for only one season.

In 1978-79 Widnes won the RL Challenge Cup, the John Player Cup, the Lancashire Cup and the BBC2 Floodlit Trophy.

There are now seven trophies to be competed for by first teams. They are:

The State Express Rugby League Challenge Cup
The Slalom Lager Premiership Trophy
The Division One Championship
The Division Two Championship
The John Player Trophy
The Webster's Yorkshire Cup
The Forshaws Lancashire Cup
See ALL FOUR CUPS.

TRUMANNS MAN OF STEEL

Introduced in the 1976-77 season, the Trumanns Man of Steel award scheme is the biggest of its kind in Rugby League. The Manchester based Trumanns Steel Ltd. provide mementoes and cash prizes to players, coaches and referees within the Northern Rugby Football League. Five categories are featured in the award scheme, with the personality judged to have made the most impact on the season receiving the top cash award and the title Man of Steel. A panel of judges determine the nominations and final awards, except for the Division One and Two Players of the Year, which are decided by a ballot by the players. The award ceremony is staged in May each year as part of a Rugby League gala evening at a northern theatre club.

Award winners to date are:

Division One Player of the Year
1977:   Malcolm Reilly (Castleford)
1978:   George Nicholls (St Helens)
1979:   Mick Adams (Widnes)
1980:   Mick Adams (Widnes)

Division Two Player of the Year
1977:   Ged Marsh (Blackpool Borough)
1978:   John Woods (Leigh)
1979:   Steve Norton (Hull)
1980:   Steve Quinn (Featherstone R.)

Young Player of the Year
1977:   David Ward (Leeds)
1978:   John Woods (Leigh)
1979:   Steve Evans (Featherstone Rovers)
1980:   Roy Holdstock (Hull KR)

Coach of the Year
1977:   Eric Ashton MBE (St Helens)
1978:   Frank Myler (Widnes)
1979:   Doug Laughton (Widnes)
1980:   Peter Fox (Bradford N.)

Referee of the Year
1977:   Billy Thompson (Huddersfield)
1978:   Billy Thompson (Huddersfield)
1979:   Mick Naughton (Widnes)
1980:   Fred Lindop (Wakefield)

Trumanns Man of Steel
1977:   David Ward (Leeds)
1978:   George Nicholls (St Helens)
1979:   Doug Laughton (Widnes)
1980:   George Fairbairn (Wigan)

TWO DIVISIONS

Two-division League football was first introduced in the 1902-03 season when 18 clubs competed in the First Division and 18 in the Second Division.

The experiment was staged for three seasons, with 18 clubs always featuring in the First Division. However, the Second Division was reduced to 17 clubs in the 1903-04 season, and further reduced in the 1904-05 campaign.

In 1905 the single division was reconstituted with 31 clubs.

In those three trial years the First Division Champions were Halifax, Bradford and Oldham respectively, while the leaders in the Second Division were Keighley, Wakefield Trinity and Dewsbury. Promotion and relegation was on a two up, two down basis.

From 1906, the League settled into a formula of one division with a top-four play off at the end of the season.

Two divisions were reintroduced for the 1962-63 season but the intended three-year trial was scrapped after only two seasons. The 30 clubs were divided 16 into the First Division and 14 into the Second Division, with the relegation and promotion being decided on the two up, two down system.

Swinton were First Division Champions in both seasons, with Hunslet topping the Second Division in 1963 and Oldham in 1964.

After returning to the one division set-up, with a new top sixteen play off at the end of the season, the League switched back to two divisions for the third time for the 1973-74 season, with a four-up, four-down formula.

With an extended promotion, the two divisions began to attract more spectators and though critics bemoaned the lack of derby matches, the two-tier League structure was given its longest period of operation.

From the 1980-81 season, the League was sponsored for three years by brewers Matthew Brown, who retitled the First Division The Slalom Lager Championship.

Division One Champions have been:
1902-03:   Halifax
1903-04:   Bradford
1904-05:   Oldham
1962-63:   Swinton
1963-64:   Swinton
1973-74:   Salford
1974-75:   St Helens
1975-76:   Salford
1976-77:   Featherstone Rovers
1977-78:   Widnes
1978-79:   Hull Kingston Rovers
1979-80:   Bradford Northern

Division Two Champions:
1902-03:	Keighley
1903-04:	Wakefield Trinity
1904-05:	Dewsbury
1962-63:	Hunslet
1963-64:	Oldham
1973-74:	Bradford Northern
1974-75:	Huddersfield
1975-76:	Barrow
1976-77:	Hull
1977-78:	Leigh
1978-79:	Hull
1979-80:	Featherstone Rovers

See also: SLALOM LAGER

TWO-LEGGED CUP TIES

Two-legged matches, decided on a home-and-away basis with the aggregate score providing the winner, have been utilised in cup ties in a bid to gain the maximum financial and promotional benefits from these popular knockout competitions. The two-legged system was first introduced during the 1939-45 war.

The Lancashire and Yorkshire County Committees decided to abolish the two-legged ties in the spring of 1954. An extraordinary general meeting of the Rugby League at Manchester on 6 Jun. 1954 decided to scrap the twin-match principle in the Challenge Cup Competition.

The two-legged system was also brought into operation for the BBC2 Floodlit Trophy to decide the Preliminary Round matches. The home-and-away scheme was utilised from seasons 1966-67 to 1974-75 inclusive, after which the sudden-death principle was applied.

Yet the financial attractions still beckoned, and the two-legged operation was revitalised again with the new-style end-of-season Premiership Trophy. Introduced in 1975, the Premiership was modified the following season to cater for a top eight play-off, with the semi-finals staged on two legs, although the pattern was interrupted by the adverse weather of 1979 which caused the Premiership semi-finals to be reduced to one-match affairs.

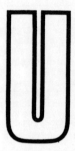

UNDER-24s

A new level of International Rugby League was introduced in 1964-65 when England Under-24s were established. Fixtures with the French League were arranged in a bid to grade the development of Britain's potential Test players.

Three matches were staged in 1965 and 1966, a fourth being played in Britain in 1969. The under-24s were then shelved until a reorganisation of International football policy in 1976 paved the way for the re-establishment of the Great Britain Under-24 team and annual home-and-away fixtures with their French counterparts.

Under the charge of ex-International Johnny Whiteley, the stature and popularity of the Under-24 team grew and the new endeavour was rewarded with the granting of an encounter with the 1978 Australian Tourists.

UNDER SOIL HEATING

Headingley, the home of Leeds RLFC, is the only Rugby League ground where under soil heating is installed. Installed in April 1963 at a cost of £6,488, the "electric blanket" consists of 38 miles of wiring at a depth of six inches. The cost for 24 hours' operation is in the region of £300, compared with the original bill of £60.

Under-24 results:

1965	England	17	France	9	Toulouse
	England	12	France	5	Oldham
1966	England	4	France	7	Bayonne
1969	England	42	France	2	Castleford
1976	Britain	19	France	2	Hull K.R.
	Britain	11	France	9	Albi
1977	Britain	27	France	9	Hull
	Britain	8	France	4	Tonneins
1978	Britain	8	Australia	30	Hull K.R.
1979	Britain	15	France	3	Limoux
1980	Britain	14	France	2	Leigh
	Britain	11	France	7	Carcassonne

UNION v. LEAGUE

Although the two codes of League and Union remain poles apart the exigencies of war-time have brought them together—on the football field at least. Many League players played in Services teams against RU teams and also in the war-time RU Internationals between 1939 and 1945.

Two representative games were played, one at Headingley, Leeds, on 23 Jan. 1943, and the other at Odsal Stadium, Bradford, in which a team of RL players opposed a RU side. Both matches were played 15-a-side and under Rugby Union Rules, the proceeds of the gate going to Services charities. The teams for the game at Leeds were:

Rugby League 15

Cpl. G. R. Pepperell (Huddersfield)
S.I. R. L. Francis (Dewsbury)
Trpr. H. Mills (Hull)

Pte. J. Stott (St Helens)
Cpl. E. W. Lloyd (Castleford)
L.Br. H. Royal (Dewsbury)

Sgm. W. Thornton (Hunslet)
SGT.I. D. R. Prosser (Leeds)

L. Cpl. L. L. White (Hunslet)
Gnr. L. White (York)
Cpl. K. Jubb (Leeds)
Cpl. E. Tattersfield (Leeds)
Pte. W. Chapman (Warrington)

Cpl. H. Bedford (Hull)
Sgt.-I. T. Foster (Bradford Northern)

Rugby Union 15

Cpl. J. Bond (Cumberland)
Lieut. T. G. H. Jackson (Army)

Capt. M. N. Walford (Oxford University)
Lieut. D. R. MacGregor (Rosslyn Park)
Sgt.-I. D. F. Mitchell (Galashiels)
2nd Lieut. L. B. Lockhart (Cambridge University)
O.Cadet H. Tanner (Swansea)
Major R. O. Murray (London Scottish)

Sgm. J. D. H. Hastie (Melrose)
Cpl. J. Maltman (Hawick)
Cadet R. C. V. Stewart (Waterloo)
Cpl. R. Cowe (Melrose)

Pte. A. Crawford (Melrose)
2nd Lieut. R. G. Furbank (Bedford)

The League team won by 18 points to 11. At a luncheon before the game the Yorkshire RU president, Mr R. F. Oakes, said that while the two codes would probably go their own separate ways after the war there could be no line of demarcation between men in uniform. The RL secretary, Mr John Wilson, said he saw no reason why the match should not become an annual event though he did not think that League and Union would ever play under one banner.

At Odsal a year later RL Combined Services beat RU Combined Services by 15 points to 10. The teams were:

Rugby League C.S.
L.-Cpl. E. Ward (Bradford N.)
Sgt.-I. R. L. Francis (Barrow)
Cpl. J. Stott (St Helens)
L.A.C. J. Lawrenson (Wigan)
Cpl. A. Edwards (Salford)
Sgt. S. Brogden (Hull)
Bdr. H. Royal (Dewsbury)
Sgt.-I. D. R. Prosser (Leeds)
Dvr. L. White (Hunslet)
L.A.C. C. Brereton (Halifax)
Dvr. D. Murphy (Bramley)
Flt. Sgt. E. Watkins (Wigan)
Sgt. I. A. Owens (Leeds)
Sgt. W. Chapman (Warrington)
Sgt.-I. T. Foster (Bradford N.)

Rugby Union C.S.
C.S.M. I. Trott (Penarth)
Lieut. G. Hollis (Sale)
Cpl. T. Sullivan (Swansea)
Lieut. H. Tanner (Swansea)
Sub-Lieut. E. S. Simpson (Bradford)
Lieut. T. Gray (Heriots)
Sqdn.-Ldr. Parsons (Leicester)
Cpl. R. J. Longland (Northampton)
Sgt. G. T. Dancer (Bedford)

Capt. R. E. Prescott (Harlequins)
Lieut. P. M. Walker (Gloucester)
Cpl. D. V. Phillips (Swansea)
Capt. G. D. Shaw (Scotland)
Capt. J. A. Waters (Scotland)
Flt.-Lieut R. G. Weighill (Waterloo)

The end of the war saw the end of the "truce". The Rugby Union's continued strict rules against professionalism hold out little hope of a get-together. An amalgamation seems an impossibility, yet there are many who believe that if the rugby game was united it could become Britain's premier sport.

The player's point of view was perhaps best expressed by the skipper of the 1943 Army Rugby Union team, Captain Walford. He said "We are concerned solely with playing rugby, and not whom we are playing with or against."

UNIVERSITIES

In 1979, one of British Rugby League's youngest institutions, the University and Colleges Rugby League Clubs Association, celebrated its tenth anniversary and it now represents one of the best vehicles for taking the game into new and influential spheres.

The seeds for the students' competition were sown during the 1966-67 season when a club was formed at Leeds University. They were closely followed by Liverpool University and the first inter-varsity fixture was staged at Widnes in 1967 ending in a 32-16 victory for the Yorkshire team.

During 1968 new teams were formed at Bradford, Manchester and Salford universities and the new League, the University Rugby League Clubs Association, was constituted in time for the 1969-70 season. The first fixture played under their control was between Bradford and Salford at Bradford University on 15 Oct. 1969 and Salford won 13-5.

More new ground was broken for Rugby League during 1969 when Sheffield University, who were coached by international referee Mr Fred Lindop, were admitted to the League. The first season ended with a clean sweep for pioneers Leeds, who won both the League Championship and the knock-out Cup competition.

Expansion was rapid and, by season 1971-72, it was necessary to form a Reserve League. The second section contained most of the Colleges of Education and

Further Education College teams so that eventually it changed its name to become the Colleges League. These teams became so important to the fabric of the Association that its name was changed in 1973-74 from the University Rugby League Clubs Association to its present title, The University and College Rugby League Clubs Association.

With the constantly shifting student population, membership of the League has never been constant and some teams have existed for short periods before dropping out, and eventually reforming. Clubs have existed at Bolton Institute of Technology, Didsbury College of Education (Manchester), Leeds Polytechnic, Moston College of Further Education (Manchester), Portsmouth Polytechnic and Surrey Universities, but they have all failed to stay in what is still a hard survival course.

One of the most important additions to the student ranks, however, was the team from Oxford University in 1977. They have found their way into the tough Rugby League world despite opposition from several sources, not least the Rugby Union establishment. One of their players, a 37-year-old Maori Bob Mahuta, found himself banned from playing Union because he played for the newly-formed University League side.

Membership for the University and Colleges League for 1978-79 was Airedale and Wharfedale College of Further Education (Leeds), Bradford University, De La Salle College (Manchester), Huddersfield Polytechnic, Hull University, Lancaster University, Leeds University, Leicester University, Liverpool University, Manchester University, Oxford University, Salford College of Technology, Salford University, Sheffield University and Wakefield Technical College.

The University and College organisation is a member of the British Amateur Rugby League Association but its biggest breakthrough came in 1976 when its existence was recognised by the University Athletics Union, the top British student sport organisation. It was a rich reward for some brave pioneering work. Expansion is still the key word for the Association, but for their second decade they are looking for more stability from newly established clubs. Moves are already in the pipeline to introduce the sport to Cambridge University and, if they succeed Rugby League will be able to boast its own Cambridge v. Oxford match. Plans are also being undertaken at Reading, Swansea and London Universities. In 1977-78 the College League was suspended because of the problems clubs were experiencing in recruiting players, and the existing clubs were taken into the University League.

Five competitions are open to the student player, the UAU knockout, the University Championship, the University Cup knockout, the College Cup knockout and the annual seven-a-side tournament. Several universities have moved outside their own competitive sphere competing in the BARLA National Cup and regional Leagues. Their success in the National Cup has been limited because they do not have the experience or forward strength of their open-age opponents.

Four clubs are trying life in the rough and tumble of open-age League football: Hull College of Higher Education play in the Humberside League, Huddersfield Polytechnic in the Pennine League, Airedale and Wharfedale College in the Leeds Sunday League and Manchester Polytechnic in the North-West Counties League. The latter team have proved the most successful so far.

The students have enjoyed more success against non-students teams in seven-a-side tournaments and the leading example of their prowess is Salford University, who reached the final of the national event in 1975. They were beaten 26-6 by the mighty Hull Dockers team.

One of the biggest attractions for the student players are their representative matches which are: An international encounter with French Universities, Lancashire Universities v. Yorkshire Universities, Universities v. Southern Amateur League and Universities v. Colleges.

Internationally the British Universities are still ambitious and their big target is to send either an all-British, or Anglo-French, student team to play university teams in Australia and New Zealand.

It has been estimated that 3,500 students have played Rugby League since the Association was formed and at least three of their players have moved on to bigger things in Rugby League. Graeme Johns, ex-Manchester University, signed as a professional for Swinton and played for Wales against Australia in 1978, John McQuire, ex-Salford University, has played professionally with Whitehaven and Workington Town and John Roberts, ex-Sheffield University, played on BARLA's South Pacific tour in 1978.

ROLL OF HONOUR

University Internationals

Apr. 1973	English Universities	11	French Universities	17	at Salford
Apr. 1974	French Universities	30	English Universities	3	at Montpellier
Mar. 1975	English Universities	8	French Universities	16	at Salford
May. 1967	French Universities	23	English Universities	19	at Albi
Apr. 1977	English Universities	12	French Universities	12	at Salford
Apr. 1978	French Universities	22	English Universities	5	at Toulouse
Apr. 1979	English Universities	11	French Universities	7	at Salford

Inter-county Matches

Nov. 1969	Lancs Universities	16	Yorkshire Universities	23	at Manchester University
Nov. 1970	Yorkshire Universities	13	Lancs Universities	8	at Odsal Bradford
Nov. 1971	Yorkshire Universities	8	Lancs Universities	6	at Fartown, Huddersfield
Nov. 1972	Lancs Universities	20	Yorkshire Universities	21	at Station Road, Swinton
Nov. 1974	Yorkshire Universities	12	Lancs Universities	3	at Belle Vue, Wakefield
Nov. 1975	Lancs Universities	21	Yorkshire Universities	2	at Naughton Park, Widnes
Dec. 1975	Yorkshire Universities	19	Lancs Universities	29	at Thrum Hall, Halifax
Nov. 1976	Lancs Universities	21	Yorkshire Universities	22	at Liverpool University
Feb. 1978	Yorkshire Universities	8	Lancs Universities	13	at Hull University
Feb. 1979	Yorkshire Universities	11	Lancs Universities	8	at De La Salle College, Manchester

UAU v. Colleges

Feb. 1977	UAU	24	Colleges	15	at Bradford University
Feb. 1978	Colleges	36	Universities	22	at Salford University

Universities v. Southern Amateur League XIII

Feb. 1970	Southern League	17	Northern UAU	16	at Hackney
Jan. 1973	URLCA XIII	19	Southern League	24	at Eastmoor, Wakefield
Nov. 1975	Southern League	15	English Universities	19	at Morden
Mar. 1977	Southern League	5	English Universities	21	at Cowley Marsh, Oxford
Mar. 1978	English Universities	32	Southern League	13	at Oxford

University Challenge Cup

1969-70	Leeds University
1970-71	Sheffield University
1971-72	Hull University
1972-73	Sheffield University
1973-74	Liverpool University
1974-75	Salford University
1975-76	Salford University
1976-77	Airedale and Wharfedale College
1977-78	Lancaster University
1978-79	Hull University

University Championship

1969-70	Leeds University
1970-71	Leeds University

1971-72	Salford University
1973-74	Sheffield University
1974-75	Salford University
1975-76	Salford University
1976-77	Lancaster University
1977-78	Hull University

Colleges Championship

1973-74	De La Salle, Manchester
1974-75	St John Rigby College, Wigan
1975-76	Airedale and Wharfedale College
1976-77	Salford College of Technology
1977-78	competition suspended, clubs now integrated Universities League

Colleges Cup

1971-72	Leeds Polytechnic
1972-73	De La Salle, Manchester
1973-74	Loughborough College
1974-75	St John Rigby College, Wigan
1975-76	Airedale and Wharfedale College
1976-77	Airedale and Wharfedale College

1977-78	Airedale and Wharfedale College
1978-79	Salford College of Technology

UAU Championship

1977	Lancaster University
1978	Hull University
1979	Hull University

Seven-a-side Championship

1970	Combined Salford Grammar Schools
1971	Manchester University
1972	Salford University
1973	Liverpool University
1974	Salford University
1975	Salford University*
1976	Hull University
1977	Hull University
1978	Airedale and Wharfedale College
1979	Hull University

*Salford University were also losing finalists in the British amateur seven-a-side championships.

See also BRITISH AMATEUR RUGBY LEAGUE ASSOCIATION.

WAKEFIELD TRINITY RLFC

Founded in 1873. Founder member of the Northern Union. Ground: Belle Vue. Colours: White jerseys with red and blue hoops, white shorts.

RL Championship Winners, 1966-67, 1967-68.
  Beaten Finalists, 1959-60, 1961-62.
Division Two Champions, 1903-04.
RL Cup Winners, 1908-09, 1945-46, 1959-60, 1961-62, 1962-63.
  Beaten Finalists, 1913-14, 1967-68, 1978-79.
Yorkshire League Winners, 1909-10, 1910-11, .1945-46, 1958-59, 1959-60, 1961-62, 1965-66.
Yorkshire Cup Winners, 1910-11, 1924-25, 1946-47, 1947-48, 1951-52, 1956-57, 1960-61, 1961-62, 1964-65.
  Beaten Finalists, 1926-27, 1932-33, 1934-35, 1936-37, 1939-40, 1945-46, 1958-59, 1973-74, 1974-75.
Player's No. 6 Trophy Beaten Finalists, 1971-72.
Club Records:
  Attendance: 37,906 Leeds v. Huddersfield (RL Cup S.F.), 21 Mar. 1936.
  Goals: 163 by N. Fox, 1961-62.
  Tries: 38 by F. Smith, 1959-60; D. Smith, 1973-74.
  Points: 407 by N. Fox, 1961-62.

WALES

Wales and the Welsh are inextricably linked with the sport of Rugby Football and it is, therefore, all the more surprising that the Principality has never been able to sustain Rugby League on a permanent basis.

The nation has provided many of the League's greatest and brightest individual stars. Ever since the code was established players from Wales have been prepared to sell their amateur status and make the journey north for professional careers. The list of converts would fill a considerable amount of space but some of the most outstanding players have been the James brothers, Bert Jenkins, Ben Gronow, Jim Sullivan, Gus Risman, Alun Evans, Trevor Foster, Lewis Jones, Billy Boston, Kel Coslett, David Watkins, Bob Prosser, Maurice Richards, Clive Sullivan, Colin Dixon, Jim Mills and Mel James.

Of course, it must be pointed out that some of the converts to Rugby League from Welsh Rugby Union were not so successful but the lure north never seems to die, despite the occasional lulls in the frequency of signings. Generally the more successful signings have been three-quarters for whom the change in styles is not quite so pronounced. The League and Union codes demand different kinds of skills from forwards.

Since 1975 a Welsh team has been playing as a national side in the European Championship and they competed as a nation in the 1975 International Championship. Several games have been played in Wales during the mid 1970s at St Helens Rugby Union ground, Swansea, but, despite an initial 20,000 plus crowd, attendances have generally not encouraged further hope for expansion.

Several attempts have been made to establish the League code in Wales. Before the First World War several clubs played under Northern Union rules and some eventually joined the Northern League. Among the more successful sides were Merthyr Tydfil, Ebbw Vale, Aberdare, Barry, Treherbert, and Mid-Rhondda. Merthyr and Ebbw Vale were the first to join the Northern League in 1907.

Mid-Rhondda were the first club side to play the pioneering Australian touring team in 1908-9 and Ebbw Vale reached the third round of the Northern Union Cup later Challenge Cup in 1909-10. Vale had, in fact, been put out of the Cup the previous season by Yorkshire amateur side Beverley, a feat not repeated until 1977-78.

By the time the First World War had been declared the Welsh clubs had all folded up. They had been forced out of business by high travelling costs and severe pressure from Rugby Union. After the war another attempt was made with a professional club at Pontypridd but it stayed alive for just one season, 1926-27.

Rugby League made another attempt to gain a foothold in Wales after the Second World War. In 1949 Huddersfield and St Helens played a number of propaganda, exhibition matches in the country, and as a result a new Welsh League was formed. The member clubs were Cardiff, Llanelli, Bridgend, Ystradgyulais, Aberavon, Amman Vale, Blaina and Neath.

During 1950 a team representing the League beat the touring Italian national side (see ITALY) 29-11 and some of their players were selected for the Welsh national side. In 1951-52 Cardiff, by far the strongest team in the League, joined the Northern Rugby League and without their strength the Welsh League collapsed. Cardiff struggled on through one season, 1951-52, before closing their doors. During 1978 the embryo of another Welsh-based team, Swansea University, appeared and the amateur League game authorities are hoping this will encourage more teams to start playing the game.

The only Welsh team to tour Australia and New Zealand played in the 1975 International Championship and their party was: D. Watkins (capt.), W. Francis, R. Mathias, C. Sullivan, D. Willicombe, F. Wilson, D. Treasure, G. Turner, P. Banner, J. Mills, A. Fisher, R. Evans, B. Wanbon, B. Butler, J. Mantle, C. Dixon, P. Rowe, M. Nicholas, E. Cunningham, K. Coslett; manager: R. Simpson; coach: L. Pearce.

WARRINGTON RLFC

Founded in 1875. Founder member of the Northern Union. Ground: Wilderspool Stadium. Colours: White jerseys with primrose and blue chevron, white shorts.
RL Championship Winners, 1947-48, 1953-54, 1954-55.
Beaten Finalists, 1925-26, 1934-35, 1936-37, 1948-49, 1950-51, 1960-61.
League Leaders Trophy Winners, 1972-73.
Club Championship (Merit Table) Winners, 1973-74.
Premiership Beaten Finalists, 1976-77.
RL Cup Winners, 1904-05, 1906-07, 1949-50, 1953-54, 1973-74.
Beaten Finalists, 1900-01, 1903-04, 1912-13, 1927-28, 1932-33, 1935-36, 1974-75.
Lancashire League Winners, 1937-38, 1947-48, 1948-49, 1950-51, 1953-54, 1954-55, 1955-56, 1967-68.
Lancashire Cup Winners, 1921-22, 1929-

18 Jan. 1930	Australia
30 Dec. 1933	Australia
12 Mar. 1949	France
16 Oct. 1963	Australia
3 Nov. 1973	Great Britain

In 1975, Wembley staged a new Rugby League event, the schoolboy curtain raiser

30, 1932-33, 1937-38, 1959-60, 1965-66.
Beaten Finalist, 1906-07, 1948-49, 1950-51, 1967-68.
Player's No. 6 Trophy Winners, 1973-74, 1977-78.
Beaten Finalists, 1978-79.
Captain Morgan Trophy Winners, 1973-74.
BBC2 Trophy Beaten Finalists, 1974-75.
Club Records:
Attendance: 34,304 v. Wigan (League) 22 Jan. 1949.
Goals: 170 by S. Hesford, 1978-79.
Tries: 66 by B. Bevan, 1952-53.
Points: 366 by H. Bath, 1952-53.

WEBSTER'S YORKSHIRE CUP

From the 1980-81 season, the Yorkshire Cup switched sponsorship from Esso to Webster's brewery, of Halifax. The Webster's Yorkshire Cup sponsorship was £42,000 over three years.

WEMBLEY STADIUM

Wembley is now the traditional home of the Rugby League Challenge Cup Final. The bold and controversial decision to stage the final of the Challenge Cup in the South of England was proposed at the Annual Meeting of the Rugby Football League in June 1928. The final decision was made in the following October, Wembley being chosen in preference to Crystal Palace or White City.

The first Wembley final was staged on 4 May. 1929, between Dewsbury and Wigan in front of 41,500, the second largest crowd in the 28-year history of the Cup. Wigan ran home winners by 13-2, the match being refereed by Mr R. Robinson, of Bradford, the Cup being presented by Lord Daresbury.

With the exception of 1932 and the 1940-45 war years, Wembley has staged the Challenge Cup Final, giving the competition national appeal and bumper attendances, the capacity being reached three times—in 1966, 1970 and 1978.

Five International matches have also been played on the famous Wembley turf:

26	Wales	10
51	Wales	19
12	England	5
28	Great Britain	2
21	Australia	12

to the Challenge Cup Final. Organised under the auspicies of the English Schools'

Rugby League, the age group is under-11, with two 13-a-side teams playing 12 minutes each way on the full Wembley pitch.

The new traditional Wembley timetable is now: music by the Guards Bands; the schoolboy curtain raiser; community singing; presentation of teams to the chief guest; the final kicking off at 3pm.

Designed to display the skills of the junior players, the curtain raiser has featured the following city and town teams:

1975:	Widnes and Wigan
1976:	Hull and Leeds
1977:	Hull and Oldham
1978:	Leigh and York
1979:	St Helens and Wakefield
1980:	Hunslet and Warrington

Also in 1975, it was decided to select an English Schools' Rugby League Association to provide the 10 ball boys for the Challenge Cup Final. The under-13 players have represented the following associations: 1975: Humberside, 1976: Oldham, 1977: Cumbria, 1978: Warrington, 1979: Huddersfield, 1980: Salford.

To boost the curtain raiser, a personality is invited to present the two teams with commemorative plaques in a special touchline ceremony. Since 1975, the role has been performed by The Earl of Derby MC, President of the Rugby Football League; John Noakes, of BBC TV's "Blue Peter"; Ed Stewart, television and radio personality; Jimmy Savile OBE, television and radio star; Rod Hull and Emu; and broadcaster Tony Blackburn.

See also CHALLENGE CUP.

WESTERN DIVISION CHAMPIONSHIP

With the re-introduction of the two-division system in the 1962-63 season, the Lancashire League was replaced by a Western Division Championship. The new title was in contention for only two years, reverting to the traditional Lancashire League with the resumption of one division football in 1964-65.

Western Division Champions were:

	Winners	Runners-up
1962-63	Workington Town	Widnes
1963-64	St Helens	Swinton

See also LANCASHIRE LEAGUE CHAMPIONSHIP CUP.

WHITEHAVEN RLFC

Founded in 1948. Joined the Northern Rugby League in 1948. Ground: Recreation Ground. Colours: White jerseys with chocolate, royal blue and gold hoops, white shorts.

Whitehaven have won no major honours.

Club Records:
Attendance: 18,500 v. Wakefield T. (RL Cup) 19 Mar. 1960.
Goals: 141 by J. McKeown, 1956-57.
Tries: 29 by W. Smith, 1956-57.
Points: 291 by J. McKeown, 1956-57.

WIDNES RLFC

Founded in 1875. Founder member of the Northern Union. Ground: Naughton Park. Colours: White jerseys, black shorts.

Division One Champions, 1977-78.

RL Championship Beaten Finalists, 1935-36.

RL Cup Winners, 1929-30, 1936-37, 1963-64, 1974-75, 1978-79.
Beaten Finalists, 1933-34, 1949-50, 1975-76, 1976-77.

Lancashire League Winners, 1919-20:

Lancashire Cup Winners, 1945-46, 1974-75, 1975-76, 1976-77, 1978-79, 1979-80.
Beaten Finalists, 1928-29, 1939-40, 1955-56, 1971-72.

Player's No. 6 Trophy Winners, 1975-76, 1978-79.
Beaten Finalists, 1974-75, 1977-78, 1979-80.

Premiership Beaten Finalists, 1977-78.

BBC2 Floodlit Trophy Winners, 1978-79.
Beaten Finalists, 1972-73, 1973-74.

Western Division Beaten Finalists, 1962-63.

Club Records:
Attendance: 24,205 v. St Helens (RL Cup) 16 Feb. 1961.
Goals: 140 by M. Burke, 1978-79.
Tries: 34 by F. Myler, 1958-59.
Points: 316 by M. Burke, 1978-79.

WIGAN RLFC

Founded in 1879. Founder member of the Northern Union. Ground: Central Park. Colours: Cherry and white hooped jerseys.

RL Championship Winners, 1908-09, 1921-22, 1925-26, 1933-34, 1945-46, 1946-47, 1949-50, 1951-52, 1959-60.
Beaten Finalists, 1909-10, 1910-11, 1911-12, 1912-13, 1923-24, 1970-71.

League Leaders Trophy Winners, 1970-71.

RL Cup Winners, 1923-24, 1928-29, 1947-48, 1950-51, 1957-58, 1958-59, 1964-65.
Beaten Finalists, 1910-11, 1919-20, 1943-44, 1945-46, 1960-61, 1962-63, 1965-66, 1969-70.

Lancashire League Winners, 1908-09, 1910-11, 1911-12, 1912-13, 1913-14, 1914-15, 1920-21, 1922-23, 1923-24, 1925-26, 1945-46, 1946-47, 1949-50, 1951-52, 1958-59, 1961-62, 1969-70.
Lancashire Cup Winners, 1905-06, 1908-09, 1909-10, 1912-13, 1922-23, 1928-29, 1938-39, 1946-47, 1947-48, 1948-49, 1949-50, 1950-51, 1951-52, 1966-67, 1971-72, 1973-74.
  Beaten Finalists, 1913-14, 1914-15, 1925-26, 1927-28, 1930-31, 1934-35, 1935-36, 1936-37, 1945-46, 1953-54, 1957-58, 1977-78.
BBC2 Floodlit Trophy Winners, 1968-69.
  Beaten Finalists, 1969-70.
War League Championship Winners, 1943-44.
  Beaten Finalists, 1940-41.
Lancashire War League Winners, 1940-41.
Club Records:
  Attendance: 47,747 v. St Helens (League) 27 Mar. 1959.
  Goals: 174 by F. Griffiths, 1961-62.
  Tries: 62 by J. Ring, 1925-26.
  Points: 372 by F. Griffiths, 1961-62.

WINNING RUNS

Wigan hold the record for most successive League wins with 31. They won their last eight League matches of 1969-70 and the first 23 of the 1970-71 season.

Wakefield Trinity had a run of 23 victories in all matches which included Cup-ties and one against the New Zealand tourists in 1961-62.

Huddersfield played 40 games in succession without defeat in 1914-15, but that included three draws. Their best winning run that season was of 21 matches.

In 1978-79 Hull won all 26 of their Division Two matches, the first time a club had won all their league matches in one season.

WOMEN

Until November 1978 women's role in British Rugby League was restricted to supporting clubs or administration. But that changed when the British Amateur Rugby League Association accepted the registration of a 14-year-old Yorkshire schoolgirl, Elizabeth Beale, to play amateur Rugby League Football. She was registered with the Kirklees Youth League by her home town club Normanton, and the BARLA authority decided that, in the light of accelerating female emancipation, they should not stand in Miss Beale's way.

Female players are not unknown in other areas of the Rugby League world, however. In Papua New Guinea there is an organised League for girls in Port Moresby. Games have also taken place in Australia and New Zealand.

In Great Britain the secretaries of three senior professional clubs Bradford Northern, Wigan and Workington Town are women. Mrs Renee Anderson of Workington was appointed to the full-time post during 1976, Mrs Bessie Higgins of Bradford Northern in March 1977 and Miss Jacqui Makinson of Wigan in August 1977.

WORKINGTON TOWN RLFC

Founded in 1945. Joined Northern Rugby League in 1945. Ground: Derwent Park. Colours: white jerseys, with blue band, white shorts.
RL Championship Winners, 1950-51.
  Beaten Finalists, 1957-58.
RL Cup Winners, 1951-52.
  Beaten Finalists, 1954-55, 1957-58.
Lancashire Cup Winners, 1977-78.
  Beaten Finalists, 1976-77, 1978-79.
Western Division Championship Winners, 1962-63.
Club Records:
  Attendance: 17,741 v. Wigan (RL Cup) 3 Mar. 1965.
  Goals: 138 by A. Risman, 1953-54.
    I. MacCorquodale, 1977-78.
  Tries: 49 by J. Lawrenson, 1951-52.
  Points: 306 by I. MacCorquodale, 1977-78.

WORLD CUP COMPETITION

The proposal to stage a World Cup competition first came from France just before the Second World War (see FRANCE) but it was not acted upon. It was revived in the post-war years and put to the English Rugby League Council by their secretary Mr W. Fallowfield at their meeting on 3 Jan. 1952. They agreed that the idea should be placed before the International Board when they met at Lyon, France, on 12 Jan.

The French received the idea enthusiastically, but the Australians were not quite so sure, believing that the tournament would not find favour with their powerful clubs.

Led by their president M. Paul Barriere the French went to the next meeting of the International Board, held in Blackpool during Nov. 1952, with an offer to stage the first World Cup Competition with a guarantee of £25,000. This was accepted.

The first series was staged in Oct. and Nov. 1954 and proved to be a great success. The British, written off as no-hopers because their team had been hit by withdrawals of players who had just returned from the 1954 Australian tour, emerged as shock winners.

Since then the competition has been staged six times but it has never realised its full potential as a major crowd attraction, particularly in Britain. It is a very costly tournament to stage and, after the 1977 series, it was decided to revert to the system of extended tours.

The 1975 tournament—it was renamed the International Championship—was run in two halves, one in the southern hemisphere and the other in the northern. Five teams competed: Australia, England, France, New Zealand and Wales. But the idea did not catch on and the 1977 series was organised on the original qualifying League and Grand Final system.

Wales, whose strength had proved erratic, were eliminated from the Championship after pressure from the Australians and the British played under the banner of Great Britain.

The World Cup Trophy was presented by the French Rugby League in 1954. It is 2ft 6in. high and weighs more than half a hundredweight.

Results of Competitions:
1954 Winners: Great Britain (Played in France)

Date					Venue	Attend.
30 Oct.	France	22	New Zealand	13	Paris	13,240
31 Oct.	Great Britain	28	Australia	13	Lyons	10,250
7 Nov.	Great Britain	13	France	13	Toulouse	37,471
7 Nov.	Australia	34	New Zealand	15	Marseilles	20,000
11 Nov.	Great Britain	26	New Zealand	6	Bordeaux	14,000
11 Nov.	Australia	5	France	15	Nantes	13,000
Play off						
13 Nov.	Great Britain	16	France	12	Paris	30,368

Final Table

	P.	W.	D.	L.	For Pts.	Against Pts.	Pts.
Great Britain	3	2	1	0	67	32	5
France	3	2	1	0	50	31	5
Australia	3	1	0	2	52	58	2
New Zealand	3	0	0	3	34	82	0

1957 Winners: Australia (Played in Australia)

Date					Venue	Attend.
15 June	Great Britain	23	France	5	Sydney	50,000
15 June	Australia	25	New Zealand	5	Brisbane	28,000
17 June	Great Britain	6	Australia	31	Sydney	58,665
17 June	New Zealand	10	France	14	Brisbane	28,000
22 June	Australia	26	France	9	Sydney	35,000
25 June	Great Britain	21	New Zealand	29	Sydney	14,263
29 June	Australia	20	The Rest	11	Sydney	20,000

Final Table

	P.	W.	D.	L.	For Pts.	Against Pts.	Pts.
Australia	3	3	-	-	82	20	6
Great Britain	3	1	-	2	50	65	2
New Zealand	3	1	-	2	44	60	2
France	3	1	-	2	28	59	2

1960 Winners: Great Britain (Played in England)

Date						Venue	Attend.
24 Sept.	Great Britain	23	New Zealand	8		Bradford	20,577
24 Sept.	Australia	13	France	12		Wigan	20,278
1 Oct.	Australia	21	New Zealand	15		Leeds	10,773
1 Oct.	Great Britain	33	France	7		Swinton	22,293
8 Oct.	Australia	3	Great Britain	10		Bradford	33,026
8 Oct.	New Zealand	9	France	0		Wigan	2,876
10 Oct.	Great Britain	33	The Rest	27		Bradford	3,908

Final Table

	P.	W.	D.	L.	For Pts.	Against Pts.	Pts.
Great Britain	3	3	–	–	66	18	6
Australia	3	2	–	1	37	37	4
New Zealand	3	1	–	2	32	44	2
France	3	–	–	3	19	55	–

1968 Winners: Australia (Played in Australia and New Zealand)

Date					Venue	Attend.
25 May	Australia	25	Great Britain	10	Sydney	62,256
25 May	France	15	New Zealand	10	Auckland	18,000
1 June	Australia	31	New Zealand	12	Brisbane	23,608
2 June	France	7	Great Britain	2	Auckland	17,000
8 June	Australia	37	France	4	Brisbane	32,600
8 June	Great Britain	38	New Zealand	14	Sydney	14,105

Final Table

	P.	W.	D.	L.	For Pts.	Against Pts.	Pts.
Australia	3	3	–	–	93	26	6
France	3	2	–	1	26	49	4
Great Britain	3	1	–	2	50	46	2
New Zealand	3	–	–	3	36	84	0

Final

10 Jun.	Australia	20	France	2	Sydney	54,290

1970—Winners Australia (Played in England)

Date					Venue	Attend.
21 Oct.	Australia	48	New Zealand	11	Wigan	9,586
24 Oct.	Great Britain	11	Australia	4	Leeds	15,084
25 Oct.	New Zealand	16	France	15	Hull	3,900
28 Oct.	Great Britain	6	France	0	Castleford	9,150
31 Oct.	Great Britain	27	New Zealand	17	Swinton	5,609
1 Nov.	France	17	Australia	15	Bradford	6,215

Final Table

	P.	W.	D.	L.	For Pts.	Against Pts.	Pts.
Great Britain	3	3	–	–	44	21	6
Australia	3	1	–	2	66	39	2
France	3	1	–	2	32	37	2
New Zealand	3	1	–	2	44	89	2

Play off Final

7 Nov.	Australia	12	Great Britain	7	Leeds	18,776

1972—Winners Great Britain (Played in France)

					Venue	*Attend.*
28 Oct.	France	20	New Zealand	9	Perpignan	20,748
29 Oct.	Great Britain	27	Australia	21	Marseilles	6,300
1 Nov.	Australia	9	New Zealand	5	Paris	8,000
1 Nov.	Great Britain	13	France	4	Grenoble	5,321
4 Nov.	Great Britain	53	New Zealand	19	Pau	7,500
5 Nov.	Australia	31	France	9	Toulouse	10,332

Final Table

	P.	*W.*	*D.*	*L.*	*For Pts.*	*Against Pts.*	*Pts.*
Great Britain	3	3	–	–	93	44	6
Australia	3	2	–	1	61	41	4
France	3	1	–	2	33	53	2
New Zealand	3	–	–	3	33	83	0

Play off final

11 Nov.	Great Britain	10	Australia	10	Lyon	4,500

No further score after extra-time so Great Britain took championship because they had scored the greater number of points in the qualifying League table.

1975—Winners Australia (home and away basis)

Date	*Match and Result*				*Venue*	*Attend.*
16 Mar.	England	20	France	2	Leeds	10,482
1 June	Australia	36	New Zealand	8	Brisbane	10,000
14 June	Australia	30	Wales	13	Sydney	25,386
15 June	New Zealand	27	France	0	Christchurch	2,500
21 June	New Zealand	17	England	17	Auckland	12,000
28 June	New Zealand	13	Wales	8	Auckland	18,000
28 June	Australia	10	England	10	Sydney	33,858
22 June	Australia	26	France	6	Brisbane	9,000
10 June	Wales	12	England	7	Brisbane	6,000
20 Sept.	England	22	Wales	16	Warrington	5,034
27 Sept.	New Zealand	8	Australia	24	Auckland	18,000
6 Oct.	Wales	23	France	2	Salford	2,247
11 Oct.	France	2	England	48	Bordeaux	2,000 app
17 Oct.	France	12	New Zealand	12	Marseilles	18,000 app
19 Oct.	Wales	6	Australia	18	Swansea	11,112
25 Oct.	England	27	New Zealand	12	Bradford	5,937
26 Oct.	France	2	Australia	41	Perpignan	10,440
1 Nov.	England	16	Australia	13	Wigan	9,383
2 Nov.	Wales	25	New Zealand	24	Swansea	2,645

Final Table

	P.	*W.*	*D.*	*L.*	*For Pts.*	*Against Pts.*	*Pts.*
Australia	8	6	1	1	198	69	13
England	8	5	1	2	167	84	12
Wales	8	3	5	–	110	130	6
New Zealand	8	2	2	4	121	149	6
France	8	1	6	1	49	204	2

1977—Winners Australia (Played in Australia and New Zealand)

						Venue	Attend.
29 May	Australia	27	New Zealand	17		Auckland	
5 June	Great Britain	23	France	4		Auckland	
11 June	Australia	21	France	9		Sydney	
12 June	Great Britain	30	New Zealand	12		Christchurch	
18 June	Australia	19	Great Britain	5		Brisbane	
19 June	New Zealand	28	France	20		Auckland	

Final Table

	P.	W.	D.	L.	For Pts.	Against Pts.	Pts.
Australia	3	3	–	–	72	21	6
Great Britain	3	2	–	1	53	40	4
New Zealand	3	1	–	2	52	77	2
France	3	–	–	3	33	72	0

Play off final

25 June	Australia	13	Great Britain	12	Sydney

YORK RLFC

Founded in 1868. Joined the Northern
Union in 1896. Ground: Wiggington Road.
Colours: Amber and black jerseys, black
shorts.
RL Cup Beaten Finalists, 1930-31.
Yorkshire Cup Winners, 1922-23, 1933-34,
    1936-37.
    Beaten Finalists, 1935-36, 1957-58, 1978-
    79.
Club Records:
    Goals: 146 by V. Yorke, 1957-58.
    Tries: 34 by G. Smith, 1962-63.
    Points: 301 by V. Yorke, 1957-58.

YORKSHIRE CUP

Season	Winners		Runners-up	
1905-06	Hunslet	13	Halifax	3
1906-07	Bradford	8	Hull KR	5
1907-08	Hunslet	17	Halifax	0
1908-09	Halifax	9	Hunslet	5
1909-10	Huddersfield	21	Batley	0
1910-11	Wakefield Tr.	8	Huddersfield	2
1911-12	Huddersfield	22	Hull KR	10
1912-13	Batley	17	Hull	3
1913-14	Huddersfield	19	Bradford N.	3
1914-15	Huddersfield	31	Hull	0
1915-16 to 1917-18 *Competition suspended*				
1918-19	Huddersfield	14	Dewsbury	8
1919-20	Huddersfield	24	Leeds	5
1920-21	Hull KR	2	Hull	0
1921-22	Leeds	11	Dewsbury	3
1922-23	York	5	Batley	0
1923-24	Hull	10	Huddersfield	4
1924-25	Wakefield Tr.	9	Batley	8
1925-26	Dewsbury	2	Huddersfield	0
1926-27	Huddersfield	10	Wakefield Tr.	3
1927-28	Dewsbury	8	Hull	2
1928-29	Leeds	5	Featherstone R.	0
1929-30	Hull KR	13	Hunslet	7
1930-31	Leeds	10	Huddersfield	2
1931-32	Huddersfield	4	Hunslet	2
1932-33	Leeds	8	Wakefield Tr.	0
1933-34	York	10	Hull KR	4
1934-35	Leeds	5	Wakefield Tr.	5
(replay)	Leeds	2	Wakefield Tr.	2
(replay)	Leeds	13	Wakefield Tr.	0
1935-36	Leeds	3	York	0
1936-37	York	9	Wakefield Tr.	2
1937-38	Leeds	14	Huddersfield	8
1938-39	Huddersfield	18	Hull	10
1939-40*	Featherstone R.	12	Wakefield Tr.	9
1940-41*	Bradford N.	15	Dewsbury	5
1941-42*	Bradford N.	24	Halifax	0
1942-43*	Dewsbury	7	Huddersfield	0
	Dewsbury	0	Huddersfield	2
	Dewsbury won on aggregate 7-2			
1943-44*	Bradford N.	5	Keighley	2
	Bradford N.	5	Keighley	5

	Bradford Northern won on aggregate 10-7			
1944-45*	Halifax	12	Hunslet	3
	Halifax	2	Hunslet	0
	Halifax won on aggregate 14-3			
1945-46	Bradford N.	5	Wakefield Tr.	2
1946-47	Wakefield Tr.	10	Hull	0
1947-48	Wakefield Tr.	7	Leeds	7
(replay)	Wakefield Tr.	8	Leeds	7
1948-49	Bradford N.	18	Castleford	9
1949-50	Bradford N.	11	Huddersfield	4
1950-51	Huddersfield	16	Castleford	3
1951-52	Wakefield Tr.	17	Keighley	3
1952-53	Huddersfield	18	Batley	8
1953-54	Bradford N.	7	Hull	2
1954-55	Halifax	22	Hull	14
1955-56	Halifax	10	Hull	10
(replay)	Halifax	7	Hull	0
1956-57	Wakefield Tr.	23	Hunslet	5
1957-58	Huddersfield	15	York	8
1958-59	Leeds	24	Wakefield Tr.	20
1959-60	Featherstone R.	15	Hull	14
1960-61	Wakefield Tr.	16	Huddersfield	10
1961-62	Wakefield Tr.	19	Leeds	9
1962-63	Hunslet	12	Hull KR	2
1963-64	Halifax	10	Featherstone R.	0
1964-65	Wakefield Tr.	18	Leeds	2
1965-66	Bradford N.	17	Hunslet	8
1966-67	Hull KR	25	Featherstone R.	12
1967-68	Hull KR	8	Hull	7
1968-69	Leeds	22	Castleford	11
1969-70	Hull	12	Featherstone R.	9
1970-71	Leeds	23	Featherstone R.	7
1971-72	Hull KR	11	Castleford	7
1972-73	Leeds	36	Dewsbury	9
1973-74	Leeds	7	Wakefield Tr.	2
1974-75	Hull KR	16	Wakefield Tr.	13
1975-76	Leeds	15	Hull KR	11
1976-77	Leeds	16	Featherstone R.	12
1977-78	Castleford	17	Featherstone R.	7
1978-79	Bradford N.	18	York	8
1979-80	Leeds	15	Halifax	6

* Emergency Competition

See also ESSO YORKSHIRE CUP.
WEBSTER'S YORKSHIRE CUP

YORKSHIRE FEDERATION AWARDS

The Yorkshire Federation of Supporters' Clubs sponsor an annual award, the James Harrison Trophy, presented to fairest and most loyal player from the White Rose clubs. In memory of the Bramley forward and member of the Federation, the award is a trophy and canteen of cutlery, the winner being chosen by a judges panel of referees for his club loyalty, regular training and sportsmanship.

The James Harrison Trophy roll of honour is:
1958 E. Cooper (Wakefield Trinity)
1959 F. Williamson (Hunslet)
1960 E. Slevin (Huddersfield)
1961 G. Owen (Halifax)
1962 W. Hargreaves (York)
1963 L. Jones (Leeds)
1964 G. Gunney (Hunslet)
1965 J. Hainsworth (Bramley)
1966 A. Keegan (Hull)
1967 D. Metcalfe (Wakefield Trinity)
1968 C. Renilson (Halifax)

1969	S. Gittins (Batley)	1975	K. Rushton (Doncaster)
1970	J. Scroby (Halifax)	1976	P. Goodchild (Bramley)
1971	R. Batten (Leeds)		J. Newlove (Featherstone Rovers)
1972	J. Woolford (Bramley)	1977	J. Martin (Halifax)
1973	T. R. Lowe (Dewsbury)	1978	D. Topliss (Wakefield Trinity)
1974	G. Idle (Bramley)		

YORKSHIRE LEAGUE CHAMPIONSHIP CUP

Year	Winners	Runners-up
1907-08	Hunslet	Halifax
1908-09	Halifax	Batley
1909-10	Wakefield T.	Halifax
1910-11	Wakefield T.	Hunslet
1911-12	Huddersfield	Hull KR
1912-13	Huddersfield	Hull KR
1913-14	Huddersfield	Hull
1914-15	Huddersfield	Leeds
1915-18	*Competition Suspended*	
1918-19	Hull	Leeds
1919-20	Huddersfield	Hull
1920-21	Halifax	Hull
1921-22	Huddersfield	Batley
1922-23	Hull	Huddersfield
1923-24	Batley	Huddersfield
1924-25	Hull KR	Leeds
1925-26	Hull KR	Batley
1926-27	Hull	Leeds
1927-28	Leeds	Featherstone Rovers
1928-28	Huddersfield	Leeds
1929-30	Huddersfield	Leeds
1930-31	Leeds	Huddersfield
1931-32	Hunslet	Huddersfield
1932-33	Castleford	York
1933-34	Leeds	Hunslet
1934-35	Leeds	Hull
1935-36	Hull	Leeds
1936-37	Leeds	Castleford
1937-38	Leeds	Hunslet
1938-39	Castleford	Leeds
1939-40	Bradford N.	Huddersfield
	(Emergency League Championship)	
1940-41	Bradford N.	Hull
	(Emergency League Championship)	
1941-45	*Competition Suspended*	
1945-46	Wakefield T.	Huddersfield
1946-47	Dewsbury	Huddersfield
1947-48	Bradford N.	Huddersfield
1948-49	Huddersfield	Bradford N.
1949-50	Huddersfield	Halifax
1950-51	Leeds	Halifax
1951-52	Huddersfield	Bradford N.
1952-53	Halifax	Huddersfield
1953-54	Halifax	Hull
1954-55	Leeds	Halifax
1955-56	Halifax	Hull
1956-57	Leeds	Hull
1957-58	Halifax	Hull

1958-59	Wakefield Trinity	Hunslet
1959-60	Wakefield Trinity	Hull
1960-61	Leeds	Wakefield T.
1961-62	Wakefield Trinity	Featherstone Rovers
1962-63	Hull KR	Huddersfield (Eastern Division)
1963-64	Halifax	Castleford (Eastern Division)
1964-65	Castleford	Halifax
1965-66	Wakefield Trinity	Castleford
1966-67	Leeds	Hull KR
1967-68	Leeds	Hull KR
1968-69	Leeds	Castleford
1969-70	Leeds	Castleford

YOUNGEST PLAYER

It is generally accepted that the youngest player to appear in a first team match was Harold Wagstaff, the Huddersfield centre who went on to captain his country on tour.

Wagstaff was 15 years and 175 days when he made his debut at Bramley on 10 Nov. 1906. He played for Yorkshire and England at the age of 17.

A player cannot now be registered as a professional before his 17th birthday.

Index